# coltrane

## the story of a sound

### benratliff

*Farrar, Straus and Giroux / New York*

*Farrar, Straus and Giroux*
*19 Union Square West, New York 10003*

*Copyright © 2007 by Ben Ratliff*
*Distributed in Canada by Douglas & McIntyre Ltd.*
*Printed in the United States of America*
*First edition, 2007*

*Title-page photograph reprinted with permission of Michael Ochs Archives.com;*
*part one photograph © Lee Friedlander, courtesy Fraenkel Gallery, San Francisco;*
*part two photograph © Riccardo Schwamenthal/CTSimages.com*

*Library of Congress Cataloging-in-Publication Data*
*Ratliff, Ben.*
    *Coltrane : the story of a sound / Ben Ratliff.— 1st ed.*
       *p.   cm.*
    *Includes bibliographical references and index.*
    *ISBN-13: 978-0-374-12606-3 (hardcover : alk. paper)*
    *ISBN-10: 0-374-12606-2 (hardcover : alk. paper)*
    *1. Coltrane, John, 1926–1967. 2. Jazz musicians—United States—Biography.*
    *3. Saxophonists—United States—Biography. I. Title.*

  *ML419.C645R37 2007*
  *788.7'165092—dc22*
  *[B]*

                                                    *2007004362*

*Designed by Abby Kagan*

*www.fsgbooks.com*

*10  9  8  7  6  5  4  3  2  1*

for kate and henry and toby

coltrane

# contents

# introduction

The common wisdom about the saxophonist
John Coltrane is that he was the last major figure in the evolution
of jazz, that the momentum of jazz stalled, and nearly stopped, after his death at age forty in 1967.

What was the essence of Coltrane's achievement that makes
him so prized forty years after his death? Why have so many musicians and listeners been so powerfully drawn to him? What was it
about his improvising, his bands, his compositions, his place within
his era of jazz? What were the factors that helped Coltrane become
who he was? And what would a John Coltrane look like now, or are
we wrong to be looking for such a figure?

From the outside, one keeps wondering which musician will
take the next decisively evolutionary step, as all those who seem to
be candidates repeat themselves, become hermetic or obvious, fail
to write compelling original material, sell out in some form, or begin to bore their audiences. And then one wonders whether evolutionary models should be applied to jazz at all. It seems to be
the case that jazz loops around, retrenches, makes tiny adjustments
that don't alter the basic language. The problem, though, is that

Coltrane certainly made it seem as if jazz were evolving. He bar-
reled ahead, and others followed. Some are still following.

His career, especially the last ten years of it, was so unreason-
ably exceptional that when he became seen as the representative
jazz musician, the general comprehension of how and why jazz
works became changed; it also became jagged and dangerous with
half-truths. Every half-truth needs a full explanation.

This is not a book about Coltrane's life, but the story of his
work. The first part tells the story of his music as it was made, from
his first recordings as a no-name navy bandsman in 1946 until his
death as a near-saint of jazz in 1967. The second part tells the story
of his influence, starting in his lifetime and continuing until today.
The reason that the two stories are separated—even though one
will cross over into the other's territory now and then—is because
the work and its reception have had distinct, different, and individually logical lives.

This is a book about jazz as sound. I mean "sound" as it has long
functioned among jazz players, as a mystical term of art: as in,
every musician finally needs a sound, a full and sensible embodiment of his artistic personality, such that it can be heard, at best,
in a single note. Miles Davis's was fragile and pointed. Coleman
Hawkins's was ripe and mellow and generous. John Coltrane's was
large and dry, slightly undercooked, and urgent.

But I also mean sound as a balanced block of music emanating
from a whole band. How important is this? With Coltrane, sound
ruled over everything. It eventually superseded composition: his
later records present one track after another of increasing similarity, in which the search for sound superseded solos and structure.
His authoritative *sound*, especially as he could handle it in a ballad,
was the reason older musicians respected him so—his high-register
sound, for example, in "Say It Over and Over Again." But it was
also the reason younger and less formally adept musicians were
drawn to him, and why they could even find themselves a place on
his bandstand.

Coltrane loved structure in music, and the science and theory of harmony; one of the ways he is remembered is as the champion student of jazz. But insofar as Coltrane's music has some extraordinary properties—the power to make you change your consciousness a little bit—we ought to widen the focus beyond the constructs of his music, his compositions, and his intellectual conceits. Eventually we can come around to the music's overall sound: first how it feels in the ear and later how it feels in the memory, as mass and as metaphor. Musical structure, for instance, can't contain morality. But sound, somehow, can. Coltrane's large, direct, vibratoless sound transmitted his basic desire: "that I'm supposed to grow to the best good that I can get to."

What Coltrane accomplished, and how he connected with audiences for jazz around the world, seems to elude any possible career plan, and is remarkably separate from what we have come to understand as European-based, Western-culture artistic consciousness. This book attempts to track the connections of his work—how and why he proceeded from A to B to Z—and then, later, to ask why Coltrane has weighed so heavily in the basic identity of jazz for the last half century.

Coltrane—whose music is marked by remarkable technique, strength in all registers of the tenor and soprano saxophones, slightly sharp intonation, serene intensity, and a rapid, mobile exploration of chords, not just melody—made jazz that was alternately seductive, mainstream, and antagonistic. Among his recordings were the high-speed harmonic étude "Giant Steps" (1959); the exotic, ancient-sounding modal versions of "My Favorite Things" (1960) and "Greensleeves" (1961); the headlong, sometimes discordant, fifteen-minute blues in F, "Chasin' the Trane" (1961); the devotional suite *A Love Supreme* (1964); the mournful ballads "Soul Eyes" (1962) and "After the Rain" (1963); and the whirligig free-jazz duet performance with drums alone, *Interstellar Space* (1967).

His work became unofficially annexed by the civil rights movement: its sound alone has become a metaphor for dignified perseverance. His art, nearly up to the end, was not insular, and kept signifying different things for different people of different cultures and races. His ugliest music (to a certain way of thinking) is widely suspected of possessing beauty beyond the listener's grasp, and the reverse goes for his prettiest music—that it is more properly understood as an expression of grave seriousness. There is more poetry written about him, I would guess, than about any other jazz musician. And his religious quests through Christianity, Buddhism, Kabbalah, and Sufism are now embedded, ex post facto, in his music. In pluralistic America, it has become hard not to hear Coltrane's modal music—in which an improviser, freed from chordal movement, becomes free to explore—as a metaphor for a personal religious search.

Coltrane, particularly from 1961 to 1964, sounds like the thing we know as modern jazz, just the way that Stravinsky sounds like the thing we know as modern classical music. Young bandleaders, especially saxophonists, find him a safe place, *the* safe place. Some musicians may disagree on the basis of their own experiences—jazz is hundreds of microclimates—but here it is: the sound of so many jazz gigs I've heard in the past fifteen years, as a jazz critic in New York, is usually the sound of albums like *Coltrane's Sound* or *Coltrane Plays the Blues*, the Coltrane quartet just before or in the first stages of a modal-jazz style, just tightening, still before *A Love Supreme* and that later music that is so personal that to borrow from it would be obvious. (Not that it isn't sometimes borrowed from, and not that such borrowing isn't usually obvious to the point of vulgarity.) He has been more widely imitated in jazz over the last fifty years than any other figure.

Some musicians have told me that after a period of immersion, they could not listen to him anymore. Listeners, too. I have played other kinds of music in bands, and studied with a jazz pianist, but I am a writer, not a jazz musician. When I first heard Coltrane's records as a teenager in the 1980s, the 1956 Prestige sessions with the Miles Davis Quintet—"Tune Up" and "If I Were a Bell" especially—he sounded to me like a great lake whose dimensions I knew I wanted to trace. Next was *Giant Steps*, with its brightness, concision, harmonic acuity, and strong original melodies. It did me no harm—not until later, when I began to hear a rote mathematical stiffness in his playing that I reacted against. I wasn't alive in the early sixties, and perhaps for that reason *The European Tour*, a double-LP set of Coltrane's band recorded live in 1962 and 1963, first seemed to me the stylization of modal music, a soft, snake-charming lob toward the progressive, self-congratulating audiences accruing around Coltrane after his radio hit, "My Favorite Things." I rejected it, pretty much.

But when I got to *Live at the Village Vanguard*, particularly the track "Spiritual," I developed a block against it. This music was no half-stepping: deep and correct and serious, harder and more violently swinging and slightly ancient-sounding, the intimations of Coltrane's modal style before it hardened as a gesture. This band was the supreme consortium of live jazz, the one most related to jazz-as-it-is-currently-played. It seemed that you could go in there and not be able to find your way out.

I did have some sort of index for seriousness in jazz at that point. I was hearing a lot of music in New York that tried to be profound and occasionally was. The guitarist Sonny Sharrock and his loud band with two drummers made sense to me by its natural connections both to rock-and-roll and post-Coltrane free jazz—specifically to Pharoah Sanders's records of the late 1960s. The tenor saxophonist Charles Gayle and his trios played a kind of highly expressionistic collective improvisation, whose main factors were its manipulation of rhythmic chaos and the unpredictable charisma of Gayle himself. Another tenor player, David S. Ware, led a quartet which took the example of Coltrane in about 1965 to the next plane of loud-and-lugubrious; it was all density. On the other hand, David Murray's trio with Wilber Morris and Andrew Cyrille was more spindly and playful and pretty, with nice original lines, and a completely different story from Coltrane's. (Murray's allegiance was to melodic improvisation, the Sonny Rollins line of playing, as opposed to Coltrane's way of implying whole chords in his sweep.)

But those Coltrane records I shrank from faced up to the idea of density and noise without fetishizing it, and didn't stop there. Coltrane connected his own learned harmonic patterns with many outside approaches, picked up from other jazz musicians and various folk cultures—a thoroughly willed, nearly maniacal method of inclusion. And he built a groove with his bassist Jimmy Garrison and drummer Elvin Jones that grew stronger, even as the rest of the music became heavy with super-extended soloing, the overload of individual will. The various sounds of *Live at the Village Vanguard* became some of jazz's most revisited majority languages, connecting schools of players who would otherwise have little to do with each other, formalists and non-formalists.

Anyway, two years went by before I tried listening seriously to Coltrane again. Now it was twenty-eight years after *Live at the Village Vanguard* was recorded, and the bohemian interior of the jazz audience in New York had become, as far as I could see, smaller and more self-conscious. Jazz's early-sixties identity as protest material for Americans who had a hard, bitter road out of the Great Society had since been celebrated, fetishized, and nostalgized; since the beginning of the 1980s, the music-as-music had been studied as an academic subject. Jazz, too, had crept into pop and hiphop. And a jazz-classicism movement, which exercised withering skepticism toward most of the loose-form and nonacoustic music that had happened in jazz after the mid-sixties, had gained fully funded legitimacy through house orchestras at Lincoln Center and Carnegie Hall and the Smithsonian.

The point I am making is that there were so many entryways to jazz by 1989 that I didn't necessarily want to deal with the most serious, uncomfortable, and perhaps necessary way in: immersion in John Coltrane's recordings. Part of that discomfort came from the fact that it had become totally unclear how to think of them. They form a path, but was it a path toward a new language or nonsense?

The trumpeter Wynton Marsalis, the artistic director of Jazz at Lincoln Center, as well as his brothers Branford (the saxophonist) and Delfeayo (the trombonist), and the critic Stanley Crouch—who

wrote a great deal of combative opinions associated with them—
had become extremely potent cultural commentators by that point.
Wynton was in the business of selecting what was good and lasting across the entire history of jazz. Serving as faction boss, he
talked persuasively about what had been watered down or lost in
jazz: four-four swing, ballads, constructive competition, a sense of
boundaries and exclusivity. He really loved to argue, and the gist of
his arguments was always responsibility: whether you are doing
good or harm to the music. (And not just to jazz, but, by extension,
to American culture.) He talked about jazz as if it were a patient on
a table. He prescribed the necessary measures musicians *ought* to be
taking if they wanted jazz to survive at all.

Suddenly the life's work of Coltrane, and his gradual trajectory
toward non-swing, non-ballads, non-competiveness, non-boundaried
inclusion, could seem dangerous. But the fact remained that if you
could stand to listen, really listen hard, to "Spiritual," or the rest of
*Live at the Village Vanguard*, both sides of the argument seemed
shallow, and imposed from without by parties with an agenda. A
record like that one indicated that the common-room of jazz was
also, paradoxically, its darkest and most mysterious place.

The rhetoric surrounding jazz has changed a great deal since
Coltrane's time. The notion that jazz is the music of the underdog's
liberation, that it is intrinsically radical, is not to be found in most
serious discussions about jazz today. That is now seen as a philosophy of its time, associated with the 1960s and early seventies.

The best jazz playing (and the best jazz criticism) has made
room for the notion that this music makes its own meaning without
the superimposition of any political or intellectual one, that it will
advance by slow degrees, and that it will go around and around in
further understanding and refinement of itself, eating its own tail.
Structural newness, genre newness, is not necessarily what we are
looking for; what we want is the musician's individual expression:

honor the past while being yourself. If a genuinely individual expression comes inside a familiar-sounding package, that shouldn't reduce its value.

But what about that hippie myth in which jazz is "tomorrow's music" forever and ever, the result of a radical process? The structural innovations of jazz really did slow down precipitously after Coltrane. Yet the surrounding rhetoric traveled on and on and on, disembodied from its context, like a rider thrown headlong from a horse. It would be easy to say that this sort of future-mongering—the kind of thing you hear especially from young musicians and those excited about the various bohemian free-jazz scenes around the world—has to do with Coltrane's death from liver cancer, which took him so unexpectedly. He was only forty, and many who were close to him hadn't known how ill he was. He did die a kind of martyr, he did die a kind of seer; and for all those who agree, whatever descends from Coltrane must be holy, and in some sense, unimpeachably true.

But that's still too neat. If we are to see Coltrane as an impetus for so much jazz that followed him—both in the main body of straightforward jazz and its abstract, outlying territories—I think the answer is to be found in the pattern of his last ten years, not just his ending.

Nobody in jazz has traveled further and more effectively, in a chartable, linear sense, during such a short period, than Coltrane. Miles Davis is the most famous paradigm-changer of jazz, but his refashionings of his music every five years or so had much to do with his inexhaustible competitiveness and self-regard. It was easier to understand Davis changing in order to confound and challenge his peers and his audience. With Coltrane, the reason to change seemed to come more from the inside.

This much seems certain: if John Coltrane had continued to progress clearly and intelligibly, pointing at both the road behind and the road ahead—as he had done in such an exemplary way from 1957 through, let's say, *Transition* in 1965—this progress would have deep and practical consequences for jazz. Instead, during those last two and a half years, he went inside himself. You could go there if you wanted, but not without either changing some of your root ideas about music or finding some intemperate notion of perfection which you might later want to renounce. Albums like *Stellar Regions* or *Live in Seattle*, from that late period after *Transition*, are expressions of blazing single-mindedness; they can express what the poet Robert Lowell, one of Coltrane's contemporaries, once called "the monotony of the sublime." But Lowell was from a Boston Brahmin family: he lived within a strict historical definition. Coltrane, evidently, was looking for a music that stepped outside of history. In the face of such striving, even-tempered criticism usually breaks down. You either accept it not just as music but as a kind of aesthetic philosophy, or you hear it once and say never again.

Thinking in the terms of traditional Western rationalism, one can feel that Coltrane, in 1965, dived into a trap. A historically relevant trap, but a trap all the same, a trap of the age—records and performances that might only seem significant inasmuch as they are of a piece with many other things that happened around it. Those "things" including: the world championship in boxing being won and successfully defended by Muhammad Ali, a new kind of culture hero; the African independence movement (thirty-six independent republics in Africa established during Coltrane's life, almost all of them in Coltrane's last ten years); the growth of a new sense of black folkloric heritage in those and other formerly colonized black areas; and the decline of American urban social services and public education, coterminous with the rise of cheap street drugs in the years after the assassination at the Audubon Ballroom of Malcolm X. And still, even if you internalized all of this, even if it were the story of your life, you might want to look away from the music's harshness.

In his final three years, Coltrane indicated a new way of thinking about music, not a way for everyone. The typical example of Coltrane's audience turning against him comes from 1965, when Coltrane's quintet played at Soldier Field in Chicago. The music was harsh and aggressive, and managed to divide the audience during the performance—this for a man who was used to drawing overflow audiences at jazz clubs. (But gauging the importance of Coltrane takes strange routes: his Detroit gigs in 1961, at his moment of highest concentrated nationwide success, were sparsely attended, and his last live performance, at the Olatunji Center of African Culture, in Harlem, when his newest music was screaming, palpitating, at its most difficult to absorb, drew three thousand people.) If you look closely, you can see that Coltrane in his late, "free" period continued to reuse what he had, to connect his instinctual present with his craftsman past. He didn't get to finish cementing the connection in more obvious ways, and since his death it has taken jazz musicians more than thirty years to find a consensual, mainstream language of rapprochement between free jazz and the more traditionally based kind.

Coltrane was a man of unusual stamina, phlegmatic temperament, and stoic charisma, who found ecstasy in his labor but otherwise was difficult to excite—a John Wayne, a Gary Cooper, a Lou Gehrig, a John Henry, a Yankee woodsman. (In *American Humor*, published in 1931, Constance Rourke paraphrases the legend of the early 1800s Yankee woodsman thus: "I'm a regular tornado, tough as hickory and long-winded as a nor'wester. I can strike a blow like a falling tree, and every lick makes a gap in the crowd that lets in an acre of sunshine.") Maybe, even, Coltrane was the cool, spirit-filled archetype of West African Kongo culture. At the end, when his public pronouncements swerved away from music and settled on God—as he variously put it, he aspired to be a saint, or at least to become "a force for real good"—one notices the matte finish on the zeal, the sense that his ecstasy is impenetrable, unquestionable, ironbound. In some sense, he hadn't changed much; he had just increased the seriousness that was already abundant within him. But now the seriousness worked in the service of a blanketing religious ecstasy rather than the hard-bitten mannerisms of the post-bop jazz language.

Still, he did provide links for you. Nothing in Coltrane's work comes out of the blue. Despite the thinness of explication (he wasn't a good interview, and came off sounding disappointingly mundane for a would-be saint), he recorded and performed so much in the last years of his life that we can trace foreshadowings, arrivals, and departures.

That path toward the sublime, which is the point of the first half of this book, really starts in 1958, the year Coltrane rejoined Miles Davis after taking a year and half off. Before joining the Davis group again, he had been playing with Thelonious Monk, subjecting himself to new challenges of chords and melody and tempo; he had quit using heroin and quit drinking. What he made in 1958 was victory music, Rocky music. It is quite unlike the music of Dexter Gordon and Charlie Parker, his two major early influences.

"Straight, No Chaser," from February 1958 (on Miles Davis's *Milestones*) and "Dial Africa," from June 1958 (on Wilbur Harden's *Jazz Way Out*) show this Coltrane: he has discovered how to concentrate, how to reconcile speed with melody, and how to exult—in the way that a preacher, and not merely a passive dandelion in the congregation, learns to exult. (Both his maternal grandfather, in whose house he grew up, and his paternal grandfather were ministers in the African Methodist Episcopal Zion Church; in an interview with August Blume, Coltrane described his maternal grandfather's religiosity as "militant.")

One of the general listener's major misperceptions of jazz is that when improvisers work at their best, they pluck ideas out of the sky, channeling heaven. No. Even at their least inhibited, Coltrane's solos still show the stamina that comes of hard, solitary practicing; it is immensely worked-out music. You can pick out dozens of devices in his solos that he was reusing and would continue to reuse.

For Coltrane, much of what had come before 1958 was a language of faltering, of finding his way. Young jazz players were (and are) interested in this, because they falter themselves. But the larger public had less use for it. It was when he got over himself, and his struggle to find his sound, when he took himself seriously as both a commercial proposition and a "force for real good," that he didn't allow himself to falter any longer, that his sound opened widest and his music began to make sense on a large scale.

Any artist—writer, painter, filmmaker, dancer—can hide for a long time in the wilds of his own language, never rising above the vegetation. "Any successful style is a spell whose first victim is the wizard," the critic Clive James has written. Still, people come to Delphi and attach themselves to the utterances, grateful to have heard one firsthand. They generally don't need to know if the oracle has magicked himself.

Coltrane got beyond the language of the utterances. He was stable and trustworthy; he said he doubted himself, even as he kept playing more forcefully and originally. He struck people afresh, and caused aesthetic change. Many people, from Wynton Marsalis to the most disengaged jazz fan you know, can tell you a story about how John Coltrane altered their lives or at least their way of looking at art, strengthened their resolve, made them see that jazz isn't an exercise book, or a father's record collection, or music as a closed-off thing-in-itself.

The other half of the Coltrane narrative, its posthumous mirror, begins before his death. The second part of this book is the story of Coltrane's influence on other musicians, and on all those who established the surrounding philosophy and discourse of jazz starting in the late 1950s.

Because his words were so indirect, because he said so little and represented such enormous ideas, because of his risks, entire careers have drafted in his tailwind. And artistic imperatives that may or may not have been his in the first place have been accepted as articles of faith. Those who have set stock in the notion of jazz-as-future often cite Coltrane as their inspiration. I thought of this when I heard fifteen young saxophonists competing in the Thelonious Monk Institute's International Saxophone Competition a few years ago. Coltrane was everywhere in their playing, that weekend. If these saxophonists wanted to imply sophistication, depth, stamina, fervor, tenderness, they used Coltrane language.

At last—for reasons that the story of Coltrane's influence should make clear—this is beginning to change. While we're still under the yoke of Coltrane but in the process of slipping it off, it seems a good time to try to analyze what he did in his life, through the sensibility of the critic, rather than the biographer. And, at the same time, to analyze why his appeal has held fast for so many years after his death.

# partone

# 1 who's willie mays?

On July 13, 1946, John William Coltrane, sea-
man second class, recorded eight songs with four other musicians,
drawn from the ranks of the Melody Masters. The Melody Masters
was a large navy band, stationed in Oahu, Hawaii; navy bands were
segregated in those days, and this one was all white.

Quiet Coltrane came from a very religious Methodist family.
Both his grandfathers were ministers. As a preteen he liked to
draw, and as a teenager he idolized Johnny Hodges, the Ellington-
band alto and soprano saxophonist. He was born in Hamlet, North
Carolina, moved to High Point, North Carolina, in his infancy, and
moved again to Philadelphia after finishing at William Penn High
School in High Point. He was two months shy of turning twenty
when the four Melody Masters invited Coltrane to jam with them.

Coltrane, a lean figure in round shades whose tall Afro flattened
out on the sides, was not a full-time navy bandsman (no blacks
were), and the Melody Masters were not officially allowed to play
with black musicians. With Coltrane as guest, escaping the knowledge of their superior officers, they made a private recording,
eventually pressing four copies of a 78 RPM record.

One tune from that amateur session was Tadd Dameron's "Hot

House," a song that later became known as one of the great compositions of early bebop. "Hot House" is a 32-bar song that first borrows from the chord changes of the standard "What Is This Thing Called Love?" before cleverly altering them. And the seamen try an effortful replication of Dizzy Gillespie and Charlie Parker's version of the tune, cut a year earlier—except that the navy trumpeter doesn't solo, as Gillespie did.

Instead, Coltrane does. In fact, Coltrane, on alto saxophone, takes the only solo—a hideous, squeaking, lurching thing. But perhaps it didn't matter to the thoroughly preprofessional Melody Masters, because Coltrane had met Bird.

Some jazz musicians are off and running at nineteen—Charlie Christian, Johnny Griffin, Art Pepper, Clifford Brown, Sarah Vaughan. John Coltrane was not. He had started playing at thirteen, on alto horn and clarinet, as a member of the school band in High Point. At fourteen, he switched to alto saxophone. The first instrument he owned was an alto bought for him by his mother when the family moved to Philadelphia; he was sixteen then. He took a year of theory lessons at the Ornstein School of Music. At eighteen, he started playing in Philadelphia clubs, working with big bands at dances or in a trio at nightclubs. According to his friends and some of the bandleaders he worked with, he was a perfectly indistinct musician.

He saw Charlie Parker perform for the first time on June 5, 1945, in Dizzy Gillespie's group.

So did his friends Jimmy Heath and Benny Golson. Golson remembered: "John just sat there, taking it all in. All over the hall, people were standing up and shouting, clapping their hands and stamping their feet. Imagine being a saxophonist and never having heard this kind of music before." Following the afternoon performance, Coltrane and Golson accompanied their hero toward the Blue Note club, where Parker had an evening gig. Golson asked if he could carry Bird's saxophone case. The three walked together: Golson on the right, Coltrane on the left, Bird in the middle. Golson, a talker, asked Bird what kind of horn he used, what mouthpiece, what number reeds. It was a scene of total adulation. Golson wasn't embarrassed by it, but Coltrane evidently was. In 1947, Coltrane met Bird again in Los Angeles, while on tour with King Kolax. He didn't remind him that they had met in Philadelphia.

On the Oahu recording of "Hot House," made a year later, Coltrane starts his solo by echoing the melody line from the bridge section of "A Night in Tunisia," which was the big bebop record of the previous year. It may have been fresh in Coltrane's ears from hearing Dizzy Gillespie's septet version of "Tunisia," recorded February 22, 1946, on Victor. Or perhaps he heard the Charlie Parker Septet version, recorded March 28, on Dial.

Musicians working within this common 32-bar song structure can find a way to begin a solo with a quote of a bridge; it's not impossible. It's just tricky. Where the solo begins is the start of a journey, whereas the bridge—in the 32-bar song form, it's the channel of music after the main theme is played and repeated, and which contrasts against that main theme—represents the middle. Coltrane doesn't play inapposite notes to the chords, but the 8-bar bridge melody naturally leads him to a psychological ending place, and he still has 24 more bars to fill. It is incumbent upon him to scramble for something new to propel himself again. Sure enough, the second 8-bar stretch of the 32-bar solo chorus grows disastrous. On the song's actual bridge, bars 17 to 24, he has an even worse time; on the final 8, he achieves adequate redemption, though certainly not poise, with a Charlie Parker lick, a curling flurry of sixteenth notes.

Moving back to Philadelphia after his discharge in August 1946, Coltrane did what any self-respecting alto saxophonist of the time would do: he tried to follow Charlie Parker's movements, because Parker was the king soloist.

At this point in jazz, when big bands and dance-hall jobs were beginning to disappear and small groups were taking precedence, solos really mattered. It was first under Lester Young, and then more decisively under Charlie Parker, that the cult of the solo had emerged. Finally, to Parker's cohort, the solos were king, subjugat-

ing the stuff around them. Even the worst examples of Parker's solos were fetishized. The earliest scholarly writing on jazz solos appeared in the 1930s, but the hagiographic approach toward jazz
soloing may have started with Elliot Grennard, a *Billboard* writer
who witnessed Charlie Parker's infamous recording session of July
1946. This was when Parker was experiencing heroin withdrawal
that caused him to suffer involuntary muscle spasms, making him
sound sick and adrift, particularly on the tune "Lover Man." Grennard wrote a fictionalized account of the "Lover Man" sessions for
*Harper's Magazine* called "Sparrow's Last Jump"; it was published
in 1948 and won the O. Henry Prize for short fiction. Ever since,
"Lover Man" has had its morbid admirers. Ross Russell's book
*Bird Lives!*—Russell was the producer whose label, Dial, put
out the "Lover Man" sessions—created a fascination for Dean
Benedetti, a Parker fan who took a tape recorder to club gigs and
recorded only Parker's solos, not what happened before and after
them.

In Philly, Coltrane played with the pianist Ray Bryant, among
others; he went on a short tour with a band led by Joe Webb, which
included the blues singer Big Maybelle. On his G.I. Bill benefits,
he studied at the Granoff School, a local music school, specifically
with Dennis Sandole. Sandole, who died in 2000 at the age of
eighty-seven, was a swing-band guitar player who eventually let
his own music take second place to his teaching. He focused on
scales, as Coltrane would before long. He used exotic ones, and created his own, yet by all accounts, tailored his lessons to the individual student.

Coltrane worked hard, to the exclusion of any other interest. "I
used to practice a lot with Trane," said his friend Jimmy Heath,
who was then also an alto saxophonist before making his name on
tenor. Everybody called him Jimmy. Coltrane called him Jim. Nobody else did. "He'd be in his shorts, we didn't have any air condi-
tioning in those hot tenement houses; he lived with his mother.
He'd be practicing, sweating, man. Practicing all day. Nobody practiced that much at that time that I knew. He was practicing all the

things he eventually perfected. Lines, harmonic concepts that we were learning together, things we had transcribed."

Heath also remembers Coltrane practicing so hard that he made his reeds red with blood.

Coltrane lived not far from the Woodbine Club, at Twelfth and Master streets in North Philadelphia, an after-hours place where jam sessions would take place, with musicians including the saxophonists Heath, Jimmy Oliver, and Bill Barron, the trumpeter Johnny Coles, and Coltrane. He would work along Columbia Avenue (now called Cecil B. Moore Avenue) in the same part of town, where there was a club on nearly every block.

Heath had gotten his hands on a transcription of Charlie Parker's solo on "Don't Blame Me"; the transcription had been made by Howard Johnson, the lead alto saxophonist in Dizzy Gillespie's band. They studied from sources like that, and used the Philadelphia Public Library to listen to classical music, for "harmonic possibilities," Heath says. "We knew that Bird carried around the *Firebird Suite* score." They didn't play the Stravinsky score per se. "We were extracting the cadenzas," he remembered, "and turning them around to fit our own groove."

A few years later, Heath mentioned something about a play Willie Mays had made in a baseball game the day before. Coltrane replied, "Who's Willie Mays, Jim?"


Work came Coltrane's way. He joined up with King Kolax, a Chicago-based trumpet player, singer, and crowd-pleasing bandleader in the jump-blues style.

Jazz has its connector-pieces, more notable for who they hired and what happened around them than for their own musical accomplishments. In his early years, Coltrane played with many of them. King Kolax, by most accounts an outgoing and funny presence on stage, left no extraordinary artifacts; the most significant recordings he played on were with Billy Eckstine's big band in 1946, as part of a four-man trumpet section that included Miles

Davis and Hobart Dotson. Kolax takes no solos. Bird, as a teenager, had played with Kolax's group in 1939—a time when Kolax had one of the hottest bands in Chicago. A few years later, in 1941, Gene Ammons was the alto player in Kolax's band. Johnny Griffin saw that band at his grade-school graduation dance at the Parkway Ballroom in Chicago, emerged stunned, and thereupon resolved to play saxophone. Coltrane was the next soon-to-be-major player in line, touring with Kolax during the first few months of 1947.

Coltrane also gigged with his friend Jimmy Heath, who led his own big band in Philadelphia, a kind of third-string version of what the Gillespie band was playing ninety miles to the north. And then he played with Eddie "Cleanhead" Vinson, a bandleader of a kind not dissimilar from Kolax: killingly dressed, singing, playing saxophone, entertaining.

Upon joining Vinson's band—it was for a long string of one-nighters in the winter of 1948–49—Coltrane took up the tenor saxophone in earnest. Vinson wanted someone who could play like Bird over rhythm-and-blues tunes. Coltrane could, but the open spot was for tenor, not alto. He took the opportunity. And now that he was on a different instrument, Coltrane—a born student—began casting about for the great tenor player who could suggest avenues for him on tenor the way Bird did on alto.

At the time, among the major contenders was Lester Young, who had become famous playing lovely, light-gauge melodic lines on tenor saxophone with Count Basie. There was also Ben Webster, who played fat, sweet, rich notes on tenor, and could subtract pitched sound until all you heard was elusive hissing; he was a super-artful manipulator of timbre and ballad phrasing. Coltrane also admired Tab Smith, a master of pitch and tonal control, a swelling-romance tenor player who descended from Johnny Hodges.

And then there was Coleman Hawkins. Coltrane liked the arpeggios Hawkins played, the articulation of a whole scale-pattern where for other musicians just a few notes would do. Hawkins seemed to have a more sweeping, kaleidoscopic vision of music than most of the other top soloists in jazz: instead of using a thin-nibbed pen to trace out melodies, he used a paint-roller. Resourcefully, he made all these notes, all these references to passing chords, sound virile and natural.

In the early 1960s, Eddie Vinson was asked about Coltrane. "Yeah, little ol' Coltrane used to be in my band. He never wanted to play. I used to have to play all night long. I'd ask him, 'Man, why don't you play?' He'd say, 'I just want to hear you play . . .' That ol' boy was something. He changed his playing every six months almost." A character trait: Coltrane may have been diffident with others, but apparently not with himself.

Then Coltrane's break came. Dizzy Gillespie's piano player, James Forman, knew Coltrane from jobs around Philly; they were both members of the musicians' union. Forman recommended Coltrane to Gillespie, who asked both Heath and Coltrane to join his big band. The job began in late fall 1949.

Bebop, in the forties, was a new language of blues-based modernism. It came to be associated with fast tempos, asymmetrical melodic lines, and chord harmonies inspired by Stravinsky, Debussy, and Bartók. It was developed in New York in the early 1940s by Parker, Gillespie, and the musicians around them, and it naturally stole into popular big bands over time: this was simply what young musicians were playing. But in 1949, the very idea of a Dizzy Gillespie big band—and in the minds of anyone reading about jazz back then, that proposition equaled a bebop big band—was problematic. First, big bands were for dancers, and bebop tempos could be fast, and harder to dance to. Second, America was recovering from a wartime economy, which had already debilitated the great touring big bands through gas and rubber shortages and a rise in travel costs; the preeminence of these bands in the national musical culture was lessening. And the proof was in the music itself. Cropped, curling bop lines, tritone-heavy bop harmony, fast and spiky bop rhythm: they were all better executed by a four- or five-piece group than by an orchestra.

But Gillespie, who along with Charlie Parker had come to be

synonymous with bebop as a movement, had an advantage in realizing a difficult proposition. He came from the Cab Calloway band of the early 1940s, which had popularized the image of strong, modern music and witty clowning; he had to do something with his show knowledge. More important, he was thinking about another big-band model: the Latin kind. He had learned about Latin music largely through his association with the Cuban trumpeter Mario Bavza, a section-mate in the Calloway group; in 1942 he had sat in with Machito's Afro-Cubans, and started learning ways to improvise jazz over the Cuban clave rhythm.

Gillespie's orchestra lasted from 1946 to 1950. He had graduated from the small labels of the first bebop experiments; RCA was recording him then. In 1947 the orchestra created "Manteca," one of the most important pieces of jazz ever—the starting place of modern Afro-Latin jazz. But by the time Coltrane joined, sharing with Heath the role of lead alto saxophone (the top voice of the alto saxophone section, playing written lines), the end was in sight. Bookings were shrinking. By the end of the decade the orchestra had been sized down to six or seven members.

Some of the radio broadcasts by the small group in 1951 survive on bootlegs, and these are the next significant recordings of Coltrane, after Oahu. Here and there you hear him on a solo feature, strong and true and improvising: he is not erased by the thundering of a big band, or relegated to the background on a singer-with-orchestra date. His growth has been remarkable, and why shouldn't it be—five years have passed, a long time for a young man. He has access to more notes, yet the logic of his playing is still jumbled, still chaotic. But what do we hear of the later, mature Coltrane in 1951? Bits and dots. And for the next four years, until he joined Miles Davis's band, there was only the refinement of a basic set of skills.

Coltrane seems not to have played any tenor saxophone with Gillespie's big band. But offstage, he was practicing the bigger horn assiduously, building on the work he had done with Vinson, using scale-book exercises by Czerny and Hanon, running various arpeggio and interval patterns, some of them jumping registers, through all the keys of Western music. They were meant for pianists, as finger-strengthening exercises; they weren't typically practiced by any kind of horn player.

By the time of the 1951 recordings, he had developed his own style, if a barely coherent one—one that mixed exotic scale patterns and rhythm-and-blues rhetoric, stubborn long tones, and the beginnings of a serious interest in the low and high registers.

The best solo on the 1951 bootleg recordings with Gillespie—there had not yet been any official studio recordings from this time featuring a Coltrane solo—is in Gillespie's "A Night in Tunisia," recorded on January 6.

We already know of Coltrane's connection to "A Night in Tunisia" from his quoting of its bridge section in the 1946 Oahu "Hot House." One can assume that it was a song he practiced on; he may have grown used to improvising over its seesaw motion between minor chords.

This "Tunisia" solo, one chorus long, has problems: some fluffed notes and hesitations. But there is character here. It begins with a break—literally, a sudden drop-out of all musicians but the soloist. When Parker recorded the tune, five years before, his break was four bars long, and came out as a swarm of sixteenth notes centering around the concert key of F. It is a famous break, and it is generally not played in any length less than four bars. But Coltrane's, weirdly, is only two, and conceived in longer notes, with a harmony that immediately pulls toward minor. As the band joins in, his swing feeling warms up, but only gradually. It has a character of patience, even of dissociation; of endurance, of waiting out the band and the audience for a kind of artistic truth to start crawling out of its shell, of a seriousness that borders on the inscrutable. It is the outsider entering an open plain where the attacks could come from any angle, defensively correct, slow, and wary.

It is a kind of trance state, and an American romantic type. It is a disposition that operates outside of historical markers; it favors staring over blinking. Johnny Cash, Clint Eastwood, Waylon Jennings had it; so did Tommy Duncan, the great western-swing baritone from Bob Wills's Texas Playboys. Walt Whitman, with his long lines, putting his feelings on the outside but still cloaking himself in whirling-dervish repetitions, had it. Gertrude Stein had a version of it, with her repetitions in clipped American rhythm. (T. S. Eliot, disapprovingly, said that her writing suggested a "peculiar hypnotic pattern not met with before. It has a kinship with the saxophone.") Natty Bumppo, in James Fenimore Cooper's Leatherstocking tales, had it, and so did John Wayne as Ethan in *The Searchers*: they took on the movements of the American Indians, and figured out a way to exist outside of the way their race, class, and status fixed them.

Jazz both encourages and discourages this disposition. It is a social music, operating in a commercial context, surrounded by hustle; you play to make your rent money, the club owner gives you a fixed fee or a percentage of the door, and you'll be booked again if the patrons drink more during your set. You play in the slotted context of a band, in a section or as a soloist-leader, and you give the audience what you think it wants. At the same time, you improvise, and try to bring out the part of you that is least like anyone else.

"What I didn't know with Diz was that what I had to do was really express myself," Coltrane told *Down Beat* reporter Ira Gitler in 1958. "I was playing clichés and trying to learn tunes that were hip, so I could play with the guys who played them." This is not strictly true if we consider the "Night in Tunisia" solo; it is considerably different from the norm. But remember, we are talking about John Coltrane—one of the primary musicians in American jazz to establish the tradition of not sounding like anybody else. And it is true that in an overall sense, in the bedrock of his note and pattern choices, he was drawing from the platform of 1940s saxophonists who had adapted Charlie Parker's alto language to the tenor: Dexter Gordon, Wardell Gray, and Gene Ammons.

Those players used Parker's rhythmic feel, but built upon it a gruffer, more earthbound edge; they were easier to follow than Bird. They found their way back to the melodic sureness and ballad sensitivity of Lester Young, and they got close to the artful honk-a-thons of Illinois Jacquet, who became famous for earthy extremes, parceling out solos in thrown bricks and blown kisses. All of them found their audiences while touring through the country with big bands, away from the intellectual core of the New York bop scene. They found the low end in bebop—both literally, in pitch terms, and metaphorically, in sensibility (low as in earthy, low as in rootsy). It is not insignificant that they created a dialect of the new music which appealed to black audiences.

At the heart of bebop, in its first apotheosis in Parker (alto saxophone) Bud Powell (piano), Dizzy Gillespie (trumpet), and the load of first-wave drummers (Kenny Clarke, Max Roach, Art Blakey, Stan Levey, Roy Haynes), there were three primary elements of sound. There was the ride cymbal, which carried so much of the fast rhythm (with bass-drum "bombs" dropped at irregular intervals); there was the pianist's right hand—Powell's, most permanently, the single notes dancing like a kite in the air, with intermittent downward tugs from stabbing left-hand chords; and there were the high registers of the alto saxophone and trumpet, with their improvised, expansive dashes into ninth, eleventh, and thirteenth intervals. (Parker was paraphrased as explaining his eureka moment this way: "I found that by using the higher intervals of a chord as a melody line and backing them with appropriately related changes, I could play the thing I'd been hearing. I came alive." He frequently explained in later interviews that his interest in Debussy and Bartók, who also used these intervals, came *after* he and Gillespie figured out their new language for themselves.)

Bebop was a high-frequency music that shot forward, then suddenly went mute in the middle of a melody chorus; it was highly aware of its own weight and shape. It didn't have the conversational quality of swing playing, of Lester Young and the daddy of them all, Coleman Hawkins, unless you mean a conversation under the influence of amphetamines. Amphetamines properly accompanied bebop, as gin accompanied stride piano.

Gordon, the key member of this transitional crew between Charlie Parker and Coltrane, added something much different: a middle- and low-register language, and a secure, natural way of playing with an underlying feeling of more even eighth notes. It is the feeling of walking at your own pace, feeling your own time— even at the risk of looking funny—rather than running to keep up.

Dexter Gordon was based in New York, as were most of the young first-call musicians. But he came originally from Los Angeles, which accounted for a basic difference in the man's temperament. (Los Angeles, then, was truly the West, where people moved and talked more slowly.) In the early forties, Gordon left home to play with Lionel Hampton, then a patient of his physician father's. And he came under the shadow of Illinois Jacquet, the star tenor saxophonist of that band. Jacquet took a solo on their 1942 hit record *Flying Home*, with Gordon in the band, which became his signature, and albatross. Over rhythm changes, the solo gathered steam through Jacquet's accreting masculine, low-register riffs, becoming a bucket of stylistic matter for jazz and rhythm-and-blues saxophonists alike. Except that Jacquet's playing had more of a common touch: it was consciously antivirtuosic. His fundamental riff-grease was adapted as a new urbane meme of jazz, a way to bring together roadhouse music and more rarefied, studious stuff. It got passed around: from Jacquet to Gordon to Coltrane.

Von Freeman, the tenor saxophonist who spent the 1950s playing in Chicago clubs, has said that Coltrane's achievement was that he absorbed the three important ways of playing the tenor saxophone: the cutting-contest style, rapid and aggressive and bebop-oriented, with a lot of darting high notes; the Lester Young soft and melodic style; and Dexter Gordon.

Again, Coltrane wasn't completely formed until much later. But during his hard-core, workmanlike bebop period, playing as a sideman for Dizzy Gillespie, a couple of his major stylistic devices are in place. One (heard on "Good Groove," a radio broadcast made in Detroit in March 1951) is the length and weight of his long tones. He plays an R&B solo as if he's waiting you out; he refuses to move quickly. Another (heard in the third chorus of his solo on "Congo Blues") is a short but strident upward phrase leaping an octave. It sounds like a sigh in reverse.

# 2 not much happens

More or less, Coltrane was on his way. But the major fact of the period between Coltrane's finishing up with Gillespie in the spring of 1951 and his joining Miles Davis in the fall of 1955 is that *not much of consequence happens*. He was still learning, and thinking subordinately.

He was drinking, and using heroin, which was not uncommon at the time. In a landmark sociological study conducted in 1954 and 1955, Charles Winick concluded that of the 357 New York jazz musicians he'd formally interviewed, 16 percent were heroin addicts. If that percentage were applied to the total number of jazz musicians in New York, which Winick estimated at roughly 5,000, you might have found more than 750 regular users of heroin among working jazz musicians in the city in 1954–55. (Winick's study deserves a little bit of skepticism. Never mind his methodology: consider what subterfuges a jazz musician might have been using with a clipboard-holding member of the straight world, and what kind of personality would have submitted to such an interview in the first place.)

Coltrane was also studying, alone and with Dennis Sandole at the Granoff School of Music in Philadelphia. One-third of the veterans of World War II used the G.I. Bill's education benefits to go to college; Coltrane was an ex-serviceman bent on self-improvement. He played in bands, some fairly popular and some not at all, whose work didn't last. He wasn't particularly making his way as a soloist. His gigs were learning jobs, rather than profile-cutting jobs.

Briefly in 1952 he played with Gay Crosse, a bandleader who was a third-tier jump-blues singer and kind of a fraudulent saxophonist; Crosse played regularly at the Club Congo in Cleveland, and had some local jukebox hits in that area.

In 1953 he played for a time with the alto saxophonist Earl Bostic. Bostic was a rarity: an R&B hit maker who played with impeccable time and control over rock-and-roll backbeats. His biggest song, "Flamingo," had hit two years before; it was a raunchy version of a creamy Ellington ballad (written by Ted Grouya and Edmund Anderson), originally sung by Herb Jeffries. Bostic, squat and solid with horn-rimmed spectacles, looked like a black middle-school principal; his sound was a more beefed-up, excitable version of Johnny Hodges. Hodges himself took a solo on Ellington's 1940 version of "Flamingo," but Bostic transformed it. If Hodges's tightly jacketed lyricism and subtle growls suggested a man watching a beautiful woman, Bostic's suggested the same with X-ray glasses; his ballad tone amped up into spitfire buzzing.

Bostic was the envy of any technical-minded saxophone player. He would spend downtime on the road tutoring his musicians in the subject of how different fingerings produce better sounds on different makes of saxophone. His realm of assured, controlled, jukebox-record making and impeccable technique was Coltrane's academy during the spring, summer, and fall of 1953.

To hear Coltrane's development on the tenor, a better place to look are the two songs he cut around 1954 with James "Coatesville" Harris, the Philadelphia-area drummer (he had been Louis Armstrong's drummer for a time in the forties). "Hamhocks and Hominy" is an average R&B honking-and-shouting record about a girl who keeps her man "like a fish on a line" with her cooking.

Coltrane comes in for a solo, and presto: there's his sound. You can hear the breadth and strength of his line. Away from alto now, where the temptation to slip into Johnny Hodges's language may have been too appealing, Coltrane is left with his own seriousness. These are records where one expects the saxophonist to repeat a note over and over, as was the style. Instead, he builds a solo in a measured pace, situating himself well behind the beat.

Coltrane had now been with two of the technique gods among young musicians—Gillespie and Bostic. Next, he'd encounter a third: Johnny Hodges himself.

Hodges was a protégé of Sidney Bechet. He started off playing Bechet's instrument, the soprano saxophone, imitating his tone and his growl (which Bechet called "Goola," after his dog's name). Bending Bechet to his own purposes, keeping the breadth of the sound and subtracting the rhythmic hustle, Hodges found his own voice. With his over-the-top stylization—unbroken alto saxophone glissandi shifting in dynamics from willowy to overpowering, dainty rhythmic pirouettes—Hodges created a new kind of masculine sensuality in jazz. It perfectly suited his long-term employer, Duke Ellington, who remains jazz's grandmaster at projecting different kinds of masculinity through music, from the almost parodically effete to the unforgivingly tough.

Hodges was particularly good at slowing the second hand. He never hurried, and this enabled him to lodge small, poignant excitements in easy, flowing lines amid the long tones; they hardly sounded improvised, even when they were. Though it took Coltrane a long time to deal with ballads—he wasn't a commanding, original ballad player until his mid-thirties—he found that Hodges's super-relaxed, darkly erotic tempos worked for him, too, and could create another mood altogether, a balance between holiness and practicality, one that jazz hadn't known before.

"Smoke Gets in Your Eyes" was Coltrane's special solo number while he played with the Hodges band; perhaps it is the otherworldliness of that song, shaded by the otherworldliness of Hodges's own sound, that showed him the way to go, pointed him toward the darkness. And on "Castle Rock," his featured blues—a rock-and-roll song, basically—he was hard, masculine, cathartic; he had to expand his tone to honk out the full-throated, raspy, hollering low notes. His rhythm was coming together: he found a nice groove with the drummer in "Castle Rock," too.

Benny Golson, who had seen Coltrane in all his phases, noticed that his friend was on to something new. Golson remembers Coltrane polishing an obvious Dexter Gordon fascination in the period just before this. But now, on the road with Hodges, he developed "a style that had no name, but was a hopping-and-skipping kind of a thing." Coltrane was beginning to play original shapes and rhythms.

"I really enjoyed that job," Coltrane said later. "I liked every tune in the book. Nothing was superficial. It all had meaning, and it all swung. And the confidence with which Rabbit [Hodges] plays! I wish I could play with the confidence that he does."

Coltrane left Hodges in the fall of 1954, and worked around Philadelphia for the next year for short terms with a number of groups. One of them was led by Jimmy Smith, the organist, but Coltrane was beginning to want to hear his own playing, and Smith's loud organ sound—"those chords screaming at me," as he later described it—blotted him out.

There were also jobs with Miles Davis, who had hired Coltrane (when in Philadelphia), and Sonny Rollins (when in New York) on and off through the early 1950s. Both Davis and Rollins, until 1955, were using heroin.

By 1955, the year that Charlie Parker died, something new needed to happen in jazz. Heroin had been sitting on it, causing death and holding patterns. Much of the core of the new small-group jazz in New York revolved around Parker's standards of rhythm, harmony, and performance practice, his particular logic of asymmetrical eighth-note phrasing. So many saxophonists studied his solos note-for-note, and brought his speed, tone, and licks into their sound, that jazz had momentarily stalled. Finally, for his hard-shell acolytes, it was his solos that mattered above all, more than the ensembles, more than anything.

Parker himself, wrecked physically and emotionally by heroin and alcohol, a stout hill of bleeding ulcers, spent kidneys, and ravaged liver, could seem to symbolize the exhaustion of bebop. Davis, instinctive about playing against type, put a new group together.

Davis had kicked heroin for the first time, and talked about it to the press, in the winter of 1953–54. He had become suddenly fascinated by the trio led by the pianist Ahmad Jamal, who was writing neat, understated set pieces for a band that could macro-improvise—through form (meaning structure), not just through content (meaning solos). Davis played a mesmerizing, full-of-character performance at the Newport Jazz Festival in the summer of 1955, and it was widely considered a "comeback" concert. (In those days, many jazz musicians were legitimate social heroes, and the drugs they took were considered part of their world. Unlike now, jazz musicians were seen as mysterious creatures, subject to their own laws and language; they were taken on their outside-of-history terms—which is not to say they were understood any better. And certain well-situated concerts, with the right people in attendance, could, and did, acquire mythic status. Today, most great jazz concerts are too quickly contextualized and become instantly average.)

Columbia Records signed Davis for a $2,000-per-year advance against a 4 percent royalty rate, which finally amounted, by the terms of the contract, to a $4,000 advance. It was a lot of money for jazz.

Davis probably would have chosen Sonny Rollins as the group's tenor player, according to his own memoirs and consistent with Rollins's high reputation at the time. But Miles felt nervous about the fact that Sonny Rollins was undecided about staying in New York. Rollins was powerfully intelligent, and absorbent; he was still searching, and yet a bandleader already. Born in 1930, he grew up in Harlem—partly in Sugar Hill, a neighborhood full of the city's best jazz musicians. Developing amid the jazz culture he venerated, he had a leg up on Coltrane. At thirteen, Rollins had already met Coleman Hawkins: it was just a matter of waiting on his doorstep on 153rd Street with a pen and a glossy photograph. By the age of twenty, he was recording for Prestige.

Finally Davis settled on hiring Coltrane. Philly Joe Jones, Davis's drummer, knew Coltrane from their teenage years in Philadelphia, and recommended him to the boss. Coltrane wasn't a completely unknown quantity, however, having sat in with Davis's band at least once before, at the Audubon Ballroom in New York in 1950. (Rollins remembers that concert as similar to many of the larger shows the beboppers played: a show for dancers, with a small detachment of stationary watchers near the lip of the stage.) Coltrane also knew a good amount of the Davis band's tunes already. He may have been the dark-horse pick, but at least he wouldn't require remedial work.

"Now," Davis wrote in his autobiography, "we had Trane on sax, Philly Joe on drums, Red Garland on piano, Paul Chambers on bass, and myself on trumpet. And faster than I could have imagined, the music that we were playing together was just unbelievable. It was so bad that it used to send chills through me at night, and it did the same thing to the audiences, too. Man, the shit we were playing in a short time was scary, so scary that I used to pinch myself to see if I was really there."

# 3 prestige

From 1955 to 1957 Coltrane's life changed. Days before starting a busy series of club dates with the Miles Davis Quintet, he married another North Carolinian whose family had moved to Philadelphia. Naima Coltrane was a Muslim, born Juanita Grubbs. Coltrane, at this time, was still addicted to heroin, and in a more noticeably public manner than before. He had his work cut out for him.

Coltrane's first solos with the band were on a recording for Columbia, in October 1955. They came in Charlie Parker's "Ah-Leu-Cha," John Lewis and Dizzy Gillespie's "Two Bass Hit," Jackie McLean's "Little Melonae," and Miles and Bud Powell's "Budo." (These can be heard on Miles Davis's album *'Round About Midnight.*) They have been praised, but they don't quite produce the chills Davis suggested.

In "Ah-Leu-Cha," Coltrane gives a better-than-decent performance, with a crisp, Gene Ammons–like sense of swing and his still-retained Dexter Gordon qualities; it is an orderly solo, setting up lines through diminished scale patterns and then responding to them before moving on to the next line. In "Two Bass Hit," he quotes and requotes Dizzy Gillespie's opening line from the song's

1947 original version for the first 8 bars. (He was showing his studiousness, as he did back in Hawaii.) He also gets hung up on rhythmically confident but rather tedious eighth-note patterns. In "Budo," he upends the tune's bright tonality with stuttery meandering.

Miles Davis was under contract to the small Prestige label, as well as to Columbia, and the first Davis-quintet recording with Coltrane for Prestige happened in November. On "Stablemates," a piece by Coltrane's younger friend Benny Golson, Coltrane plays what is probably his first decent, coherent recorded solo. But there is still a drifting, noncommittal feeling to it, and that feeling seems to infect the rest of the group.

The Prestige sessions proceeded without rehearsal, and most of the tunes were not part of the band's regular bandstand book; Davis and Bob Weinstock, the head of the label, quickly scrounged from standards and film-song repertoire (like "Diane" and "Surrey with the Fringe on Top") for more material. Davis spoke proudly about wanting to preserve mistakes in his music as proof of humanity; still, it's doubtful that Coltrane's fluffed notes in "Just Squeeze Me" (from November 16, 1955) and "Diane" (from May 11, 1956) would have made the master take in a Columbia session.

At this point it may have been possible to see the hiring of Coltrane as a setback for Davis. If you compare two versions of Dave Brubeck's "In Your Own Sweet Way," both made by Miles's group for Prestige in 1956, one featuring Coltrane and the other featuring Rollins, and put yourself in Miles Davis's head, you still want Rollins. The Rollins performance is succinct, rhythmically tough, confident, pleasingly modern, coherent in its narrative. Coltrane's may suggest a broader vision of harmony, but it is shabbier in execution and seems, in a narrative sense, to stay in one place; the patterns are punched out without much grace.

The sessions recorded for Prestige Records by the Miles Davis

Quintet including Coltrane—especially the all-day sessions of May 11 and October 26, 1956, with the group recording enough tunes (all first takes) to fill out the remainder of Davis's four albums owed to the label—were marathons. Had they turned out to be mediocre (which many shorter and less-pressured Prestige sessions did turn out to be) then Miles Davis, trying to make his comeback, could have seriously stalled his own progress by having *four* mediocre albums on the market. Despite the flaws, which are easy to hear and rather benign, these are excellent sessions. They made great records. Not masterpieces; just great records.

By the spring of 1956, the group had grown into itself. Aside from Coltrane, who shared the front line, the rhythm section was killer-elite; these recordings were the pinnacle of a style later called hard bop.

The music from the sessions has aged well, especially the October 26 session, and, taken as a whole, represents an early concept album for Miles Davis—possibly even one to be considered alongside later ones like *Miles Ahead, Porgy and Bess,* and *Sketches of Spain.* (The eventual titles put on the records from these sessions reinforces their sense of belonging together. In order of catalogue number, they are *Cookin' with the Miles Davis Quintet, Relaxin' with . . . , Workin' with . . . ,* and *Steamin' with . . .*) Since Davis had a vested interest in getting through a lot of material quickly, he performed what were essentially in-studio concerts, starting a new tune quickly after the last. He gambled that he could create the casual atmosphere of a live set rather than the boxed-in, clinical feeling of a studio session, while executing his contract responsibilities at the same time; he wanted to think about a long sequence of music, rather than the normal studio convention of punching out one track at a time. He won his gamble.

Casual meant that on a few of the best Prestige tracks— "Surrey with the Fringe on Top" and "If I Were a Bell"— Coltrane rushes in from off-mike, clearly not yet ready for his turn. It meant that there were fewer fixed arrangements and framing devices for the sections of the tune. It meant that tunes could simmer down organically rather than end with a controlled pop.

The bassist Paul Chambers created the grooving armature of the group, with his strong pizzicato phrasing deep at the instrument's bottom end; some of his solo passages, bowed and plucked, demonstrate a rhythmic command that puts him in line with Jimmy Blanton and Oscar Pettiford. But basically he was an anchor. ("A bassist of Paul Chambers's stature is hard to find in New York," Coltrane said, "because he understands the junction: he hears the piano and the drums, and all his work consists in improvising in the service of these instruments. His melodic line is kind of a result of the melodic lines of the two other musicians.") The drummer, Philly Joe Jones, stamped out loud, sharp, self-contained fills, and played everything, from soloing to tipping behind a bass solo, with a strict, secure sense of time. The pianist, Red Garland, has become most famous for his neat block chords, but rhythmically he was earthy and elegant, a more temperate version of Horace Silver, illuminating a similar area behind the beat.

Garland found Coltrane's entrances and exits a step more modern than he was willing to go, yet finally trackable, manageable. "I've always been struck by the continuity of his ideas and by his unique way of handling changes," Garland told Nat Hentoff. "He can start a chord in the strangest place. The average cat might start on a seventh, but Coltrane can begin on a flatted fifth. And he has the damnedest way of breaking chords down, but I have no trouble accompanying him because of that sense of continuity I was talking about."

"Continuity" is a revealing word for Coltrane's cast of mind: just as he was connecting phrases that seemed harmonically distant, he was also making connections between bodies of knowledge that might seem unrelated.

David Amram, the French-horn player, met him for the first time in early 1956 outside the Café Bohemia on Barrow Street in Manhattan's West Village. Amram had just finished a set with

Charles Mingus's band, and Coltrane was sitting outside the club, eating a piece of pie.

He said, "How are you?" I said, "Everything's fine." And then he said to me, "What do you think about Einstein's theory of relativity?"

I don't think he was so interested in what I knew about it; I think he wanted to share what he knew about it. I drew a blank, and he went into this incredible discourse about the symmetry of the solar system, talking about black holes in space, and constellations, and the whole structure of the solar system, and how Einstein was able to reduce all of that complexity into something very simple.

Then he explained to me that he was trying to do something like that in music, something that came from natural sources, the traditions of the blues and jazz. But that there was a whole different way of looking at what was natural in music.

"Surrey with the Fringe on Top," from May 11, is probably Coltrane's first recorded solo with a coherent personality—the first to combine his provocative routes through chord progressions, odd-numbered rhythmic note groupings, alternation between slow and fast sequences, and so forth, in the service of a musical persona that you might want to spend time with rather than simply study. He has lost some of his experimental coldness. He has learned how to steer to an elegant resolution, rather than impatiently bailing out of an improvisation while it's still aloft. There are still shortcomings, however: his articulation still sounds pinched in the fast passages; one feels a general lack of comfort.

Still, by the October 26, 1956, session, from the first track—"If I Were a Bell"—Coltrane's phrasing, his strange, blobby note groupings, had developed their own comfortable dimensions, turning into clarion calls. He has become better at using space; only very recently he had become a ballad player. Perhaps hedging his bets, Davis had asked him to sit out the ballads of the May 11 session. But here he is heard on "'Round Midnight" and "You're My Everything."

Coltrane's transformations define the story of his work; they are the theme of this book. This one—from the math-struck, eighth-notes-to-the-moon of "Ah-Leu-Cha," exactly one year earlier, to "If I Were a Bell"—amounts to a major leap. As Eddie "Cleanhead" Vinson said, even in Coltrane's days of raw anonymity, he changed his style almost every six months.

The Miles Davis Quintet worked on the road nearly nonstop, and started acquiring a little myth around them.

Like almost all serious jazz groups at the time, they dressed up; Davis especially wanted his bandmates to look sharp. For his own part, post-comeback, he dressed Ivy League: he ordered neatly cut tweed suits tailored for him by the Andover Shop in Harvard Square. Coltrane was a little off. He looked too earnest. He was big-boned, as opposed to the birdlike Miles, and he wore dark suits with loose jackets and thin ties. He didn't look sharp; he projected a deep, spacey interiority, a disinterest in surfaces.

In the five and a half months between the first and second long sessions for Prestige, the Davis quintet played a two-week hit at the Café Bohemia in New York, two weeks at the Crown Propellor Lounge in Chicago, a week at Peacock Alley in St. Louis, a week at the Café Bohemia again, a week at Storyville in Boston, and two more weeks at the Bohemia. Though jazz initiates were aware that the group had become special, enough to stand alone, the band played typically multitiered bills in typical clubs. A nightclub ad in the *Chicago Defender* from Christmas week of 1955, for instance, lists "Miles Davis and his Combo" at Birdland, on the same bill with Marimack's Calypso Dance Team; "Kaloh, Exotic Dancer (First Time in Chicago)"; and "The Incredible Billy Gamble, M.C., Singing, Dancing, Comedy."

It isn't surprising that Miles, performing that much, would

have felt inclined to adopt the rhetoric of a live performance in the studio. It is also little wonder that Coltrane's playing would move forward so abruptly at this point: he was under not only a general pressure as the tenor player in one of the country's most popular new small bands (the Clifford Brown–Max Roach Quintet was contemporaneously celebrated and often compared to it), but also a specific performative kind of pressure. Miles habitually walked offstage to let him solo. Coltrane, alone and under the spotlight, had to strengthen his language.

Coltrane joked that Davis gave him little guidance. (Responding to a question about whether Miles had specifically told him to play as far out as he could, Coltrane responded, "Miles? Tell me something? That's a good one!") But Davis could be imposing about the level of quality he demanded from his band. When the saxophonist John Gilmore—whom Coltrane greatly admired— once sat in with the band, Coltrane left the stage at one point to let Gilmore solo alone with the rhythm section. Davis berated Coltrane for it. "Miles eventually cursed Trane out," Gilmore recalled. " 'Don't you ever let anyone come on my bandstand and look like they're superior to you.' "

Coltrane never, ever disparaged another musician on the record. (Perhaps he did among friends, but if so, they have drawn the veil of honor tightly around him.) The worst stories are mild. One night, after a gig at the Bohemian Caverns in Washington, D.C., long after Coltrane had left Miles, a young college-radio disc jockey on WAMU named Eric Kulberg told Coltrane how gracious he'd been to give him an on-air interview that evening at the club. "Miles Davis came through here, and he wouldn't do it," Kulberg added. "Well, Miles can be a bit of a prick," Coltrane replied.

Had John Coltrane and Sonny Rollins been inclined to team up and take their show on the road, they might have gotten a lot of work. But they worked out of divergent sensibilities; they were never going to be a two-tenor team, sharing a front line and alter-nating solos over a rhythm section.

Double-teaming was a perennial fallback recording and tour-ing concept, from the high years of bebop through the mid-sixties. It started out as collegial rivalries in the popular big bands: the first pair of tenors to score equal notoriety off a presumed rivalry was Dexter Gordon and Wardell Gray, who canonized their compe-tition on *The Chase*, a six-minute, double-sided record made for Dial in 1947. Later came Johnny Griffin and Eddie "Lockjaw" Davis, Sonny Stitt and Gene Ammons, Zoot Sims and Al Cohn. It was always two men who were reasonably equal in age and ability, and who were rooted in a similar style.

Coltrane and Rollins were more mulishly independent. They were close friends, mutually respectful. Coltrane named Rollins in a list of influences he provided to *Down Beat* in a musicians' survey around that time, and Rollins was the only personal friend on the list. Both Coltrane and Rollins saw Coleman Hawkins as a primary influence—not just the popular, romantic Hawkins of ballads, but Hawkins the harmonic daredevil, the saxophonist who thought in sets of moving chords. Both were developing reputations as thinkers and hard workers; they would go on to remake the model of the practicer in jazz, as well as the performer.

The two saxophonists had played together onstage with Miles from time to time—one of those times was at the Audubon Ball-room in 1950, the "dance job" when Coltrane first shared a stage with Davis—but they only met in the studio once, on May 24, 1956, for a single track. "Tenor Madness" was the tune. It hap-pened simply because Rollins was using Miles Davis's rhythm sec-tion for what would be his next record. Coltrane, in those days, was hanging out a lot with Paul Chambers and Philly Joe Jones, and he came along for their ride to Rudy Van Gelder's studio in Hacken-sack, New Jersey. Typical for a Prestige session, their impromptu duet was simply a song somebody remembered at the date: "Royal Roost," originally recorded by Kenny Clarke in 1946. Composer credit went to Sonny Rollins.

The meat of the song—a 12-bar blues—is the fifteen choruses of improvisation at the beginning, divided into seven for
Coltrane and then eight for Rollins. Coltrane's sequence shows a
logic growing more continuous, and a greater number of his own
licks, including his upward octave glissandi and small, bunched
arpeggios repeated in downward stepwise motion. One of the crucial steps in this early-stage development of Coltrane's was his
learning how to evenly alternate fast passages and long tones; it
gave him the multilingual feeling he was after, as if two voices
were coming through the horn at once. But too much of one or too
much of the other didn't work; the trick lay in artfully switching
back and forth.

Rollins, when his turn arrives, sounds more self-assured. His
tone is calmer, broader, deeper than Coltrane's acrid grapeshot
bursts and long tones; he uses an eighth-note language instead of
Coltrane's needling sixteenths, and swings them with control after
the manner of Louis Armstrong, pausing and giving weight to individual notes.

For its uniqueness, "Tenor Madness" has been too highly rated.
It isn't a particularly special recording. It shows the language of
each player in a less-than-inspired context.

Coltrane told Rollins that he wanted to record with him again,
but it didn't happen; they both had enough drawing power and
artistic ambition to become bandleaders. Necessity, which generally decides one's fate in popular music, didn't will it. But that still
doesn't completely explain why they stayed away from the obvious
temptation to package the rivalry between them (even if that rivalry existed only in the public imagination) and take it on the
road.

Solitude does. Rollins and Coltrane had both arrived in the
early 1950s, when isolation and solitude had begun to assume a significant place again in American art, really for the first time since
the Industrial Age had started, a century before. Jazz people, in reality, spent a great deal of time together, as a subculture; they were
cabalistic, setting themselves apart through shared wit and habits

and attitudes toward race relations and prideful indifference to consensus. Rollins and Coltrane were part of this subculture, but they each had solitary interests. They were practicers, readers, scholarly minded.

In the new mentality, jazz was no longer a youth-culture movement, not a naïve horde activity. Big bands had already begun to seem antiquated, and small ensembles had taken their place. Charlie Parker and the myth of the black intellectual antihero—which only took hold in earnest after Parker's short, confusing life ended—were largely responsible for this change. Rollins and Coltrane took their first serious steps as bandleaders the year that Parker died; still young enough to learn and change, they separately colonized the post-Parker universe.

"Sonny Rollins, you heard him recently?" Coltrane asked August Blume in 1958. "Yeah, like some guys, you know, you call *great*, man. Sonny, he's one . . . he's just reached that great status, man."


There exists a collection of John Coltrane's work for Prestige from 1956 to 1958, as a sideman and a leader, called *John Coltrane: The Prestige Recordings*. When it first appeared in 1990, it took up sixteen discs, and it is proof that even some great artists must endure their own tedium, or perhaps that a great artist must realize all by himself what he must do to break out of all the rigmarole, the formalities, the business-as-usual in any given field at any given time.

Prestige made a lot of records that were barely more than documentaries, placeholders, calling cards made cheaply.

Bob Weinstock used looser quality-control standards than other label heads, and he stockpiled. He was concerned with getting material in the can, so that he could make more than one record out of each session. He went in big for easy ideas, and consequently celebrated the supergroup and the "blowing session," records with hastily assembled heads or arrangements and long spaces for the musicians to jam. (He believed in jam-session recordings: on Fridays throughout the mid-fifties, he would round up groups of musicians and send them off to Rudy Van Gelder's studio in Hackensack, appointing Mal Waldron to write simple charts for the band.) The Prestige catalogue had strokes of luck, good timing, and genius—Sonny Rollins's *Saxophone Colossus*, Eric Dolphy's *Live at the Five Spot*, Lucky Thompson's *Lucky Strikes*—as well as a lot of records subtitled "Part One" and "Part Two," like yesterday's lunch scraps reheated for another meal. If a musician wanted to try out new things, Prestige sessions were a good place to do it.

It was on Prestige, for example, that Coltrane became known as a ballad player. Coltrane recorded his first ballad solo against a slow background, without the rhythm section switching to double-timing, in "How Deep Is the Ocean?" for a four-tenor record on Prestige called *Tenor Conclave*, with Zoot Sims, Al Cohn, and Hank Mobley. The solo begins prettily, leading in with sweeping, lingering statements, but by his second chorus he seems to run out of the proper compassionate spirit. The improvisation reverts to his own tics, the quick-note flurries and phrases chopped off at odd-counted junctures, and it sits uneasily with the mood of the tune. (Hank Mobley, whose solo directly followed Coltrane's, demonstrates a better grasp of the situation.)

He made another ballad solo on Tadd Dameron's *Mating Call* album in late November 1956. What he played on the tune "Soul-trane," his own composition, was smoother and more ballad-conscious than his "How Deep Is the Ocean?" performance, but more monochromatic, the sort of pristine candlelight music that Johnny Hodges could redeem but Coltrane couldn't.

Prestige began using Coltrane more often as a result of his new recognition from touring with the Davis quintet, and all the reviews he got, both positive and negative. The critic Bill Coss wrote in *Metronome* magazine about the first Miles quintet record on Prestige: "There is too much echo on the soloists, the ensembles are generally bad; the tenor on the Rollins-Stitt kick is even more out of tune." In *Down Beat* a year later, a critic wrote of the Davis quintet's *Relaxin'* LP that "there is a hesitancy and lack of melodic content in Coltrane's playing at times here that hampers his effectiveness for me and lowers the rating of the LP." (He gave it four stars out of five.) "This is particularly true on the first two tracks, on which his solos seem to be rather aimless and somewhat strident."

He appeared on Prestige records led by Elmo Hope, Tommy Flanagan, and, on a leaderless date called *Interplay for Two Tenors and Two Trumpets*, by the pianist Mal Waldron. He cut an excellent version of Jimmy Heath's "C.T.A." for an Arthur Taylor album, and recorded a number of strange, evocative pieces in a front line with two baritone saxophonists on an album called *Dakar*.

Back to the Prestige sessions. In May 1957, with the tenor saxophonist Paul Quinichette, Coltrane made *Cattin' with Coltrane and Quinichette*, a wan little record with forced-march rhythm-section accompaniment; at its most expansive moments, which are Coltrane's solos in "Anatomy" and "Vodka," Coltrane nearly sounds as if he's practicing alone, squeezing diminished-scale patterns to the limit of their usefulness. Mal Waldron, who wrote the tunes for the session and acted as pro forma musical director, plays as if he's got mittens on, grinding short gray phrases around middle C into the keyboard. (Waldron had a heroin addiction at the time, but he was always a musician with strange emotional absence. An overdose in 1963 erased his memory for playing the piano; once it was restored, three years later, he retained more or less the same style.)

In September 1956, Davis's bassist, Paul Chambers, included Coltrane as part of his own quintet for what would be *Whims of Chambers*, a record for Blue Note. It would include two Coltrane originals, "Nita" and "Just for the Love," the first recorded tunes under Coltrane's own authorship. They are self-consciously progressive in design, without shattering the earthy swing feeling produced by the rhythm section of Horace Silver, Chambers, and Philly Joe Jones.

"Nita" is a 30-bar tune that uses ii–V–I chord cycles—a favored and much-used chord progression in jazz, much used in part because it can establish a new key so quickly. In "Nita," those cycles followed each other a third apart, and this is the beginning of Coltrane's using a kind of harmonic motion based on third-related chord movement that would find its master's thesis in "Giant Steps," a few years later. "Just for the Love," a curious blues in F, is a bebop line that sounds as if it begins in the middle of a thought. The mood of the piece remains abrupt to the end.

Finally Prestige put Coltrane under contract to make his own albums, with some of his own compositions, which had seemed so intriguing in their first exposure on the Paul Chambers record. The contract, dated April 9, 1957, was for peanuts: $300 per album, and three albums per year.

While critics in 1957 regarded him as the number two new tenor player behind Sonny Rollins (in the "New Star" category of *Down Beat*'s summer critics' poll), Coltrane still didn't have an album under his own name. Rollins, meanwhile, had more than ten.

It had been a period of general change and improvement for Coltrane. In April he was fired by Miles Davis, for generally unprofessional behavior—coming to gigs high, drinking in between sets, looking ragged. If we are to believe Miles Davis's autobiography, Coltrane picked his nose and ate his own snot onstage. Sonny Rollins took his place as a part-time replacement starting in June. It is dangerous to make presumptions about an artist's psychological state in relation to his art. But with Coltrane it makes a little more sense: his periods of the greatest clarity and ambition came when he was not only off drugs and alcohol but emotionally focused. An article came out a little while later in a Cleveland newspaper quoting Coltrane referring to his own condition, before the spring of 1957, as "depression."

In May, back home in Philadelphia and aided by his family and friends, he quit heroin and, for the most part, alcohol. (He later made reference to drinking late-night scotches with Thelonious Monk that summer—though possibly it was only Monk and his friend Baroness Nica de Koenigswarter on the scotch.) Coltrane detoxed the cowboy way, shutting himself up at home and going cold turkey.

On the last day of May, in New York City, he made a respectable album for Prestige, to be titled *Coltrane*, his first record as bandleader. From the first track, "Straight Street," the attitude is clear: Coltrane was self-improving. He wasn't going to skunk his chances. He surveys and shuffles through his runs, his technical tics in nearly every solo on the album; but there is a greater variety of them, and he plays them with more gusto and precision. For half the album he chose the deep hue of Sahib Shihab's baritone saxophone to harmonize with him; in general, he made the record distinct, his own.

"Straight Street," a reference to sobriety, contained curiously structured writing (an AABA piece with 12 bars to each section instead of the normal 8) and idiosyncratic chord changes. Bronislaw Kaper's theme from "While My Lady Sleeps" became a favorite tune of Coltrane's: though he was generally not a quoter, he would quote from it while improvising in other pieces. It shared a harmonic atmosphere with one of Kaper's other famous standards, "On Green Dolphin Street," which also became a Coltrane favorite, and its wide intervals might have been the germ of Coltrane's own later exotic, hymnal ballads, like "Dear Lord" and "Lonnie's Lament."

In the early summer of 1957, Coltrane was invited by Thelonious Monk to join his quartet. The job was to play through the summer at the Five Spot, on the Bowery just south of Astor Place in New York's East Village, at the north end of what was thought of as Manhattan's ultimate skid row. The summer gig extended through the end of the year.

It is tempting to try to figure out exactly, down to the atom—in terms of harmony and rhythm and melody—what John Coltrane got from Thelonious Monk, since that year has often been described as Coltrane's turning point.

In interviews, Coltrane talked around the answer. "Working with Monk brought me close to a musical architect of the highest order," he said in 1960. "I felt I learned from him in every way—through the senses, theoretically, technically . . . I would talk to Monk about musical problems, and he would sit at the piano and show me the answers just by playing them. I could watch him play and find out the things I wanted to know. Also, I could see a lot of things that I didn't know about at all."

The answer lies here, in a way: since "the things he wanted to know" included "things he didn't know about at all," perhaps Coltrane wasn't so much after specific phrases and changes to orient himself around, but much larger areas of music-making that he hadn't considered. It became a kind of unlocking-the-giant-within seminar. And Monk gave him lots of his own time; they spent entire days together that summer.

Monk held up a better mirror to Coltrane than anyone else did. Monk's own musical style was enormous, imposing, but it wasn't his style that changed Coltrane; it was the total suggestion of possibility within Monk's composing, arranging, and improvising that opened Coltrane's eyes to what he already *could* play. "Monk was just another iron in the fire for John," Benny Golson has insisted. "John already had his sense of direction."

The A sections in the 32-bar Monk songs of this period are rather unusual; the harmonic motion of the bridges (the B sections) are much more so. Sometimes it is a matter of chord voicings: without completely distorting functional harmony, the left-hand chords turn harmony relationships upside down, boxing the saxophonist who plays with him into the strict dimensions of the composer. "I always had to be alert with Monk," Coltrane said, "because if you didn't keep aware all the time of what was going on, you'd suddenly feel as if you'd stepped into an empty elevator shaft."

After this winding-up, Monk would let Coltrane go, sometimes leaving the stage and letting the band play for twenty minutes at a time. Even more than what Miles had done, this was coaching, not teaching, instruction by hypothesis: *suppose you could be the kind of player that fulfilled such demands.* Either because of this greater responsibility, or for some other reason, Coltrane changed reeds during the period of playing with Monk. Having gotten used to a very hard reed, he started using softer ones. As a result, a greater flexibility opened up within his playing. And his new comfort with the music was palpable.

After he had shaken loose of his early heroes—Lester Young, Charlie Parker, Dexter Gordon—Coltrane started to learn in a more indirect sense, rather than simply by storing up phrases in his bank. The same goes for his time with Miles Davis. Coltrane told Valerie Wilmer that Miles gave him "an appreciation for simplicity," and that before joining his band he used to dream of playing tenor saxophone the way Miles played trumpet. "But when I joined him," he explained, "I realized I could never play like that, and I think that's what made me go the opposite way"—toward mosaics of sixteenth notes, toward stacking chords on top of chords.

By the same reasoning, clearly it wasn't only Monk's individual soloistic style itself that reshaped Coltrane that summer. It was Monk's absences: the times he got up from the piano and walked away from it, or moved in a circle to hear the music from all angles, leaving Coltrane alone for fifteen or twenty minutes to improvise, with only the bassist Wilbur Ware to provide some kind of harmonic companionship. A piano—or a guitar, or a vibraphone, or any chordal instrument—sets up a framework for a monophonic, one-note-at-a-time instrument like the saxophone; the saxophonist must always operate within the imposed logic of the piano chords. Take the piano away, and the saxophonist is freer to create his own harmonies.

Ware, too, was looser than any bass player he had experienced before. "A bass player like Wilbur Ware, he's so inventive, man,"

Coltrane told August Blume, in June 1958. "Like, he doesn't always play the dominant note. He . . . plays the *other way* sometimes. He plays things that are kind of—they're *foreign*. Well, if you didn't know the song, you wouldn't be able to find it, because he's superimposing things, he's playing around and under or over or something . . . Sometimes he would play—he would be playing altered changes, and I would be playing altered changes. And he would be laying some other kind of altered changes from the type I'd be playing. And neither one of us playing the changes of the tune until we reach a certain spot and then we—if we get there together, we're lucky . . ."

As for Monk, Coltrane told Blume about his conviction in playing things that didn't sound conventionally correct. "He's always doing something back there that sounds *so* mysterious," Coltrane said. "And it's not mysterious at all, when you know what he's doing. Just those little things, just like simple truths. Like he just—he might take a chord, a major chord, a *minor* chord, and leave the third out. Well, he says, 'This is a *minor* chord, man!' [I'd] say, 'You don't have the minor third in there, so you don't know what it is.' He says, 'How do you know it's a minor chord? Well, that's what it is, a minor chord with the third out!' And when he plays the thing, man, it will just be in the right place and voiced the right way to have that minor feel."

Monk was both more specific with answers to Coltrane in questions about music and less direct in his style of bandleading. The Monk quartet with Coltrane recorded three songs together, later released on *Thelonious Monk with John Coltrane*. The record hinted at what was going on, even if it didn't live up to the highs going on nightly at the Five Spot.

On that record, however, Monk's "Trinkle Tinkle" contains the general idea. It's one of Monk's gnatlike pieces ("Four in One" would be another) governed by a humorously, almost absurdly, fast and fragmented theme. Coltrane lets the character of the theme shape his solo, which appears in great twisted skirls of notes, with all the effort apparent, including squeaking high notes and gruff low honks. Monk contributes quite a bit of accompaniment in Coltrane's first chorus, a total of four chords in the second, and none at all in the third.

Coltrane was twenty-nine—still young—and fresh with a great new group; the heat of his ambition can be heard here. (As weird as "Trinkle Tinkle" may seem, it is also, after the theme, in straight, standard 32-bar AABA song form; when Charlie Rouse soloed through it during Monk's concerts in the 1960s, he created a much smoother, more singing music.)

Very little else has emerged from Coltrane's six-month period with Monk in 1957. Nearly half a century later, however, in 2005, fifty-five minutes of live music materialized at the Library of Congress. It had been recorded by Voice of America at Carnegie Hall, as part of a long benefit concert that also included Ray Charles, Billie Holiday, Sonny Rollins, and Zoot Sims's quartet with Chet Baker. Here, on November 29, 1957, Coltrane sounds pressurized, but up to the job: he strung together rows of his original licks, all of them making sense within Monk's harmonic language. Mostly, he is executing beautifully, leagues beyond the anxious, fractured feeling of his long solos from only a few months before (such as, for example, "Bass Blues," recorded on August 23 and released on the Prestige record *Traneing In*). Only sporadically, as in his ten blues choruses during "Blue Monk," does he let his guard down, going back to what one of his reviewers from the previous year described as "hesitations," but which deserves here to be described as a personal voice.

On the Carnegie recording the band is relaxed, limber, magnetic; the tempos are more wakeful. Compare the tune "Nutty" from the May studio version, on *Thelonious Monk with John Coltrane*, with this stage version, and you hear it quickly. Coltrane has become agile, finding a flexible way of running his original patterns—patterns based on whole tones, on dominant sevenths, on diminished scales. Monk balances an inscrutable serenity against driving, almost violent rhythmic figures. And everything coming from Shadow Wilson, the drummer, is to be savored: he guards and upholds the groove, while building small, richly detailed accents around it. It is a magic record, mellifluous in its provocations.

The album *Thelonious Monk with John Coltrane* didn't appear until late 1961. It contains only five pieces with the two musicians together; the three pieces with the quartet were recorded on the down-low because of contractual complications. (It may have been personal animus, too: Orrin Keepnews, who ran Riverside, the label that Monk recorded for, has said that Monk didn't want to work again with Prestige's director, Bob Weinstock, as he had before; Coltrane was recording with Weinstock at Prestige, and the only way the labels would agree to lend one musician to the other was if they made recordings for both labels, with the Prestige album being marketed as a Coltrane record and the Riverside album being marketed as a Monk record. In any case, no records were officially issued at the time.)

Had the group been able to make a proper record—or had the Carnegie Hall concert been released then—it might have proved a peak achievement for both musicians. But it seems fair to assume that it wouldn't have appreciably altered the course of public opinion about either musician.

Coltrane was called in to the studio repeatedly through the summer: suddenly, he was the desired tenor player.

The Blue Note label had passed on signing him the year before, when he came by its office to ask for some Sidney Bechet records. But this summer he had been given a small advance, and he went in to make a record for Blue Note, while he was hot. With rehearsal time paid for by the company, as was its custom, the preparation in the music is obvious. Coltrane organized five tunes, including four of his own, making it the most forthright display of his own music up to that point.

For *Blue Train*, the Blue Note record, he was back with his old friends Paul Chambers and Philly Joe Jones in a band of his choosing, and the first track, "Blue Train," sounds like an extension of Coltrane's playing mood from "Trinkle Tinkle" a few months before. It is agitated, driving, splintered music, reaching to the very end of his lung capacity. It was also a blues, and for a player with progressive tendencies, Coltrane had begun to establish himself as a specialist in the blues—possibly, at that time, the most inventive blues player in jazz. "Moment's Notice" and "Lazy Bird" are the first of Coltrane's études—short and perfect pieces with quickly moving chords connected in unusual relationships.

With the Jerome Kern–Johnny Mercer song "I'm Old-Fashioned," Coltrane showed that he was also growing rapidly as a ballad player. Consider where he had come from: only a year before, he had made considerable strides, for example in his halting version of "'Round Midnight," with Miles Davis for Columbia. By now he was making his spooky, thick-textured, long notes in the middle register, with their minimal vibrato—the iconic center of what was to be Coltrane's sound.

# 4 theory-mad

At the end of Coltrane's gig with Monk, Miles Davis immediately rehired him. The last day at the Five Spot was December 26, 1957; the first day back with Miles was January 2, 1958. He was a different musician. He had found a guide-rope to lead him forth from his own research and practice, toward his own voice. Here is what he said to various people about what had happened to his playing since the last tenure with Davis:

I was trying for a sweeping sound.

I thought in groups of notes, not one note at a time.

I was beginning to apply the three-on-one chord approach, and at the time the tendency was to play the entire scale of each chord. Therefore, they were usually played fast and sometimes sounded like glisses. I found there were a certain number of chord progressions to play in a given time, and sometimes what I played didn't work out in eighth notes, sixteenth notes, or triplets. I had to put the notes in uneven groups like five and sevens in order to get them all in.

I got interested in [the harp] around 1958, when I was interested in playing arpeggios instead of straight lines.

. . . due to the direct and free-flowing lines in [Davis's new 1958 music], I found it easy to apply the harmonic ideas that I had. I could stack up chords—say, on a C7, I sometimes superimposed an E♭7, up to an F♯7, down to an F. That way I could play three chords on one. But on the other hand, if I wanted to, I could play melodically. Miles' music gave me plenty of freedom.

In February, Coltrane showed up at Columbia's Thirtieth Street studio—a converted Armenian church near Third Avenue on the East Side—to begin work on Miles Davis's new album, as part of what had become the Miles Davis Sextet. The sixth member was Julian "Cannonball" Adderley, the alto saxophonist. Adderley was a consummate blues player with a honey-dripping sound and an eighth-note rhythmic attack that had a reassuring and almost comic regularity. He wasn't bunching notes together in odd numbers the way Coltrane was, but he and Coltrane rubbed off on each other. Overgrown, note-stuffed patches began to show up in Adderley's sensible style, ranging over the full expanse of the horn. They had in common a slightly sharp tone; this is why some new listeners to jazz frequently get confused, hearing Coltrane as Adderley and vice versa.

"Straight, No Chaser," from the February 4 Columbia session—it would end up on the LP *Milestones*—is one of the great Coltrane moments. He enters after a solo by Adderley and then a deftly cute improvisation by Davis, picking up the last note of Davis's solo; he assumes the blues form of the well-known Monk tune and then explodes it, getting beyond the form.

At first he announces himself, getting comfortable with some long tones in his first chorus. But most of the second and third are expressed in sixteenth notes, skidding through extensions of chords and implying several chords simultaneously; it's like dirty motocross. The critic Ira Gitler, right around this time, in the liner notes to Coltrane's 1958 *Soultrane* LP on Prestige, had called this kind of playing "sheets of sound." (Coltrane's practicing from harp books—probably Carlos Salzedo's *Modern Study of the Harp*—led him toward extravagant and rapid arpeggios and scale patterns.) When Red Garland follows with his solo, concluding with a block-chord rendering of part of a Miles Davis improvisation from his 1945 recording with Charlie Parker of "Now's the Time," it is a model of crisp swing and precision within traditional tonality. One feels a weird moment of disjunction, an uncomfortable juxtaposition.

This is the beginning of Coltrane's trance music, his practice of ignoring the limits of conventional harmony, and the beginning of what would turn so many listeners almost violently against him.

There is a kind of self-indulgence in this Coltrane solo, but with a breadth and level of facility that didn't preclude soul. (A straight-up rhythm-and-blues holler starts off his fourth chorus.) He had declared war on the common definition of coherence. The abundant performance tapes from this period, passed among collectors, consistently show that Coltrane was the only one in the group running up against standard tonality. But it was a role that the group came to accommodate. When Wynton Kelly joined the band in early 1959, he would support these tendencies, accompanying with chords appropriate to Coltrane's tonality-stretching, but clashing against Chambers's walking bass.

In his solos on "Dial Africa" and "Gold Coast," recorded with the trumpeter Wilbur Harden later that year, again Coltrane plays lavishly around and outside simple changes. As a matter of lesser interest, but supplying more evidence of his systematic growth, the pattern he plays at the beginning of his second chorus of "Dial Africa" foretells what he will play eight months later, in the beginning of his second chorus on "So What," from *Kind of Blue*.

Speaking of *Kind of Blue*, *Milestones* contained another clue to

Miles's next step, and one of Coltrane's later steps. It was in his tune "Milestones," which had very little harmonic motion.

Remember that Miles and Coltrane had come up as beboppers, who as a breed prided themselves on racing through fast and difficult chord changes. But Miles, always ready to shift into the open lane, had worked on transcending the stereotype. He had found ways to soften the sharp turns of bebop's chordal movement by playing fewer notes and making each one more deluxe, more important. If you were a gender-theory musicologist, you might call this a feminine approach. If you were any other kind, you might call it a popular approach. Sweetness is usually popular; severity is usually not. In any case, the new theory expressed in "Milestones," modal writing, was a kind of opposite of bebop.

Miles Davis had borrowed a piece of music theory to deepen his own proclivities toward simplicity and lyricism. The theory was authored by George Russell, a jazz drummer, composer, and arranger, and it appeared in his book *The Lydian Chromatic Concept of Tonal Organization*. Russell, the son of railroad workers, grew up in Cincinnati. After some apprentice work with Benny Carter, he early on took himself out of the running as a band musician. He wrote "Cubana Be/Cubana Bop" for Dizzy Gillespie's big band in 1947, and went on to write the book in the early 1950s, while laid up for sixteen months with tuberculosis. Even before the book appeared, Russell had already talked with Miles about modes—in the late 1940s, by his own account.

The book was suggestive, not prescriptive. Russell analyzed the relationships between chords and scales, taking into account major scales, bebop scales, the music of the French Impressionist composers, and ancient church modes. Observing that the Ionian mode in the key of C had become the preeminent scale for Western music five hundred years ago, he suggested that perhaps the Lydian mode might be more useful. It would encompass more chords, and offer jazz musicians scale choices that they might not have considered before. And soloing within a mode for longer stretches of time, they wouldn't have to keep jumping through chord changes and reorienting themselves harmonically; they could go further in one direction, develop their ideas at greater length.

As Miles Davis put it in a 1958 interview with Nat Hentoff that appeared in *The Jazz Review*:

> When you go this way, you can go on forever. You don't have to worry about changes and you can do more with the line. It becomes a challenge to see how melodically inventive you can be. When you're based on chords, you know at the end of 32 bars that the chords have run out and there's nothing to do but repeat what you've just done—with variations.

He went on: "I think a movement in jazz is beginning away from the conventional string of chords. There will be fewer chords but infinite possibilities as to what to do with them. Classical composers—some of them—have been writing this way for years, but jazz musicians seldom have."

"Milestones," a brooding song with a bright medium tempo, has an AABBA structure—an expanded, 40-bar version of the standard 32-bar cycle of American popular song. It also sounds different, more ancient: it is modal. While Red Garland outlined three chords in the A section, they were all in the key of F major, outlining part of an F-major scale. When he switched to the B section, the three chords outlined the C-major scale.

Miles, knowing about modes, had written a piece which would encourage the horn improvisers to swing between two modes for the whole piece: G Dorian (stretching the F-major tonality a bit) and A Aeolian (stretching the C-major tonality a bit). Not having to move so quickly through new chords helped the players improvise more calmly, and, one hoped, more soulfully. And Paul Chambers had a brilliant idea to accompany the modes. In the B section of "Milestones," instead of playing the usual walking-bass patterns, he played a gestural, plucking phrase between two notes, leaving silence during the "one," and sounding African, like a thumb piano. He got it perfectly: the figure confirms the tune's ancient feeling.

Yet Coltrane was still besotted with chord changes; he wasn't done studying the science of harmony. A few days after making *Jazz at the Plaza*, Coltrane played on a George Russell recording date, for music that would end up on the album *New York, New York*. He ran through the complicated chord sequence on Russell's "Manhattan"—according to Russell, he got up just before recording began and took a forty-five-minute time-out on the studio clock to study the harmony, while fourteen top-level musicians waited in irritation—and he blew through the solo brilliantly, "making substitutions on my substitutions," Russell said. In other words, he stuffed in all sorts of way stations on the route back to the beginning of each chord cycle.

He was in a new kind of mixed company here, with musicians like Doc Severinsen, Ernie Royal, Milt Hinton, and Hal McKusick—studio professionals, rather than his own gang of friends. And despite all the substitutions, he created a more measured solo. He may have put more chords into the moving harmony, but he didn't play as many notes as he was used to playing. This was a sign of growth; whenever Coltrane either started playing more notes or fewer, something was happening inside him.

That Coltrane solo on "Straight, No Chaser," the note-splattering one, the one that seems to lift itself up by its own incantations: this was the extremism listeners were beginning to associate with Coltrane. It was just the sort of thing to make casual listeners feel that jazz had become hopelessly elitist, a murky, difficult caterwaul. Coltrane's contributions to the live recordings *Miles Davis at Newport 1958* and *Jazz at the Plaza*, recorded in mid- and late summer of that year, have a deadening effect: solo after solo, he's just too fast, registering too many notes, too much information. He's playing everything he knows.

In a review of the Newport concert published in *Down Beat*, the writer Don Gold called this playing "angry"; and to anyone who might have been taken aback by a black man talking at length and with force, then, yes, such music could have been the equivalent of angry speech.

Beginning in the late fifties, Coltrane opened himself wide to larger issues of music, philosophy, and language. His friend Zita Carno remembers that at home Coltrane was listening hard to contemporary symphonic music: Ravel's *Daphnis and Chloe*, Stravinsky's *Rite of Spring* and *Dumbarton Oaks Concerto*, Debussy's *La Mer*, and a lot of Paul Hindemith.

In the late summer of 1959, he invited Wayne Shorter to visit him and his wife at their apartment on West 103rd Street in Manhattan. Coltrane was thirty-two, and the younger Shorter (he was twenty-five), who had just joined Art Blakey's Jazz Messengers, looked up to Coltrane as an "adult," someone who had organized his sound and style and was living a responsible life.

Coltrane had already told a journalist—Russ Wilson of *The Oakland Tribune*—that he intended to leave Miles. That summer he told Shorter that striking out on his own was becoming increasingly necessary. "I have to leave Miles," he said. "What I'm playing with him sounds wrong."

Coltrane asked Shorter if he'd ever heard about *om*. (Thinking of the smell of the tomato sauce Naima was cooking in the kitchen, Shorter thereafter equated "om" with "home.") Later, Coltrane and Shorter sat together near the piano, with their saxophones out of their cases. Coltrane laid his whole forearm on the keyboard: *dronggg*. "See how many of those notes you can grab," he said to Shorter. Shorter played as fast as he could, trying to match the tones hanging in the air. Coltrane asked Shorter to do the same for him. Later, they talked about improvising and language, and how it might be ideal to start a sentence in the middle, then travel backward and forward, toward both the subject and the predicate, simultaneously.

In the spring of 1959 had come the sessions for Miles Davis's *Kind of Blue*—which would prove the most popular jazz record since World War II, a lyrical record that sits almost formally isolated in jazz history, one more turning point for Coltrane in a five-year stretch that was already full of turning points.

It is sweet and expressive music, but it lays out its formal intentions quite plainly. "The way Miles used these modes on *Kind of Blue*," George Russell said, "he was inspired by the Lydian concept. He just said, 'Here are five modes, play on them as long as you want to.' " (It is important to note that this freedom is only truly exercised on one track in the album, "Flamenco Sketches"; all the rest have a more predetermined form.) "That meant that the musician didn't have to meet any kind of chord deadlines, because those modes are chords, too. They're chord modes. 'Instead of there being two beats on every chord,' Miles said, 'play on this chord as long as the soloist plays.' "

The strange new wrinkle on *Kind of Blue* as a whole is that it doesn't contain any of the funk and the rapid swing that "Milestones" did. With "So What" as its first chapter—8-bar chunks of one scale at a time, swinging between D Dorian and E-flat Dorian—the record is a quiescent thing, moving along lightly. It is more chamberish, more folkish, or even European, than before. In his fascinating, maddening, posturing autobiography, Davis revealed two extramusical inspirations for the feel of *Kind of Blue*: one from childhood in Arkansas, of walking home from church with a cousin; and one from not long before the recording, of watching the Ballet Africaine in New York, where a thumb piano had accompanied the dancers.

The drummer Jimmy Cobb—on board since May 1958—was part of the reason for this new somnolence on *Kind of Blue*. Davis seemed to prefer his drummers to play up on the beat rather than settling back, but Cobb was even stricter: he played an almost scientifically steady beat with a cushioned groove. It didn't get in the way, nor did it sound like Philly Joe Jones's cracking snare hits that had helped shape the sound of Miles's band. Bill Evans, the new pianist, also had a lot to do with the feeling of the music. He knew how to play in chary whispers, voicing his left-hand chords without the root notes, or gently sounding a right-hand chord with the upper notes first.

One month after recording it for *Kind of Blue*, the Miles quintet recorded "So What" again, during a television broadcast on *The Robert Herridge Theater Show*, for CBS. It showed how unusual a recording session *Kind of Blue* had been, how intent Miles had been on making a subdued recording. This latter "So What," with Wynton Kelly instead of Evans, and without Adderley, has a brighter tempo; it swings harder, and it is more indicative of what Miles and Coltrane were playing in regular situations. Miles's solo stays in the pocket; it amounts to one of the most businesslike, swinging, mid-tempo solos he ever recorded. Coltrane's solo is less melodic, more vertical and obsessive—one of his great ones, exercising nearly all his idées fixes, from long tones to repeated clumps of scale notes and simple triads that then extend into longer arpeggiated nuggets, turned this way and that, played up and down and over.

In 1959 Coltrane started moving toward independence from Davis. It wasn't easy, even when Miles helped him do it. Because he valued Coltrane dearly, Miles pointed him in the direction of escape, and in the process drew him closer. Davis was dismayed by Coltrane's public avowal of his need to leave the band. Yet he must have facilitated the process, because during that year, Harold Lovett, Miles's manager, became Coltrane's manager, too, securing a recording contract for him with Atlantic Records. And Jack Whittemore, Miles's agent, started to find bookings for Coltrane's band when the Miles Davis group was off the road.

Coltrane's first session with Atlantic was on April Fools' Day 1959, one month after the session that produced the bulk of *Kind of Blue*. Among the tunes he recorded was a preliminary take of "Giant Steps." The day after that would bring the television recording of "So What," with the Davis group, on *The Robert Herridge Theater Show.*

"Giant Steps" and "So What"—two of the most famous and important songs in jazz; a psychic hemisphere apart. Coltrane, involved in both, must have gained some confidence from the realization that his feet were planted in shifting tides.

"So What," composed by Miles Davis, is an experiment. It uses familiar dimensions to contain the floating somnolence of modal playing. It is in the 32-bar AABA form, the basic structure of American popular song. Each part of the AABA is a single scale (or chord, if you like), each lasting 8 bars. It runs at easy medium tempo, and the implications of the mode mean that the player has more room to stretch without going outside of tonal harmony. He isn't being pushed along by the chord changes.

"Giant Steps," composed by John Coltrane, is another experiment. At a much higher-cranked tempo than that of "So What," it calls for a new chord on every other beat; the descending chord sequences are related by distances of a major third, which makes the piece effectively change keys three times within four bars. (These are the "giant steps" the title refers to.) Each new key center is phrased by a kind of ii–V progression, that ubiquituous motion in jazz tunes. Anyone playing "Giant Steps" is emphatically pushed along by its chord changes; the whole point of the tune, its identity, lies there.

Most jazz musicians learn that this harmonic movement has a precedent in the bridge of the standard "Have You Met Miss Jones?," whose music was written by Richard Rodgers. Coltrane would likely have known the version of it by his idol Coleman Hawkins, recorded a few years before on an LP called *The Hawk in Hi Fi*, but the trail goes back further than that.

Coltrane was theory-mad. He had studied third-related harmonic relationships with Dennis Sandole at the Granoff School, and, as we have seen, there was a hint of the device in his composition "Nita," recorded on Paul Chambers's *Whims of Chambers*, three years earlier. Exercises published in Nicolas Slonimsky's 1947 book *Thesaurus of Scales and Melodic Patterns*, which Coltrane studied closely, point to the "Giant Steps" patterns, even down to some of its melody.

The "Giant Steps" changes were the stiffest exercise he had as yet given himself as an athlete of improvising. Coltrane had authored a device that jazz musicians would use forever to sharpen their skills, just as the bridge section of Ray Noble's "Cherokee" had done for Charlie Parker's generation—although "Giant Steps" changed chords with double the frequency of "Cherokee."

He used the "Giant Steps" changes as a movable device, to create new tunes based on standards, and they showed up in many other songs he recorded over the next two-year period; for example, "26-2" (based on Charlie Parker's "Confirmation"), "Countdown" (based on Eddie Vinson's "Tune Up"), "Central Park West," "Satellite" (based on "How High the Moon"), "Sweet Sioux" (based on "Cherokee"), "Fifth House" (based on Tadd Dameron's "Hot House"), the Gershwins' "But Not for Me," and the bridge sections of the standards "Body and Soul" and "The Night Has a Thousand Eyes."

The tempo of "Countdown" was faster still than that of "Giant Steps." It was frightfully controlled music—the next thing to geekdom—distinguished by Coltrane's broad, passionate tone, his fantastic sense of rhythm, and the smart arrangement idea of beginning with a drum solo and ending, after a furious two minutes and twenty-one seconds, with the tune's melodic theme.

All the rest was chord changes. Pure changes moving this rapidly can block out the tune; Tommy Flanagan, the pianist on "Giant Steps," and a supreme melody player, remembered his task in playing the title song as a matter of all changes and no melody.

Why did Coltrane do this? Playing jazz well and being able to outline every chord change are not the same thing. Evidently, from the trail of self-criticism, he felt he needed the exercise; he wasn't good enough. But even after he had written a series of jazz's all-time great études, mastered them, made a watertight album out of them (*Giant Steps*), he remained discontented. He admitted as much on the *back cover of the album itself.* "I'm worried that sometimes what I'm doing sounds like just academic exercises," he told Nat Hentoff, the album's annotator, "and I'm trying more and more to make it sound prettier."

In a later interview, he expanded on the same idea:

> *Giant Steps*, everything I did on that was harmonic exploration, harmonic sequences that I wasn't familiar with prior to that. I was working strictly from a chordal-sequential progression-pattern, and not melodically. It was easy to soon exhaust that harmonic thing. To write melodically is really the best way, because then you're not going by this set rule or that set rule; it takes everything. It's much more flexible and more far-reaching, for me, to write like that than to write from a harmonic basis. Now that I'm trying to write melody first, the melody will be that more important. Eventually I may derive some melodies which maybe have some quality, some lasting value of some sort.

Atlantic would let him record again and again over the next two years, from March 1959 to May 1961. The label also allowed him a layoff: during the summer of 1959, the time of his philosophical encounters with Wayne Shorter, when he had to rebuild his embouchure after dental surgery. He had gotten an upper bridge replacement in May 1959, after recording the master take of "Giant Steps," and didn't record again for six months. Perhaps it is no wonder that *Coltrane Jazz*, recorded mostly in November, had more tentative-sounding themes.

It seems that Coltrane started to change his mind about the exclusive uses of original melody. He had just formed a publishing company to copyright his songs, but suddenly these songs were all floating into each other. Listening to his constant stream of hard projection on the Atlantic records, you can experience momentary confusion about what track you're in. A little bit of a pattern from "Like Sonny" got into "Village Blues"; "Mr. Knight" and "Mr. Day" had similar motifs (just as, two years later, would the beginning of "India"). Many great musicians—Ali Akbar Khan, Björk, James Brown—essentially create their art as chunks of an ongoing discourse. The stronger the work is, the more it becomes a matter of sound rather than notes, the more unabashedly similar one piece is to the next.

*Giant Steps* was the first album to be issued from Coltrane's Atlantic sessions. All the Atlantic releases were organized with great thought; Nesuhi Ertegun, Atlantic's master of artists and repertoire for jazz, didn't want to put forth a crass or casual projection of the jazz musician's daily work, preferring to arrange it carefully into sets after the fact.

The album contained Coltrane's thirds-relationship writing—proof of his study—presented both fast ("Giant Steps") and faster ("Countdown"). It had a couple of memorable hard-bop blues lines, so à la mode at the time due to Art Blakey's influence ("Mr. P.C." and "Cousin Mary"), and an original, hymnlike ballad of the "While My Lady Sleeps" variety ("Naima," which remained a favorite of his own pieces). What was missing on "Giant Steps" was a blues of any profound consequence—something like a step in the direction of "Blue Train," but further.

Coltrane, and Ertegun, got around to it. His disquisitions on the blues would be released together, in a clump: "Village Blues," from October 21, 1960; and then from the fruitful day of October 24, 1960, "Mr. Syms," "Mr. Knight," "Mr. Day," "Blues to You," and "Blues to Bechet." Tenor players of Coltrane's generation thought about the blues form either in the context of bebop or R&B. But Coltrane forced down the tempo of the blues, and put drones in it; he made it minor, or led it through both major and minor tonalities. The sound he was after seemed to go back much further than bebop, or jazz itself. It was around this time that he was seen traveling with books of Negro spirituals.

*Coltrane Plays the Blues*, the resulting album of those original blues pieces, turned out to be one of the great records in jazz. It was nevertheless overshadowed by other material he recorded during the same sessions in October.

That other music was *My Favorite Things*, Coltrane's first popular breakthrough. If it seems freakish or accidental that his true hit record came from a reworked sentimental show tune (the song comes from *The Sound of Music*, which was then in the middle of a successful Broadway run) played with an Eastern-sounding tonality, there are two things to understand. One is the force of novelty: instead of tenor, Coltrane was playing the soprano saxophone, which wasn't at all a common sound. The other is the power of the band. In jazz, finally, the band is the thing.


In the summer of 1960, Coltrane toured Europe with Miles Davis. But Coltrane did not want to tour Europe with Miles Davis. He informed Miles before leaving that he would leave the band, without question, after the tour; he was already impatient to begin his own group.

"He didn't really want to make the gig," Jimmy Cobb remembered. "But Miles talked him into it. He sat next to me on the bus, looking like he was ready to split at any time."

Several recordings—one from Stockholm, widely circulated (though never released by Columbia), others from Paris and Zurich and Düsseldorf, less so—show an almost cartoonish representation of the musician who needed a long time to say what he had to say. He worked in split-tone screams; he repeated blues lines, he growled, he circled around one falsetto note for a minute at a time. His new sound was biting, discursive, and self-indulgent; it created an aggressive and totally self-possessed new style of phrase-smearing.

Davis let Coltrane do what he wanted, and it could sound like meandering, especially in contradistinction to the solo that followed, invariably by the pianist Wynton Kelly, whose crisp, orderly, neat figures now sounded certifiably old-fashioned. Kelly was the younger musician, but Coltrane was the alarm signaling the end of the 1950s.

The tour also yielded the juxtaposition of Coltrane with Stan Getz. Getz, possibly the most popular saxophonist of the 1950s, had his own group on the same tour, as did Oscar Peterson. Both audio and video exist of the concert in Düsseldorf, on March 28. Miles appears to have been absent that night, and so the lineup was Coltrane with Wynton Kelly, Paul Chambers, and Jimmy Cobb. Getz joins the group on a long medley of standards. They play "What's New?" and Coltrane, in the company of the current king of melodic ballad playing, shows that he is a contender. Now his dense runs are completely embedded with lyricism; there is no paradox anymore. The meeting culminates in Monk's "Hackensack," with Oscar Peterson replacing Kelly, and the two saxophonists— both in tuxedos, neither visibly reacting much to the other, Coltrane in a higher register, Getz playing furry low notes—play their solos individually, and finally, at the end, trade fours and harmonize on the theme. Getz's phrases are self-contained, rhythmically alive within the boundaries of the bars, fastidious, almost glib. Coltrane's eighth-note rhythm seems almost awkward by comparison, but—is there any other word for it?—more honest. He is running his own scale-based patterns, ripping up and down and across through the moving harmony with his new harsh, gruff sound—a sound he did not have on the great Monk-Coltrane live performance of 1957.

His instinct, in more and more aspects of his work, was to discriminate as little as possible: try it all, do the lot, melt it together, and the message will be revealed. "I'll Wait and Pray" was one of the titles he gave one of his ballads in 1959. It seemed he could assume the pious mode until the desired information crossed his path. If you didn't like how stubbornly he was moving, that was your issue. He couldn't do anything else.

In June 1960, Coltrane had just begun recording with a soprano saxophone as well as his tenor. He had only been playing it in public for five months, after first finding one in a car that had been left behind by a musician hitching a ride, and then apparently being given one by Miles Davis, who said that he bought it as a gift for Coltrane at an antiques shop in Paris, in March, during the Davis tour. According to Jimmy Cobb, he killed a lot of time on the bus "playing oriental-sounding scales on soprano."

Coltrane used the soprano on a session with Ornette Coleman's band, for an unspectacular album called *The Avant-Garde*, which wouldn't be released until 1966. (It has been suggested among musicians that he heard Bismillah Khan, the North Indian virtuoso of the reed instrument called the *shenai*; if so, one assumes it happened around this time, given how quickly he developed his keening sound on the instrument. On the other hand, he may not have needed Bismillah Khan's suggestion at all. His sound on tenor could be keening enough.)

In the summer of 1960 he had hired the pianist McCoy Tyner, also from Philadelphia, and only twenty-one years old; in September he had hired the drummer Elvin Jones. (They had first met in 1957 when Jones went to admire Shadow Wilson play at the Five Spot one night with the Monk-Coltrane group.) Jones hung way behind the beat. Tyner rode up on it. In Coltrane's band they balanced each other.

Jones grew up in Pontiac, Michigan, the youngest of ten kids in an extraordinary family that included the pianist Hank Jones and the trumpeter Thad Jones. There were similarities between Coltrane's and Jones's family backgrounds: Jones's father was a deacon who thought jazz was the devil's music. Coltrane, too, had grown up amid constant church activity. Jones eventually became a combination of gentleman and wild man. (He was one of the most prodigious heroin users in jazz to live through the 1950s and sixties.) He had been in New York since 1956 and recorded with Sonny Rollins on *Live at the Village Vanguard* in 1957, which gives some indication of how he would later sound—especially in his solo on "What Is This Thing Called Love?" and his duets with Rollins on "Sonnymoon for Two" and "Striver's Row." But back then, he was already known for destabilizing the regular, marked rhythms of jazz. He wouldn't indicate regular beats—particularly the upbeats—simply. Instead he used concatenations of cymbal and snaredrum accents. Bobby Jaspar, the tenor saxophonist, played with him in 1957 and wrote an article about him soon thereafter in *The Jazz Review*. "I have never tired of his complex and highly stimulating playing," Jaspar wrote. "The basic tempo is there once and for all; it never varies throughout a performance (obviously this should be so; but sometimes it seems to disappear completely)."

Jaspar then applied a little criticism. "At up tempos, though, whether through intention or through flaws of technique, Elvin sometimes creates a rhythmic climate that cannot be sustained (at least when he drowns out the bass in volume). From that point of view, Philly Joe seems to be the better drummer of this school. I know of few soloists in New York who can improvise freely in front of Elvin at up tempo without falling off the stand." It was a statement that would very shortly look funny.

Tyner, from Philadelphia, was twelve years younger than Coltrane. A young pianist fascinated with Bud Powell and Thelonious Monk, he first met and worked with Coltrane at the age of seventeen, in 1955, and came to spend a lot of time with him in Coltrane's mother's house, during Coltrane's spell between tenures with Miles. Over the next three years, they talked about life and music theory (including, Tyner remembers, the "Giant Steps" changes). Coltrane told Tyner that he was looking forward to forming a quartet of his own, and that he wanted him to join it. Tyner responded enthusiastically. It took three years, but Coltrane honored the promise, and so did Tyner.

In the late fifties, Coltrane had become a heroic figure to the younger jazz community in his hometown; he validated them and their efforts, but he also sought validation himself. He needed musicians who could enter his music on its own terms, who could build up force the way he did. Steve Kuhn, the pianist he worked with during the summer of 1960, was not a perfect fit; Coltrane felt his comping was too busy. Tyner's comping, by contrast, was flatter and more monolithic, but it had an identity. He had a strong left hand, and he used it like a steady hammer; he himself has used the word "metronomic" about his time feel. He always marked the structure clearly; he always emphasized the "one" in every measure. That stability helped center the band for both Coltrane and Jones. From this point on, Coltrane and Jones complemented each other. Theirs was, in the end, perhaps the most special connection in the group.

*My Favorite Things* was released in March 1961. If Coltrane had been self-critical about "Giant Steps," he was giddy about "My Favorite Things." He told the French critic François Postif a year later that the song was "my favorite piece of all those I have recorded. I don't think I would like to do it over in any way, whereas all the other discs I've made could have been improved in some details. This waltz is great: when you play it slowly, it has an element of gospel that's not at all displeasing; when you play it quickly, it has other undeniable qualities."

Like much of the Atlantic material, it showed that Coltrane was starting to develop canny instincts as an arranger. The switch between major and minor modes gives the song traction; it worked for any jazz fan who was on the lookout for divisions between serious and light, hip and square. The E-minor section, which starts the piece, suggested mysticism; the E major brings bright and naïve relief. During the solo sections, Tyner and Coltrane each play as long and as simply as they need to in the minor, then play the melody, after which they change to the major; the melody again, then the minor. Just as Ahmad Jamal had done several years earlier in "Poinciana," switching between tempos, "My Favorite Things" came out as two different moods within one song, but tied together by the persistence of the melody.

Coltrane must have been satisfied by more than just the song. In its first week of recording together, the band had recorded a tune which, after some editing to fit a 45 RPM record, became a radio hit. (It wasn't the first time Coltrane had been put on a 45; Prestige had done it with "Traneing In," "Good Bait," "I Want to Talk about You," "I Love You," and "Star Dust." But it was the first time a single had blown up.) This was a public vote of confidence for a band, and also for a tenor player who had started to conjure around him an atmosphere of almost violent incomprehension.

There is no evidence anywhere that Coltrane ever *tried* to be provocative. But the disposition he had grown into represented a subversion of artist-to-audience relations in jazz up to that point. Primarily, jazz had been a music for working people, in cities, people who had limited time and money. A musician on a bandstand had a responsibility to get hot quickly. But given Coltrane's interest in spirituals, we can infer that he may have been importing an idea from church—not only the musical rhetoric of gospel music, but the actual worship. A religious performance could go on much longer than the typical secular entertainment. And the assumption, too, was that your interest went beyond just entertaining yourself. Otherwise, you hadn't earned the right to be there.

His position was not antisocial. There is no question that Coltrane's intent was generosity, and that he wasn't interested in the shocking-diversion aspect of modernity, or even particularly in art for its own sake. I have searched through his written and spoken comments, and unless I'm mistaken, Coltrane never used the word "art" on the record.

Coltrane read different kinds of theoretical books, about music, religion, the occult, science, mathematics. In workbooks, he made correlations between times of day, sunrises and sunsets, and musical notes. (He didn't press any of this research on his musicians, though he shared some of these interests with Sonny Rollins and Yusef Lateef.) Among the books he owned was the extended edition of *Music: Its Secret Influence Through the Ages*, by the English composer Cyril Scott, published in 1958. Scott was influenced by Theosophy, the late-nineteenth-century occult pursuit, which borrowed concepts from Hinduism. It held, among other things, that nature is infinite, and that all beings and things in nature are interconnected, made from the same essence. (The Alabama-born jazz pianist and bandleader Herman Blount, who later called himself Sun Ra, was also interested in Theosophy, and Coltrane first came into contact with Sun Ra while he passed through Chicago on tour with the Miles Davis Quintet; they would continue to meet after Sun Ra moved, with his Arkestra, to New York in the early sixties. Whatever else Coltrane absorbed from Sun Ra, it seems certain that they shared some philosophical interests.)

Scott believed that music, properly used, brings humans in touch with the Devas, the angels or gods from previous ages. He also argued that music easily and effectively changes human psychology; he argued that human behavior is affected not only by the emotional content of music but by its form, and that such forces are pervasive: one need not be within earshot of music to benefit from its effects. Scott wrote about music (even twentieth-century music) in religious and semiscientific terms, without bringing up the subject of art much. He did talk about jazz, though, with priggish, racialized scorn. (He felt that it "closely resembled the music of primitive savages.")

It seems quite possible, according to various sources, that Coltrane also read *The Mysticism of Sound and Music*, a collection of lectures written in the 1920s by Hazrat Inayat Khan, a Sufi master and former musician (he played the vina, a stringed instrument). Hazrat Inayat Khan didn't use the term "art," either, in describing music; only when referring to visual art. He wrote about music as sound, and sound as truth emerging from the depths of one's being. He wrote about repetition. ("If you repeat: flower, flower, flower, your mind will be much more impressed than if you only think of the flower.") He wrote about how music leaves "impressions" on plants and living things. (One of the chapters in the book is titled "Impressions"—is it a coincidence that this became the title of a Coltrane song and album?—and it deals with how deeply music alters the consciousness of those in earshot of it.) Unlike Cyril Scott, Khan had no problem with jazz. He admired its psychological effect.

Even if Coltrane may not have thought about his music as art for its own sake, he did prefer to see his music as closer to "classical" than popular. "I dunno, I may be wrong on this," he said much later at a press conference. "But the term 'classical music,' in my opinion, means the music of a country that's played by the composers and musicians of the country, more or less, as opposed to the music that people dance or sing by, the popular music." He asked the interviewer whether he agreed, allowed that he (Coltrane) might not be correct but that that was the way he felt, and then continued. "If you would ask me what we are playing, I feel it is the music of the individual contributor. And if you want to name it anything, you can name it classical music."

Still, one of the mysteries about Coltrane is why he so nonchalantly subjected his audiences to such a rigorous working-through process. Clearly he believed, stubbornly, that there was an intrinsic positive force in his work, something larger than music.

Coltrane was acutely self-possessed in his identity as an artist, at a time when a lot of celebrated American art had become seen as a kind of sanctuary, an escape from military conspiracies, war, and television. In painting, there was Mark Rothko's desire (as he put it) to "breathe" onto the canvas, creating deep edgeless squares floating on a larger field of color. And there was Jackson Pollock's sustained, long-form gestural graffiti. Both processes came out of a kind of trance state, a mystical belief in an artistic process quite separate from what was congealing into standard postwar American pragmatism.

As was suggested by the title of one of his Atlantic records—*Coltrane's Sound*—Coltrane cared about something larger than technique and style. The best way to describe this is "sound." Especially since picking up the soprano, with which he desired to create a big tone despite the narrower default sound of the instrument, he gradually played louder, and more powerfully, holding notes for longer. He grew interested in the partials that made up a single tone. "The playbacks haven't sounded right," he remarked of his records in November 1961. "They get too close to the horn with the mikes and don't give the sound time to travel as they should. Consequently, they don't get enough of the real timbre and they miss the *whole* body of the sound. They get the inside of it but not the outside as well."

Ornette Coleman's pianoless quartet came to New York in 1959, and, like many other musicians, Coltrane was shaken up by it; he worked hard to understand what Coleman was doing. Coleman's music, then as now, is sweet, melodic, bouncy; to a great degree it avoids the minor-seventh chords that give jazz its serious, contemplative feeling. Listened to now, it is easy to understand. But in the late 1950s it could sound almost ragtag, half-formed.

Coltrane loved the ideas operating behind Coleman's quartet: the notion of playing without a pianist or any other chord-based instrument; the band's intuitive ways of getting around strictly delineated rhythm, and changing tonality in the middle of a tune. His pronouncements about Coleman—and his tentative flirtations with Coleman's style, mostly through the album *The Avant-Garde*—are instructive in terms of how Coltrane sorted out incoming knowledge.

When Coltrane was really excited about something, he studied it, got involved, and tried not to think that he had mastered it to the point of drawing concrete conclusions. It seemed to help him to feel that he hadn't quite figured it out yet. He lived with negative capability: he sat on things, mulled them over, got closer to them by trial and error. He was not passive in his desires to change his music. In 1960, during a stint at the Village Vanguard, he would head out after his job, night after night, to hear Roy Haynes's band, playing in a club several blocks south on West Fourth Street. Haynes had Eric Dolphy and Reggie Workman in his band. A year later, Coltrane had hired all three of them. He asked Paul Motian in 1965 whether he should be playing with two drummers. (Motian said he didn't know.) Ten months later, he had two drummers.

Coltrane seemed to see Coleman, a melodist who had not studied harmonic relationships in the organized way that Coltrane had, as a source of knowledge that could move him away from his obsession with harmony, with the science of the relationships inside and between chords. Coltrane wasn't ready to declare that he wanted to be free of the "Giant Steps" changes. But he did want to make himself vulnerable to the possibility of something displacing that from the front of his brain.

"The person with whom I would have the most pleasure in making a record is Ornette Coleman," he said in November 1961. "I only played with him once in my life, and he asked me to join him. We played two pieces—twelve minutes to be exact—but I know that that was the most intense moment of my life." (Coleman believes these twelve minutes may have occurred at the Five Spot—certainly in New York—but can't quite remember.) To the Belgian bassist and critic Benoît Quersin, Coltrane said, "When [Ornette] came along, I was so far in this thing [meaning the 'Giant Steps' harmonic movement], I didn't know where I was going to go next. And I don't know if I would have thought about just abandoning the chord system or not. I probably wouldn't have thought about that at all. And he came along doing it, and I heard it, and I said, 'Well, that must be the answer.' "

In fact, Coltrane seemed to quickly determine that it wasn't re-

ally *his* answer. Coltrane grew as a composer after the Atlantic period, and that growth was in the direction of simplicity. Starting in
1961 he and his band basically didn't rehearse, even when addi-
tional members were temporarily involved, and his instructions
were minimal—usually something about a vamp and a key. He
wanted to get away from what had become a fixation on chords,
and he talked about that desired shift not in terms of imposing his
own individual will over his playing, but in terms of entering a situation where he would come upon the answer accidentally.

They were philosophical-religious terms. Coltrane was not explic-
itly saying that the best music comes from a higher power—perhaps
in 1961 this would have sounded grandiose—but that is the subtext of
his comments. He was aware that fixating on chords and the "Giant
Steps" changes was a matter of habit, the patterns of his conscious
mind, the condition of not seeing the forest for the trees. Whether he
felt that the catalyst would be the subconscious or God, he wanted to
be *led* to something new. A bandleader can do this by setting up some
ground rules that can be overridden. Vamps, modes, and drones were
suitable ground rules that can, in the right circumstances, be overridden. "Here's how I play," he said in November 1961:

> I start from one point and go as far as possible. But, unfortunately, I
> never lose my way. I say unfortunately, because what would interest
> me greatly is to discover paths that I'm perhaps not aware of. My
> phrasing is just a simple extension of my musical ideas, and I'm
> happy that my technique allows me to go very far in this area, but
> I have to add that it's always done very consciously. I "localize,"
> which is to say that I think always in a given space. I rarely think of
> the whole of a solo, and only very briefly: I always return to the
> small part of the solo that I was in the process of playing. The har-
> monies have become for me a kind of obsession, which gives me
> the feeling of looking at music from the wrong end of a telescope.

He did thereafter follow Ornette Coleman's example and begin
to play without a piano on occasion. But even while praising Cole-

man's system, he acknowledged why it didn't work for him. "My real pianist, McCoy Tyner, keeps himself to the harmonies, which lets me forget them. It's he who kind of gives me wings and lets me leave the earth from time to time." On the sessions with Coleman's band on *The Avant-Garde*, he chose tunes (one by Don Cherry, three by Coleman) that *didn't* represent the most wide-open side of Coleman's music; they had melodies that strongly implied standard changes. The fifth was Monk's "Bemsha Swing," with which he was thoroughly familiar.

Before permanently leaving Miles, Coltrane made a few last recordings with him in March 1961, for Columbia, under the direction of producer Teo Macero. On the waltz "Someday My Prince Will Come"—written in the mid-thirties for the Disney film *Snow White and the Seven Dwarves*, and a perfect example of Miles as trend-watcher (sentimental Hollywood themes recast as jazz waltzes, à la Coltrane's "My Favorite Things")—the rest of the band stays perfectly at ease; but Coltrane's playing sounds gnarled, bunched up. And "Teo," another waltz, composed by Davis, now has more of the character of Coltrane music than Miles music: as in "Olé" and "My Favorite Things," also modal waltzes, he arpeggiates and plays long tones through minor vamps. The chasm that opened on tour the previous summer was not to be closed.

Soon after the release of *My Favorite Things*, Coltrane's contract with Atlantic was bought out by Impulse, a jazz label formed within the ABC-Impulse family. (Creed Taylor was the executive who made Coltrane the first artist on the label.) Coltrane respected the logic of artists-and-repertoire, the need to give the audience something new and special. His first record for Impulse was one of the default moves a jazz bandleader makes when he wants his audience to hear him in a new way: a large-ensemble record.

*Africa/Brass*, Coltrane's first recording made at Rudy Van

Gelder's studio in Hackensack, New Jersey—he would record almost everything else there until his death—is indeed a different
sound. Coltrane had never before sounded so echoey; there were
eighteen musicians in the brass-heavy ensemble, and you hear a lot
of the room itself. It is the first intimation of Coltrane's really
oversize music, his slightly spooky grand-scale works.

It was also the first time that Coltrane implied that a single
mode was enough for an entire piece. Earlier that year he had been
stretching out his listening regimen, listening not just to classical
music now but to folk forms and foreign traditional music: black
American spirituals, Folkways recordings of Indian music, quite
possibly the 1955 record by Akbar Ali Khan called *Music of India:
Morning and Evening Ragas*, and Ravi Shankar—so much Ravi
Shankar that he desired to make a record with him. (Coltrane was
close to the saxophonist and flutist Yusef Lateef, who had been listening closely to Indian music since 1955 or so.) In Indian music
especially, he noticed how a single mode made a piece; the key it
was in, and the kinds of phrasings in it, determined the color and
gave it its individual personality. He was clearly fond of songs-qua-
songs, but from this point on they might not have been necessary.

Edited down, it was a brilliant LP. With all its extra material,
issued later on CD, it is less successful. "Greensleeves," a piece using the same major-minor strategy as "My Favorite Things," was
similarly effective. Cal Massey's composition "The Damned Don't
Cry," halting and sloppy (and not included on the LP), seems like
the first real evidence of failure on record since Coltrane started
making albums in 1957. But all in all, *Africa/Brass* didn't sound
like anything else in jazz. It was more serious and open and inclusive (or just dire, to some) than anything he had done before.

For "Africa," the most arresting piece on the LP—it took up all
of side A, and was based on a single chord—Coltrane used two
bassists, Art Davis and Reggie Workman. This was not a first in
jazz. Duke Ellington experimented quixotically with two bassists
from the mid-thirties through 1940, using them as a beefier version of a single bass line. (Ellington was after ways to make his or-

chestra sound as unique as possible.) On "Africa," Coltrane wanted something different: specifically, a drone, one low (the open E) and one high.

He would use the two-bass drone again while recording the track "Olé," two days later, as well as the following summer and fall, into the Village Vanguard sessions of November (on another new one-chord vamp piece, "India," its melody taken from a Hindu chant Coltrane heard on a Folkways field-recording album, and released as part of the album *Impressions*). The horn arrangements, by Coltrane and Tyner, are fairly simple, based on Tyner's comping. But they are not particularly well executed; in a few takes of "Africa," there's an anything-goes feeling, which we would hear more on later Coltrane records.

Eric Dolphy played alto saxophone, flute, and bass clarinet on *Africa/Brass*, and probably wrote the horn arrangements for the session, using Tyner's chord voicings. He had been talking about music with Coltrane since 1954, when Coltrane went to Los Angeles with Johnny Hodges's band, and the two had become close since 1960, when Dolphy moved to New York from Los Angeles. Coltrane very much wanted Dolphy to become part of his working group but knew that he arranged best for himself and his three musicians; he was trying to find a way to create music for five people in a way that didn't just sound like a more cluttered quartet. Dolphy was similarly obsessive about music, both as a player and a listener. (Roy Haynes remembers going by Dolphy's house in Los Angeles in the mid-fifties and finding bootlegs of unreleased live Charlie Parker recordings, when these were still hard to come by.) Dolphy didn't have quite the internal clamp on time that Coltrane did, and Tyner has long intimated that Coltrane's band found the basic quartet the special, and by far the preferable, format. But Dolphy posed another challenge to Coltrane: like Ornette Coleman, he represented new knowledge to lead him on, a new trip-wire. He was also a significant friend. Coltrane would travel with Dolphy's picture after he died, hanging it on the walls of his hotel rooms.

# 5 vanguard

The year 1961, so far, had been a time of heroism, retribution, terror, forced equality, and some resolution.

Leisure time became a higher priority: the American middle classes were spending great amounts of money on what can only be called aesthetic products; audiences were being trained in a new kind of cultural consumerism. Record numbers went to see art in institutions. Sixty-three hundred people entered the Museum of Modern Art on November 19 to see Marc Chagall's stained-glass windows depicting the twelve tribes of Israel. One week later, 86,770 spectators in four hours went to look at Rembrandt's *Aristotle Contemplating a Bust of Homer*, a new acquisition at the Met (exceeding by far the museum's previous attendance record).

Modern visual art, after the imperious, crash-through Abstract Expressionist work of the early 1950s, had become more everyday, more casual; also, more easily salable, more available to the budgets of the unaristocratic. In December, Claes Oldenburg opened "The Store" at his small studio on East Second Street, an exhibition that made art of everyday objects rendered in plaster, all of them (pragmatically) for sale. The Museum of Modern Art opened "The Art of Assemblage," a show about ways of making art that drew on more everyday material, craft-oriented areas beyond painting and sculpture: collage, photomontage, decoupage.

In the first months of 1962, the artists James Rosenquist, Wayne Thiebaud, and Jim Dine had their first solo exhibitions. The basement of Judson Church had been opened a few years earlier to show young artists including Jim Dine and Tom Wesselmann, and some of the first performance-art happenings took place there.

In 1961, Dashiell Hammett died of cancer, and Ernest Hemingway of a self-administered shotgun round to the head. Now that hypermasculine American succinctness had been eclipsed, camp could become a popular mode. *Accent*, a network television show broadcast in December that ran through the year's high points, spent considerable time fixating on Jackie Kennedy, Elizabeth Taylor (who was filming *Cleopatra* that year and nearly died of pneumonia), and Judy Garland.

Some reports claimed that Americans spent more time and money on books and music than ever before. In May 1961, almost three decades after its publication in France, Henry Miller's *Tropic of Cancer* was allowed to be sold in American stores. Americans had passed through days of intimate paranoia with the Bay of Pigs crisis in May, followed by a sense of temporary relief. But in September, the Soviet Union began a new round of nuclear weapons testing, setting off enormous explosions in Central Asia and the Arctic. America started its own tests, in retaliation.

"The Soviet Union's resumption of nuclear weapons tests last week has revived a specter that mankind had hoped might be exorcised permanently," ran a story in the science section of *The New York Times* on September 3, 1961. "The specter is that of worldwide radioactive fallout." By the end of October, rain in Tokyo was determined to be radioactive. On *If the Bomb Falls*, an instructional LP released that year, a calm, Midwestern-sounding male voice intones:

It may be safe for you to leave your house after a few hours. Or, it may be as long as two weeks or more. Two weeks with very little food or water, tension, unaccustomed closeness. Two weeks with sanitary facilities most likely not operating. No lights, no phone. Just terror. By all means, provide some tranquillizers to ease the strain and monotony of life in the shelter. A bottle of 100 should be adequate for a family of four. Tranquillizers are not a narcotic, and are not habit-forming. Ask your doctor for his recommendation.

That summer, the Yankee teammates Mickey Mantle and Roger Maris competed to out-home-run each other; Maris won and broke Babe Ruth's long-standing record. That winter, Wilt Chamberlain was averaging fifty points per game, a level of scoring that had never been seen before in basketball.

Racial tensions in America were alarmingly high in 1961, but at least a few symbolic battles were won. School desegregation had taken place without too much violence. And a remarkably straight-shooting documentary on racial inequality, *Walk in My Shoes*, was aired on the ABC network on the evening of September 20. (Some southern ABC affiliates refused to air it.) The film is punctuated with running commentary from a middle-aged black man with a soft Caribbean accent, driving a car through Harlem and turning to his right to speak to the camera. "I think the time has come when the white man's time is running out on him, just like the tide," he says, without rancor. "He's got to go. His time has come. There's no two ways about it."

That year had seen the summer of the Freedom Riders, black and white men and women who risked being beaten with chains, ax-handles, and iron bars for race-crossing on buses through the deep South, in order to protest the segregation of public facilities. On November 1, the Interstate Commerce Commission, under pressure from Attorney General Robert F. Kennedy, ended racial segregation in bus terminals.

That night, Coltrane made his first live record. On the original *Live at the Village Vanguard*, collated from four nights of recording in the second week of a two-week stand in 1961—from November 1, 2, 3, and 5—Eric Dolphy appears on only two out of five tracks as an occasional fifth player, even though he played with the group that week far more often than not, and subsequently went on tour with the band through Europe.

But limiting him to two tracks may have been about right. Coltrane had pretty well figured out the dimensions of the quartet. The formula was wrapped tight; Dolphy set it slightly out of alignment.

Coltrane had just finalized his quartet, and the music radiates self-assurance. He had become interested in a kind of babbling style of improvising, based in Charlie Parker's tight, bouncing, rhythmic phrasing. Dolphy played it, too, though more pronounced, more over-the-top; but instead of intensifying the music, Dolphy's presence made it slacker. This was a volatile, high-velocity kind of music-making, and had to be practiced carefully. Besides the slow, forgiving groove of "Spiritual," whose melody had been directly adapted from a rare version of "Nobody Knows De Trouble I See," from a book in Coltrane's library—James Weldon Johnson's *The Book of American Negro Spirituals*—most of the Village Vanguard music that *isn't* just the quartet minus Dolphy is, in one way or another, too laborious, too all-over, too much.

*Live at the Village Vanguard* brought the bassist Jimmy Garrison into the band, the fourth and last member of the quartet to click into place. This was the group that was to hold together for six years; by McCoy Tyner's estimation, it rehearsed four or five times during that stretch. All the rest of their work happened on the bandstand, in increasingly long engagements within single clubs—a key part of the group's cohesion even within its first year—and in the studios.

The great statement of Coltrane on the Vanguard tapes of late 1961 was "Chasin' the Trane," a 12-bar blues improvisation in F that starts, as most Coltrane performances did, without anybody counting off one-two-three-four: it just vaults into being. Then and thereafter, it was to be a piece for trio, with McCoy Tyner (and, in this case, Dolphy, too) laying out. The tune was recorded twice during the week, and the longer of the two versions, at nearly sixteen minutes, the one without Dolphy, made it onto the record. It is remarkable for the way it starts at absolute full intensity and retains that level without peaking or deflating.

It should not be surprising that Coltrane would construct his landmark performance of the period on a blues. He was of a generation of jazz musicians that understood the blues form, and blues harmony, from the inside: it was the main artery of truly popular jazz—jukebox jazz—from the 1930s to the fifties, and it was the music Coltrane was often required to play as an apprentice with Kolax and Crosse, Hodges and Bostic, Gillespie and Jimmy Smith. We have seen how the blues form challenged him to invent crucial differences between him and his colleagues, and how he had a gift for writing distinctive, original blues lines. There exists a Chicago nightclub tape of Coltrane playing "Trane's Blues"—a line he recorded with both Paul Chambers and Miles Davis in separate sessions in 1956—from March 1961, seven months before the Vanguard booking. It is monstrous and refined, a little less volcanic than "Chasin' the Trane," a little more insistent on a blues tonality throughout. Whatever—it is extraordinary, a musician finding his own greatest resonance, hitting his spot. Had you heard it then, you might have guessed that the blues would figure into Coltrane's next important move.

Coltrane had been comfortable in the lower-middle register of the tenor saxophone, but after he started to play the soprano saxophone, he gravitated toward wider areas of the tenor. As he put it in a conversation with Frank Kofsky, the lowest note on the soprano is one of the middle notes on the tenor—a sound within his comfort zone. But when he developed his embouchure to reach the higher notes on the soprano, he started to think in higher pitch ranges for the tenor, from the low B-flat upward. He began to play much more of his instrument, and the Vanguard recordings give evidence of the new range.

The little two-note patterns Coltrane plays with throughout the issued version of "Chasin' the Trane," turning them up and down and over, suggest Sonny Rollins, and the kind of improvising you can hear on Rollins tracks like "St. Thomas," from 1956; it may be the closest Coltrane ever got to Rollins's rhythmic language of phrasing.

But Coltrane said later that around that time he had also been listening closely to John Gilmore, the tenor saxophonist in Sun Ra's band, some of whose run-on language of short motivic cells can be heard on tracks like the up-tempo "Jet Flight," from *The Futuristic Sounds of Sun Ra*, recorded a month before Coltrane's Vanguard engagement.

There is a stretch of split-tones in "Chasin' the Trane," reminiscent of the Miles Davis European tour of the previous year; in it, he trips up the internal 12-bar logic. He causes patterns to change every bar, or stretches a single pattern across the 2nd and 3rd bar, or the 4th and 5th, or three in a row. In under a minute, Garrison, walking in hiccupped phrasing by pulling his finger off the string, loosens himself from the 12-bar structure; Coltrane (and Jones) still demarcate the end of the 12 bars by the beginning of a new melodic idea and an emphatic cymbal crash.

But at two and a half minutes in, Coltrane starts to disregard the 12-bar markers, and he's off, at large, exploring texture, fooling with short, sweet melodies. This is not quoting, at which Sonny Rollins was so adept. For a while, Coltrane may appear to be playing with the melody of the English folk song "Oranges and Lemons, Say the Bells of St. Clement's." But then again, it could just be a series of intervals. (If someone seems to be quoting "Three Blind Mice," he is also playing III–II–I.) The band's groove is there, though, planted into his playing. "Coltrane had his own drummer in here," Roy Haynes has said, pointing to his chest.

"Chasin' the Trane," as a whole, is a remarkable demonstration in balancing harmonic structure and no harmonic structure. Coltrane had heard Ornette Coleman enact it (and Garrison came from the most recent edition of the Coleman quartet)—this assumption that chord changes should be internalized by the musician, but not necessarily spelled out. That a musician should feel the freedom to play a phrase for as long as he wanted, even if the note it ended on left him at odds with the composed logic of the tune. But the sound of the Ornette Coleman quartet depended on the notion of doing away with preset chord changes; "Chasin' the Trane" stuck to the form of the blues. And as such, "Chasin' the Trane" has served as one of the most important recordings in jazz as it is currently practiced. It is a unifier. This recording, precisely, is what free jazz and straight-ahead jazz—Lower East Side, post-hippie, ragged blow-out jams, and Branford Marsalis—have in common.

*Live at the Village Vanguard* was the first Coltrane album produced by Bob Thiele, who had just started as head of Impulse. He replaced Creed Taylor, who had moved on to Verve. In less than a year, Impulse had already scored album hits twice, non-glibly, with natural crossovers: Ray Charles's *Genius + Soul = Jazz*, and Oliver Nelson's *The Blues and the Abstract Truth*.

As evidence of Bob Thiele's trust in Coltrane, and Coltrane's trust in himself, "My Favorite Things," Coltrane's hit, would not be heard on *Live at the Village Vanguard*. This was deliberate: the group didn't play the song once during the four days of recording, whereas in all their gigging before and after the Vanguard engagement, they played it every night.

The period after the success of "My Favorite Things" until the 1964 album *A Love Supreme*—Coltrane's mid-thirties—appears to be a period of trial and error, of balance.

Part of this may have been emotional. Coltrane's relationship with Naima, after a series of tensions, apparently involving a girlfriend, ended in the summer of 1963; around the same time, he began living with Alice. Another part may have been physical. Even after the installation of his dental bridge, his mouth continued to bother him. He also damaged his mouthpiece, probably by taking it to a repairman who filed it down too much, and some of his comments about his 1962 recordings suggest that he never found real satisfaction with new mouthpieces, but finally decided that mind-over-matter was the way to move on. He seemed to feel discouraged by the fact that it wasn't as easy to keep playing "that certain fast thing I was reaching for"—by which he might have meant the rapid improvising language of *Live at the Village Vanguard*, or perhaps, as Lewis Porter has suggested, the fast passages with that extra-serrated, gritty tone that characterizes the 1960 and '61 solos, but thereafter disappears for a little while.

Different mouthpieces can produce a different feeling for certain musicians. The saxophonist Michael Brecker, for instance, one of Coltrane's later stylistic descendents, intentionally used only a hard-rubber mouthpiece, as opposed to plastic, for his 2001 ballad record *Nearness of You*. But Ravi Coltrane denies the importance of Coltrane's lost mouthpiece during the early sixties.

> I don't think it was something that plagued him, that this was a cause-and-effect, shaping who he became and the way he played. He probably knew that so much of sound is internal. It wasn't a sort of desperation, "I gotta go for the ultimate sound, I gotta get a mouthpiece that will give me that." It never gets to a point where it really affects what we do musically. I can't imagine it affected John Coltrane's direction. Some people have said that he fucked up his mouthpiece and could never get that thing back, and it made him upset, so that's why he became aggressive. But this is one of the greatest musicians who ever played. He's not gonna divert because of a technical problem.

Coltrane's uneasiness could have been part of a defensive reaction, because what he brought to his public through 1961 with Dolphy, including the Vanguard engagement and the subsequent European tour, provoked the strongest negative reactions he had yet experienced. The reaction must have been based on audience disappointment rather than audience fatigue, because Coltrane would have brought no joy to anyone who was looking for a Black American Wildman. The intensity of a concert could vary from night to night, but by today's standards, it seems naïve to think that the band was trying to be perverse or willfully provocative.

The group's three-song performance on Danish television on December 4, 1961, for example, hosted by the jazz critic Joachim-Ernst Berendt, transmits absolute sober control. Wearing unassuming leisure clothes—brown jacket with no tie, a black shirt with the collar out, a white T-shirt exposed, pants tailored a little too high—Coltrane never smiles. Even executing tricky and urgent phrasing at the end of his solo in "Impressions," he appears to expend little physical effort in his solos. He plays with his eyes open for long stretches of time: he blinks less often than usual. As Berendt, a young-professor type in thick glasses, introduces "Every Time We Say Goodbye," contextualizing in Danish about Sidney Bechet and the soprano saxophone, Coltrane looks impassive, unaffected, unembarrassed.

Through the broadcast, behind Coltrane, the rhythm section locks in. Neither McCoy Tyner, Reggie Workman, nor Elvin Jones abandons the implication of a strong and constant pulse. It is Dolphy who doesn't quite fit into the picture. Playing an alto saxophone solo on "Impressions," Dolphy sputters, right out of the gate; he uses a more fractured version of a Charlie Parker rhythmic feeling. He leans forward, knits his brow; the strange bump in his forehead, like half a golf ball, suggests some tensing muscle in the brain. But after he finishes his solo, the music returns to the group's tight weave. Dolphy can be understood as an impulsive player, in contrast to Coltrane's greater sense of balance; he can be understood as a virtuosic musician in an original language.

Still, consensually, critics showed their frustration. They didn't understand what the group was trying to do. The rhythm section was more or less given a pass, but it was the saxophone soloing that challenged credulity, its length and perhaps its unwillingness to tell a traditional story.

For what it's worth, in all the existing recordings of Coltrane's group in Europe from those years (1962 and '63), Coltrane gave a spoken introduction exactly once. If there's one thing the facile critic needs to do his job, it is some verbal personality from the bandstand, some words to transcribe into the review—anything to make a thoroughly musical endeavor more literary or conversational. Coltrane would not provide it.

*C*oltrane, recorded in April 1962, again produced by Bob Thiele, is the first to feature the fully intact "classic quartet," with nobody else alternating or replacing—no Dolphy, no Reggie Workman, no Art Davis. Just John Coltrane, McCoy Tyner, Jimmy Garrison, and Elvin Jones.

The album leads sensibly out of the Village Vanguard material, without nearly as much shock but with the same implication of seriousness. This is when many songs in Coltrane's repertoire start to sound similar, if only perhaps after the statement of the melody is finished.

In one important respect, during these years, Coltrane functioned like a popular artist does: he used the feel of his successes and landmarks as his paradigms. Harold Arlen's "Out of This World," a bright mid-tempo 6/8 piece, is refashioned after the general feel of "My Favorite Things," with a similar tempo and a similar use of modal vamps. (Coltrane had a preference for the soprano saxophone on songs composed in three-beat rhythms.) "Soul Eyes" is a slow ballad with a keening melody that turns mid-tempo after two choruses—sort of a cross between "Naima" and "Every Time We Say Goodbye," from the *My Favorite Things* album. "The Inch Worm" is another bright song with a three-beat rhythm, like "Out of This World," but mellower, and with the soprano. "Tunji" is an "Africa" or "India" kind of piece, with Jones's slow groove and a bass drone, a single chord all the way underneath Coltrane's gentle introductory soloing. It's only three minutes in, at the beginning of McCoy Tyner's solo, when—surprise—the song turns into a 24-bar blues, with Tyner playing particularly beautifully, saving it from drudgery. "Miles' Mode" (also called "The Red Planet," and possibly written by Eric Dolphy), a twelve-tone melody first run forward and then retrogade, proceeds in a single mode for seven and a half minutes. The best moments come early: Coltrane solos for two minutes, mathematically cranking up the tension with the band until Tyner drops out completely, and Jones begins to hit especially hard. (At this point suddenly the room sound changes, as if the microphones have been drawn back from Jones's drum kit.)

After "My Favorite Things," Coltrane had suddenly won a large audience that didn't truly know him, and he switched up on them. It would not have occurred to a jazz musician who was specifically trying to maintain career momentum to hire Eric Dolphy after having a mainstream radio hit. And if Coltrane thought of music in any kind of political terms—that is, espousing a cultural position, staying on a point—he would not have recorded an album of slow ballads so soon after the tumultuous year with Dolphy.

*Ballads* was a contrivance, planned by Coltrane and Bob Thiele, but a balanced one that Coltrane was prepared to give himself over to. It is one of the best ballad records in jazz. Coltrane's own ballads had already become fascinatingly rich. The family of songs with strong pedal points whose atmosphere arose from his recording of Kaper's "When My Lady Sleeps" in 1957 was so far best embodied by "Naima"; it would continue through "Dear Lord" (1963) and "Lonnie's Lament" (1964).

The songs on *Ballads* were popular melodies, songs Coltrane chose himself because he liked them but that he wouldn't henceforth be performing. Of the eight tracks on *Ballads*, the band had been playing only one previously on gigs—Rodgers and Hart's "It's Easy to Remember"—and there is only scant evidence to suggest that it was played once more.

The best of the tracks on *Ballads* was Jimmy McHugh and Frank Loesser's "Say It (Over and Over Again)"—perhaps because its A section was centered around the tonic and dominant, nothing too busy, and its bridge could be underlined by one of Tyner's pedal points. This was an unusual piece for Coltrane, in a way. The sophisticated mainstream, as established by America's great song-writers, generally didn't suit him; he found his emotional pitch in benign melodies like "My Favorite Things," "The Inch Worm," and "Greensleeves," but rearranged them to make them simpler.

In "Say It," form meets content: the idea of "over and over again," a not un-Coltrane-like concept, repeated twice in the lyric, is borne out by the repeated motion of the notes. He was able to adapt the melody line of the A section to his natural phrasing, so that it sounded like a song he might have written; here is another prime example of the power and clarity of Coltrane's sound, espe-cially in the upper register.

*Duke Ellington and John Coltrane* was next—another con-trivance. The two had never met before, and came together by Thiele's planning; Ellington brought his own bassist and drummer, and they alternated as the rhythm section with Coltrane's (minus McCoy Tyner). Together, they made it work.

This was an album that attempted to bridge not only genera-tions but entire philosophies about jazz. Ellington's "In a Senti-mental Mood," his greatest ballad composition, was another standard—like "Say It"—that Coltrane could bend to suit his own purposes. (Coincidentally, Ellington claimed he wrote "In a Senti-mental Mood" after a dance in Durham, North Carolina, in 1935, to resolve a rift between two female friends who were fighting af-ter one had trespassed on the other's man.) Johnny Hodges had originally established the gravity of the song, and Coltrane revises it in his own fashion. He plays it so well, and so deeply, that it seems the best kind of tribute—one that acknowledges the aim of what's being celebrated but doesn't at all sound like it. Thiele said that Johnny Hodges later told him of his preference for Coltrane's version of "In a Sentimental Mood" above all others but his own.

Bob Thiele described Coltrane's difficulty, previous to the recording with Ellington, with letting go and moving on: he was never quite satisfied with any completed take. Ellington was the opposite, ready to part with a performance immediately and move on to the next thing. "In a Sentimental Mood" was recorded in one take. "After that meeting with Ellington," Thiele said, "Coltrane never spent that much time on a take, on a tune. He would like to get it in one or two takes and if it didn't happen we would scrap it."

The other great piece from *Duke Ellington and John Coltrane* is the blues "Take the Coltrane," a line written by Ellington for the session. Ellington lays out for Coltrane's solo, just as Tyner got out of the way for "Chasin' the Trane." It is an extension of the November '61 Village Vanguard soloing style, with many short three-, four-, or five-note clumps repeated, or joined together, or turned over, but delivered in a rapid projection and in long sixteenth-note strings, around which Jones makes his cross-rhythms jump. This is one of Coltrane's great solos, during a period when he wasn't making them regularly.

Next Coltrane collaborated with the singer Johnny Hartman. Hartman had performed and recorded on a semiregular basis with Dizzy Gillespie's orchestra between 1948 and 1949, just before Coltrane's short tenure with Gillespie. Apparently they crossed paths on Gillespie's bandstand at least once, in 1950.

Hartman had a deep, rich tenor voice; he was a long-note ballad singer with a cello-like tone, not a rhythm-tune bebop singer. Yet he made his best music with jazz musicians, which was to be the cause of much career confusion for him.

With Thiele's encouragement, Coltrane came up with the idea to record with Hartman, who had been working in Japan. Hartman later said, "I was a Coltrane fan, and although I'd never met him, I'd been listening to him for years. I didn't think we'd fit too well. But Bob told me to go to Birdland when I got back to the States. Then, after the show, when the place had closed, I tried a couple of tunes with him. I did—just me, Coltrane, and his pianist."

The following week—March 6 and 7, 1963—they recorded. Hartman worked marvelously with Coltrane, who had by this point perfected a strict-melody ballad style on tenor saxophone, staying close to the tune with little improvisation, as "My One and Only Love" demonstrates (and also the extraordinarily moody "After the Rain," a quartet track recorded about seven weeks after the Hartman session). It was a matter of full projection and long tones at low volume, of Coltrane centering himself in the horn's upper-middle register, where he could play the melody, express a feeling of vulnerability, and not get crossed up in Hartman's deeper notes. (As a ballad player, remember, Coltrane's model was Johnny Hodges, the best in the business; his own close-to-the-melody style can be understood as his answer to Hodges's.) But *John Coltrane and Johnny Hartman* uses other strategies, too; in "Lush Life" and "Autumn Serenade" Coltrane lays out until after Hartman sings the entire lyric, then improvises freely in his own language.

Coltrane had developed remarkable clarity of purpose, a sense of why he was making music and who he was performing for—not just in the professional sense, but in the philosophical sense. He had put drugs behind him: few musicians who had quit heroin only three years earlier could work confidently in a band with two active junkies, Jones and Garrison. His band had become miraculous, a buoyancy. With that part of his work done, he was on to more personal searches.

At this time Coltrane was as much of a culture hero within jazz as Charles Mingus, but, unlike Mingus, he didn't worry out loud about the place of jazz in American society. He was curiously uncompelled to publicly condemn uncomprehending listeners, whether for reasons of aesthetics, philosophy, culture, or race; he seemed to believe in his music implicitly.

In June 1962, Don DeMichael, the editor of *Down Beat*, with whom Coltrane had a friendly relationship, received this letter.

Many thanks for sending me Aaron Copeland's [*sic*] fine book, "Music and Imagination." I found it historically revealing and on the whole, quite informative. However, I do not feel that all of his tenets are entirely essential or applicable to the "jazz" musician. This book seems to be written more for the American classical or semi-classical composer who has the problem, as Copeland [*sic*] sees it, of not finding himself an integral part of the musical community, or having difficulty in finding a positive philosophy or justification for his art. The "jazz" musician (you can have this term along with several others that have been foisted upon us) does not have to worry about a lack of positive and affirmative philosophy. It's built in us. The phrasing, the sound of the music attests this fact. We are naturally endowed with it. You can believe all of us would have perished long ago if this were not so. As to community, the whole face of the globe is our community. You see, it is really easy for us to create. We are born with this feeling that just comes out no matter what conditions exist.

Later, in the same letter:

. . . You know Don, I was reading a book on the life of Van Gogh today, and I had to pause and think of that wonderful and persistent force—the creative urge. The creative urge was in this man who found himself so much at odds with the world he lived in, and in spite of all the adversity, frustrations, rejections and so forth—beautiful and living art came forth abundantly . . . if only he could be here today.

Truth is indestructible. It seems history shows (and it's the same way today) that the innovator is more often than not met with some degree of condemnation; usually according to the degree of departure from the prevailing modes of expression or what have you. Change is always so hard to accept. We also see that these innovators always seek to revitalize, extend and reconstruct the status quo in their given fields, whatever is needed. Quite often they are the rejects, outcasts, sub-citizens etc. of the very societies to which they bring so much sustenance.

Often they are people who endure great personal tragedy in their lives. Whatever the case, whether accepted or rejected, rich or poor, they are forever guided by that great and eternal constant—the creative urge. Let us cherish it and give all praise to God. Thank you and best wishes to all.

Sincerely,

John Coltrane

Between October 1962 and the recording of *A Love Supreme* in December 1964—which is the stretch that people mean when they refer to "mid-period Coltrane," the period of the group that became the most comprehensible mainstream model of small-group jazz for decades afterward—the only musician who intruded into the quartet's lineup was the drummer Roy Haynes. He and Coltrane had known each other since the late 1940s, and Coltrane brought him into the band during a three-month period when Elvin Jones was in jail on drug charges.

Haynes recorded "Dear Old Stockholm" with the Coltrane quartet in April 1963. There was more space and fragility in Haynes's sound than in Jones's. Coltrane described it in spatial terms, as a "spreading, a permeating," as opposed to Jones's forward drive. During Coltrane's long solo, when McCoy Tyner sits out, close listeners will hear Jimmy Garrison's bass playing, leaving different beats open and unstressed in each bar, better than on almost any recording made by Coltrane's quartet. Some musicians have suggested that Garrison plays so strongly here as to nearly overpower Haynes.

The quartet with Haynes also recorded, that July, at the Newport Jazz Festival, a version of "Impressions"—Coltrane's line that seesawed back and forth between the same modes Miles Davis used on "So What?"—which is faster than any other the band ever put on tape. Haynes's sound is lighter and snappier and higher-pitched; the center of gravity isn't in the interplay of snare and bass drum, as it was with Elvin Jones, but between snare and ride cymbal. (Consequently, Coltrane told Haynes that with him he could hear Tyner better than when he played with Jones.) Haynes was more precise about marking the "one" than Jones, and he was a bomb-dropper in the bebop style: he found obscure areas between the downbeats to thud a bass drum. Coltrane wanted to sustain the intensity of the music, and Haynes wanted to match him. It was the rare situation, Haynes has said, when he had to use sticks, instead of brushes, on ballads.

Haynes was fantastically happy playing with Coltrane. It was the closest thing to playing an improvised duet with the bandleader. "For a drummer, to play with Coltrane is just to accompany the guy," he said. "With others, you gotta hold down the fort. With Coltrane, I could do things I had dreamed about." When the music does in fact reduce to Haynes and Coltrane, one sees the force of the connection more clearly: the long saxophone-and-drum duet at the end of "Impressions" is stunning—the only example of a musician outside the group connecting so well with Coltrane.

"I Want to Talk about You" was the Billy Eckstine ballad that Coltrane had included on his 1958 album *Soultrane*. He loved the song so much that he kept it in his repertory for his own quartet; other than "Soul Eyes," it is the only piece from the Prestige years that Coltrane ever reused for his quartet. It is one of the pieces that makes the record *Coltrane Live at Birdland* special. But more so is "Alabama."

"Alabama," one of the album's two studio-recorded tracks, recorded on November 18, 1963, was most likely written to memorialize the infamous Sunday-morning church bombing in Montgomery, Alabama, on September 15 of that year, in which four black girls were killed. The suspect, Robert Chambliss, was found not guilty of murder; he went free after a small fine and a six-month jail sentence for possessing dynamite.

But it also could have been a generalized response to the events that had unfolded in Alabama over the previous eight years: Rosa Parks and the first Montgomery Bus Boycott of 1955, the beating of the Freedom Riders in Birmingham in 1961, Dr. Martin Luther King's imprisonment during protests in Birmingham in April 1963, and then the confrontation in May, when Birmingham's commissioner of public safety, Bull Connor, turned fire hoses on groups of young children mobilized by Dr. King to protest.

It has been suggested that Coltrane based the long, mournful, through-composed line at the beginning and end of "Alabama" on a Martin Luther King text. And it does sound like a transcription of speech; many of the rhythmic phrases seem unnatural for Coltrane. (The first three notes, in fact, could be the word "Birmingham.") But none of the obvious sources of King speeches before November 1963—"I Have A Dream," the speech at the Great March in Detroit, or the "Letter from Birmingham City Jail," or the eulogy for the victims of the Sixteenth Street Church bombing, delivered on September 18—seem to provide the source.

In any case, here was a different kind of song, almost a classical recitation with a very short improvised section in the middle; he found his natural long-tone phrases and arpeggios to build a dramatic swell before the end. It is a striking piece of music. If anyone wants to begin to understand how Coltrane could inspire so much awe so quickly, the reason is probably inside "Alabama." The incantational tumult he could raise in a long improvisation, the steel-trap knowledge of harmony, the writing—that's all very impressive. But "Alabama" is also an accurate psychological portrait of a time, a complicated mood that nobody else could render so well.

In terms of written material, and the band's sound, up until the changes suggested by "Alabama," Coltrane had been sticking with formulas since late 1961. He knew it.

He had just been through a period of relative stasis. "I'm not actually progressing right now," he told a Swedish interviewer in November 1961, while on tour with Dolphy. "[I'm] just sitting and listening, looking at the jazz scene and trying to see what has been done that I can adapt to, what I feel, to help me move out of what

I've been doing the last two or three years. You can get stagnant, you know."

He was generally pursuing either the fast style (after the model of "Chasin' the Trane"), the soprano-saxophone waltzes (after the model of "My Favorite Things"), or the modal vamping (after the model of "Impressions" and "Africa"). And he did this for two years—not so much time, really, but if we look at how quickly Coltrane moved in the 1960s, it is a significantly long period.

*Crescent*, from April 1964, is the fully developed Coltrane, and also the record that augurs a change. Here is a prime example of what Coltrane and his band could do; and, as if to prove that, every member gets a significant solo, somewhere on the record.

In the piece called "Crescent," Coltrane demonstrated an even further degree of maturity, mixing ballad playing with urgency, using practiced devices and echoes of older tunes to move him toward rawer, speechlike interjections. Its slow theme lasts for a minute and a half, and then the improvising begins, over a midtempo groove that gradually becomes harder and more cutting. At a little after three minutes, Coltrane's raw, squawking tones begin; at a little over four minutes, Tyner drops out and Coltrane starts worrying over shorter and shorter figures; at a little over five, Coltrane is playing as succinctly and powerfully as he ever did.

He kept building on what he had been playing in the past: his improvising in "Crescent" refers several times to the theme of "Miles' Mode." And the changes of "Crescent" itself are rather unusual. The point to be drawn from this is that a musician can project his will on anything: harmonic restrictions and complicated structure can coexist with simplicity and openness; lyricism can coexist with ferocity. "Crescent" is odd: very hot for a ballad, and very mentholated for what would soon be called "energy" music. It has a 12-bar form, though it isn't a blues. It doesn't behave like any species of jazz song in particular.

Coltrane gave Tyner his most extended solo of the record on "Wise One," a ballad with Afro-Latin swing, and when Coltrane returned for his solo, Tyner played in the spaces he left open. Again, Coltrane's solo evolves not toward greater enjambment and speed, but to a point of playing three- or four-note phrases in the same rhythm, which he turns upside down and sideways. He has taken just a little bit of his incantatory mode—the mode that went on for minutes at a time in the solos with Miles Davis during the 1960 European tour, and on "Chasin' the Trane"—and inserted it with a clear end point. He restrained himself; he was becoming known more and more for playing at unreasonable length, but he could achieve balance in making records.

Coltrane's solo in "Bessie's Blues," short and medium up-tempo, a casual tune marking a halfway point in a fairly somber album, includes more references to "Miles' Mode." "Lonnie's Lament" is one of the best ballads written in jazz, but it is an unusual sort of ballad: it could have been a soul song or a hymn. And "The Drum Thing," considering the athletic peaks the band reached on a regular basis, is a strangely muted piece, an extended, through-composed theme leading to a malleted solo over a bass pedal; the bass leaves, and then it is Jones himself for several minutes, switching to sticks, and using very little cymbals.

Coltrane would later intimate that his melodic lines for three pieces here—"Wise One," "Lonnie's Lament," and "The Drum Thing"—worked off the narrative rhythm of text, just as "Alabama" seems to have done. (The implication was clearly that the texts were his own poems, but they never have been found; if they existed as a single trove, they might include a text written for "Song of Praise," from *The John Coltrane Quartet Plays*, which seems like it could be a recitation-song as well.) We have seen that Coltrane wanted to be tricked out of his own thought patterns, and out of his normal phrasing; at the same time, he was also moving closer to music as actual speech.

# 6 two concepts going

Coltrane ran as far as he could in one direction, then started running quickly in another.

By late 1963, he didn't want to keep playing the same tunes; his band book started to change. Also, as we have seen, he didn't want to be controlled by harmonic exercises anymore.

These were not the only changes in his life. Coltrane had left his wife, Naima, in the summer of 1963, and shortly thereafter was living with Alice McLeod, a pianist from Detroit who played bebop and had studied informally with Bud Powell in Paris. They had met soon after she moved to New York in 1962, and made an instant connection. In the summer of 1964, John and Alice moved to a house in suburban Dix Hills, Long Island. They were raising Michelle, Alice's four-year-old daughter from her first marriage, and John Jr., their newborn and first child together.

He had peace, and time to practice continually, on many instruments: besides tenor and soprano saxophone in the house, he had Eric Dolphy's flutes, bagpipes, a harp, various drums, and an acoustic guitar. He was still using charts and graphs, based on math and astrology and architecture, to inspire composition; he had even found ways to derive song from the shape of a cathedral.

They had few visitors. "He was the type of person, he didn't care for socializing," Alice Coltrane said later. "And I don't care for socializing, so that's sort of the way it was."

Coltrane was songwriting, using this new method of composing to the written word. Ultimately he was ready to spread out—both in terms of building a bigger group, and by compounding his interest in religion and philosophy, so that it affected the structure and style of his music.

Alice Coltrane has said that on one day in the late summer of 1964 he came downstairs in his new house "like Moses coming down from the mountain," holding the complete outline for a new suite. No other Coltrane music would be so formally prepared.

A manuscript showing this preliminary musical arrangement for *A Love Supreme* surfaced in late 2004, when Alice Coltrane (they married in Juárez, Mexico, in October 1965) offered it to Guernsey's Auction House to be sold. It indicated, among other things, that Coltrane felt the piece could be arranged for a group of nine: tenor saxophone and "one other horn," piano, trap drums, two basses, two conga players, and one timbales player.

Other markings on the paper demonstrate his thoughts: toward the end of part one, he noted, a saxophone solo with quartet accompaniment should lead into "all drums multiple meters and voices changing motif in E♭mi 'A Love Supreme.'" Later, toward the ending: "Make ending attempt to reach transcendent level with orchestra . . . rising harmonies to a level of blissful stability." At the bottom of the page he writes: "last chord to sound like final chord of Alabama."

Apart from creating a nine-piece group, which he did not do— he only added Archie Shepp and Art Davis on a scrapped alternate take of "Acknowledgement"—Coltrane realized his ambitions. He recorded *A Love Supreme* in one day, December 9, 1964, and it is not just another cusp in a series of cusps but the fulcrum of his career, setting the outline for understanding both his past and future work.

Much is established in the first ten seconds of the first part,

"Acknowledgement": Coltrane plays an ascending I–II–V pattern that forms an E-major chord, and turns it into a melodic cell that he runs up and down for the major part of his improvisation. (This cell-making process—and at times these particular intervals—are in his playing from "Crescent" onward.) At the core of "Resolution" is a doleful ballad melody played with sweeping legato between notes that relates back to Kaper's "While My Lady Sleeps" and "On Green Dolphin Street," not to mention Coltrane's own "Lonnie's Lament."

It is a full-band work: all members have their own moments within the record, and the quartet's ensemble sound grows especially rich at the end of "Resolution." The record includes his fast, hard, nubby "Chasin' the Trane" style of playing, in the middle of his "Pursuance" solo. It also includes a B-flat minor blues: "Pursuance," part three of the work, which incorporates the work's unifying cell. And it includes a word-based recitation, probably his best, in "Psalm," taking off from Coltrane's poem, which was printed on the LP sleeve. ("Thank you, God" is the refrain in between lines; in that phrase, the word "God" always signals a return to the tonic.)


It seems likely that by the beginning of 1965 Coltrane was thinking of changing the quartet—probably by adding to it, as he experimented with on the *Love Supreme* sessions.

In June 1965, Coltrane recorded three sessions. The recordings resulted in quartet performances that ended up on the albums *Transition, Living Space*, and *Kulu Se Mama*. The track "Transition" shows a band running together at its highest output, like a floored car engine. It starts off with a slight rhythmic muddle before the downbeat; only on the 8th bar do you feel the full force of Elvin Jones's "one." Ninety seconds in, the music reaches its top revving, and stays there.

•   •   •

"Resolution" had been the last of Coltrane's great melodies. Beyond it, for the most part, lay something other than songs-for-the-sake-of-songs: melody lines were now a matter of intervals and cells, musical vitamins to keep the drone healthy. "Suite," recorded six months after the suite that really mattered, isn't nearly as distinctive. It marks the beginning of a late Coltrane-quartet period that amounts to one interconnected song. It is music of meditation and chant, the sound of his interior cosmos.

The music Coltrane's quartet played at New York's Half Note in the spring of 1965—often bootlegged, and not released officially until 2005—shows better than the studio albums just where the band had gotten to. A recording of "One Down, One Up," during which Elvin Jones breaks his bass pedal and plays without a bass drum for several minutes, remains one of the best indicators of the group's energy. From the midway point to the final iteration of the theme, thirteen minutes of its twenty-seven-minute duration are a duet between Coltrane and Jones, and so it belongs in that select group of Coltrane-Jones performances alone, alongside "Vigil" (from *Transition*) and a portion of "Crescent." And in it Coltrane swings, wired to the slightest accents of his drummer, delivering massive projection.

"One Down, One Up" is extraordinarily tough and coordinated music. There is not much obscure or implied about it; both the technical accomplishment and the physical endurance are of a sort that I have never experienced firsthand from any jazz group.

Those who caught it, during Coltrane's run of gigs during this time, remember it as an almost physical sensation. The saxophonist Joe McPhee saw him in 1965 at the Village Gate and felt flooded, overloaded. "I thought I was going to die from the emotion," he said. "I'd never experienced anything like that in my life. I thought I was just going to explode right in the place. The energy level kept building up, and I thought, God almighty, I can't take it." The jazz critic and historian Dan Morgenstern—whose passion runs toward swing and bebop players and who has never been known as much of a Coltrane booster—said something similar about an evening he spent watching Coltrane at the Half Note at around the same time. "The intensity that was generated was absolutely unbelievable," he said. "I can still *feel* it, and it was unlike any other feeling within the music we call jazz."

The year 1965 was a period of more concentrated excellence for Coltrane than has often been acknowledged. Its excellence is in its turbulence, its volubility. The great quartet was still intact but reaching the edge of the cliff, and Coltrane had fully absorbed Albert Ayler.

Ayler, ten years younger and several times wilder, found a purpose for naïveté in jazz, even more so than Ornette Coleman had. He was a walking example of new American transcendentalism. William James would have assigned Ayler to the "religion of healthy-mindedness"; he seemed to act out of Walt Whitman's idea that "what is called good is perfect and what is called bad is just as perfect." He had his own style, but he was the embodiment of an idea much more influential than his style: the advancing of "spirit" over craft.

Ayler wrote stirring melodies that sounded like anthems, hymns, or marches, completely subsumed in harmony: specifically, major-triad harmony. But his seeming lack of interest in tonal harmony in his improvisations (specifically, bebop harmony), his broken shrieks, his pile-driving volume, his lack of defining references to key or pulse or structure infuriated many of his elders, musicians like Johnny Griffin and Eddie "Lockjaw" Davis and James Moody. He seemed to be channeling terrors. (Harmony is rational science, and in his improvisations Ayler was effectively refuting it.) One could interpret it for days, seeing evidence of a new social order, but it really didn't need explanation. It was immediately stunning, whatever it was. (When it wasn't bluntly, forcefully stunning, it could sometimes be intricately stunning, as in his recordings in a trio with Gary Peacock and Sunny Murray in 1964.) Ayler played as if he were throwing himself at the fire, looking down into the precipice, et cetera; a legion of players and listeners oriented themselves around metaphors like that. But the music was all changeable, unpredictable, slightly anarchic. The metaphors and quick analyses never quite held fast. Was it lack of ambition? Was it grift? Magic? Supernatural visitations? Hippie vaudeville?

Albert Ayler had sat in with the Coltrane quartet at the Jazz Temple in Cleveland in the summer of 1963, during a period when he was living with his parents and defeated by lack of work in New York. Later, that winter (December 31, 1963), as a member of the Cecil Taylor Unit, Ayler appeared on the same bill with Coltrane at Lincoln Center.

Around the same time, the drummer Rashied Ali was getting ready to leave Philadelphia, where he was one of the hometown believers. (In the late 1950s he used to sometimes sit in Fairmount Park across from Coltrane's mother's house on North Thirty-third Street, in the Strawberry Mansion neighborhood, listening to the sound of Coltrane practicing on the top floor.) Ali had his own turnaround experience with Coltrane, who encouraged him to move to New York, promising him that there were people there who played in the rhythmically free style he favored.

Again—as in the case of hiring Eric Dolphy at the moment of his greatest commercial success—Coltrane demonstrated independence of mind. Like Earl Bostic in his time, Coltrane had become the ultimate saxophone student, recognized and respected as such; he practiced constantly, even regularly between sets at nightclubs, and had become astonishingly proficient at working through harmony. But he heard something powerful in Ayler, who took the very opposite approach.

Ayler was not particularly interested in keys. He was not interested in extensions of bebop. He really did want to scream through his instrument, and he had his reasons for it. Perhaps we are underestimating Coltrane's ambitiousness and competitiveness; perhaps Coltrane was in some sense threatened by Ayler. But if this were true, he wouldn't have absorbed him so quickly. After all,

Coltrane had a baseline authority. He was a master bebop player. The overwhelming percentage of jazz lovers, who as a rule do not like to hear screaming through the horn, would never have tsk-tsked him about not having come to terms with Ayler. He could simply have ignored him.

From 1963 on, Coltrane and Ayler, when both in New York, were often in the same room. Various recollections have placed Coltrane watching Ayler and Cecil Taylor at the Take 3 Coffee-house in the West Village in the fall of 1963; watching Ayler and Eric Dolphy together at the Half Note sometime that year; inviting Ayler onstage at the Half Note in March 1964; hearing Ayler's group with Rashied Ali at a little performance space at 27 Cooper Square in early 1965.

On that evening in 1965, Coltrane may have been interested in hiring Ali. Ali remembers Coltrane pulling out a chair from the row at the performance space, a building where the writer Amiri Baraka (then LeRoi Jones) and Archie Shepp were living, and putting it in the middle of the aisle so he could get a clear view of Ayler as he played. This made Ali nervous and self-conscious.

Coltrane is said to have given money to Ayler, and eventually helped him get a record contract with Bob Thiele at Impulse.

Coltrane started bringing new members into the band in 1965. The reception to this experiment had been chilly enough when he tried it with Eric Dolphy; this time his audience was even less forgiving, and as a result he undermined his own credibility. Most of his fans could go with his new music as long as band members of repute were playing it. With new members of less objectively measurable talent, some felt they were being conned.

At some point in early 1965, Rashied Ali got up the courage to ask Coltrane if he would let him play with the group at the Half Note. Later that year, possibly in May, Coltrane let him sit in for a whole night when Elvin Jones was unavailable. After that, Ali brought his friends Pharoah Sanders and Archie Shepp to the Half Note; in time they would sit in with the group as well. In return, Coltrane started coming to their gigs.

A filmed performance exists of Coltrane with his quartet, from August 1, 1965, in Comblain-la-Tour, Belgium. The setting is an outdoor jazz festival, and the weather is cold. It is a comfortable group doing a night's job, playing well-trod repertory. But that workmanlike comfort involves extremely rigorous playing. The bridge of "Naima" becomes torn, agitated, almost baleful, with Jones occupying the far back end of the beat and Garrison sketching impulsively around the tonic. At the conclusion of this superb "Naima," Coltrane—thicker and heavier now than he appeared on the Danish television broadcast in 1961, and playing with his eyes tightly shut, unlike in the earlier footage—doesn't acknowledge the applause. Even before the last beat of the song he darts off to his left to fetch his soprano saxophone, and then starts to play "My Favorite Things." It is evocative footage: the musicians are working up a sweat in their heavy dark suits—Jones especially—and the cold air causes steam to rise visibly off their figures.

His performance at Soldier Field in Chicago two weeks later, on August 15, 1965, as the headlining act of the Down Beat Jazz Festival, has been understood as a famous breaking point—a Dylan-at-Newport, or a *Rite of Spring*. As with both of those examples, the challenge put forth from the artist to the audience is half-overstated and half-real. The set was thirty-seven minutes long. The quartet, with Archie Shepp as an extra on tenor, yoked together a set out of the theme from "Nature Boy," some collective improvising, and "Blue Valse." The music grew jagged and vociferous. It aggravated a great part of the crowd, prompting, according to some witnesses, a large exodus. It has seldom been considered, however, that the first intimations of the truly wild Coltrane had already been recorded but not yet released. Or that casual jazz fans who had been in the sun all day at a free festival, listening to more straightforward performances by Woody Herman and Gerry Mulligan and Monk and Joe Williams, might well be inclined to start for home at the first splash of dissonance.

●  ●  ●

Some of his recorded music from this time shrinks his options down. "Amen," for example, from *Sun Ship*, recorded two weeks after Soldier Field, uses only a I–II–V cell—that basic harmonic relationship from the "Acknowledgement" section of *A Love Supreme.*

On the other hand, the album *Ascension*, recorded in late June 1965, before his European tour, expanded his options. Possibly as a result of his allowed sit-ins at the Half Note, seven extra musicians—Archie Shepp, Pharoah Sanders, John Tchicai, Marion Brown, Freddie Hubbard, Dewey Johnson, and Art Davis—joined the group, playing through a series of scales flowing into each other, signaled by Coltrane; the music moves through pile-ons and gradual extrusions of single soloists. The extra musicians create a weakening of the music's base; in retaliation, Jones and Tyner keep reasserting the pulse as hard as they can.

*Ascension* is not a success in particular. It is hard to get around the tremulous chaos of the group sound, not to mention the many moments of a band whose members are not in sync with one another, reaching points where they might as well stop, but don't.

Instead it is a success in general, a paradigm. First of all, it had to happen: if you intimate the loosening of structure in any art form, sooner or later you are going to have to let the opposite of form run rampant. ("Form" exists on many levels, however, and *Ascension* was by no means formless.) It broke the seal on full-bore, single-gesture, all-out, free-blowing sessions—Sun Ra's free sessions were lighter-bodied, and Ornette Coleman's album *Free Jazz* was calligraphy by comparison—as well as the notion of the jazz band as community, a collective effort to make large-scale textural music rather than an exclusive, carefully structured machine moving through smaller and more defined parts. This had obvious political implications in 1965, especially in Europe, where Marxism was strong and the memory of fascism was still fresh. The album led directly to the German saxophonist Peter Brötzmann's album *Machine Gun*, three years later, one of the major statements of European free jazz. Even if the philosophical ideas governing *Ma-*

*chine Gun* were different from those of *Ascension*—Brötzmann
carries a rich sense of himself as a product of the working-class,
steel-and-coal Ruhr Valley, and as a German born during World
War II—the sound is similar.

In terms of applicable conventions that could be crudely aped,
it was the rare example of Coltrane getting there first. (It was
more Coltrane's way to move organically toward a harmonic pattern, or a group sound, that was personal and resistant to political
metaphors.) Because he did, it became the basis for a huge amount
of free jazz after it, then and still. While Albert Ayler had been
making heart-palpitation yawps, Cecil Taylor explored pan-
tonality and the music of physical reflexes, Ornette Coleman made
Ornette Coleman–style group interaction, and the New York Contemporary Five recapped Ornette Coleman, *Ascension* was the first
major piece of work from the jazz avant-garde to valorize the idea
not only of sheer volume but of *texture* in jazz-group interaction.

However subtly, Coltrane designed and directed *Ascension*, and
he arises from it as its single impressive soloist by far. But it is an
experiment in the democratic ideal—much more than most other
works of jazz, no matter how often, and loosely, the metaphor of
democracy is misapplied to the music.

*Ascension* suggests cathartic release, but Coltrane felt anything
but released while recording it. "I was so doggone busy; I was worried to death," he told Frank Kofsky. "I couldn't really enjoy the
[recording] date. If it hadn't been a date, then I would have really
enjoyed it."

Immediately thereafter, the idea of texture would become very
basic to experimental jazz. The Association for the Advancement of
Creative Musicians, led by the pianist Muhal Richard Abrams and
including the musicians who would make up the Art Ensemble of
Chicago, compounded the emphasis on texture by bringing new
instruments into the regular mixture of horns and piano and percussion; they were the first jazz performers to use the sounds of
bulb-horns and cans of water hung on a rope. They used prag-

matic, everyday sounds: they promised an expanded but still neighborhoody new world of what they came to call "Great Black Music."

John Coltrane was releasing albums on Impulse at a rate of about one every three months. He was able to record at Van Gelder's studio even when Impulse wasn't aware of it. If being in the presence of Ellington helped him let go of each record more easily, the new unlimited opportunity seemed to make him more pasha-like. He called Bob Thiele after the release of *Ascension* and declared that the take he chose was not the take Thiele had pressed. Amazingly, Thiele complied, issuing a new, correct (and longer) take. A few months later, in September 1965, Coltrane recorded *Meditations*, a rather beautiful new suite with serene echoes of the ballads from *Crescent* but clearly in the direction of condensed cells over developed melody. He decided not to release it—this first version would not appear until 1977—and rerecorded the suite at the end of November with Rashied Ali added on drums and Pharoah Sanders added on tenor saxophone.

This one-foot-in, one-foot-out phase was characteristic of Coltrane, who resisted making qualitative decisions about his music. Essentially, he wanted it all: he wanted to mash the old players and the new players together, without losing anyone. "There was a thing I wanted to do in music, see," he said. "I figured I could do *two* things: I could have a band that played like the way we used to play, and a band that was going in the direction that the one I have now [in 1966] is going in—I could combine these two, with these two concepts going. And it could have been done."

One assumes that Coltrane was talking about combining the two into one unit, rather than keeping two groups going separately, so that the combinations could produce some positive tension in his work.

As he implied, it wasn't done, or at least not to his satisfaction.

Miles Davis would do it, however, a few years later, during the two-year transitional period between his albums *Nefertiti* and *Bitches Brew*. He fused groups, combining his old people and his new people. Being sandwiched between completely different approaches to music isn't just a psychological or critical challenge: it is a technical challenge. Some of the musicians closest to Coltrane found free jazz difficult, necessitating a whole new language; Jimmy Garrison said he had to learn "to phrase, rather than to walk," in his new role. And Coltrane's newer recruits were not up to the challenges of his old material and his old band. Some of Davis's newer recruits, on the other hand, were.

Sanders was a rhythm-and-blues journeyman who had met Coltrane in 1961 and moved to New York in 1962. If Ayler was a free agent, a self-conscious, original naïf, a post-everything player and a weird kind of old-fashioned melodist at the same time, Pharoah Sanders (fourteen years younger than Coltrane) was specifically the first major post-Coltrane saxophonist: his pan-tonal musical personality came straight out of modal pieces like "Africa." He essentially became Coltrane's new Eric Dolphy, a wilder trip wire who helped the leader more than he helped the group as a whole.

*Live in Seattle* features a sextet, with an extra bassist (Donald Rafael Garrett) and Pharoah Sanders, and its versions of "Out of This World" and "Body and Soul" are effective returns to the contours of Coltrane's older work.

This "Body and Soul" is more soul than body. It keeps part of the arrangement from *Coltrane's Sound*: the "Giant Steps" changes remain in the bridge. But this was a slower and more ancient-sounding version of the song, as if its original source was one of Coltrane's collections of spirituals, as if Coltrane wanted to melt the song down to liquid. Donald Rafael Garrett bows long tones on the bass during Tyner's solo, and Tyner becomes more insistent on sounding the bass-clef tonic, hard; he gives the piece a thick upper layer of drone.

Jones's 4/4 ballad swing-rhythm had deepened since he joined the band; his tempo gravid and lovely, the snare feels even more small and precise; the loud smacks of Tyner's fifths in the left hand sustain a ringing on the first beat of every measure. Coltrane begins the tune after thirty seconds of vamp, plays it fairly straight in the first 8 bars of the melody chorus, begins to improvise broadly on the second 8, barely refers to the melody of the bridge yet stays in tonality, and starts propelling himself in the final 8. The second chorus, before Tyner's three-chorus solo, is where the action really starts—the short, low-register bursts, the gargled hunks of scales. The bridge on the second chorus, going into the final 8 of the second chorus, darkens, growing thick with fluttering notes.

Tyner gives one of his thundering, sustain-pedal improvisations, playing modal within chords; Pharoah Sanders enters, in the hard spot of having to follow such heavy-gauge expositions, uninterested in the chord movement in the bridge, playing weakly and generally off-microphone, chary about getting in deeply until the very end, when he delivers pure sound: low, capacious blasts. Finally, at the end, the band gathers itself up for a quiet, final flourish, with the drums dropped out.

"He was a deep, great artist, even if he was rather a sententious man," D. H. Lawrence wrote of Melville in *Studies in Classic American Literature*. Lawrence might have been describing the Coltrane of late 1965. Coltrane continued to play for his audience in suit and tie; talked with gracious sensitivity to interviewers, politely refusing to elaborate on his split-focus beween the old jazz reality (Johnny Hodges) and the new jazz reality (Albert Ayler); became physically heavier and less easy to parse; stayed available by telephone to his circle of musicians, but did not enter into deep friendships; bought a Jaguar; maintained a middle-class home life in Long Island with Alice and their two children.

At the same time, to a certain way of thinking, he represented America's tribal subconscious, its attraction to sublimity. He was reportedly taking LSD during this period, and the day after the show at Seattle's Penthouse, he recorded *Om*, with the quartet plus Pharoah Sanders, the multi-instrumentalist Donald Garrett, and the percussionist and flutist Joe Brazil. *Om* cannot be held up as an ideal example of what Coltrane was working toward. It is a fairly disjointed, agitated, muddy, twenty-nine-minute catharsis, culled from a six-hour jam session.

"Om" is a Vedic mantra meant to suggest the sound made at the moment when God created the world. The Coltrane record begins and ends with thumb piano, wood flute and bells, and this recitation from the Bhagavad Gita:

> Rites that the Vedas ordain, and the rituals taught by the scriptures, all these am I, and the offering made to the ghost of the fathers, herbs of healing and food. The mantram. The clarified butter. I, the oblation and I, the flame to which it is offered. I am the sire of the world, and this world's mother and grandsire. I am he who awards to each the fruit of his action. I make all things clean. I am om. Ommmm, ommmm, ommmmm, ommmm . . .

"He was a real American in that he always felt his audience in front of him," Lawrence continued, about Melville.

> But when he ceases to be American, when he forgets all audience, and gives us his sheer apprehension of the world, then he is wonderful, his book commands a stillness in the soul, an awe . . . It is the same old thing as in all Americans. They keep their old-fashioned ideal frock-coat on, and an old-fashioned silk hat, while they do the most impossible things . . . Their ideals are like armour which has rusted in, and will never more come off. And meanwhile in Melville his bodily knowledge moves naked, a living quick among the stark elements. For with sheer physical vibrational sensitiveness, like a marvelous wireless-station, he registers the effects of the outer world. And he records, also, almost beyond pain or pleasure, the extreme transitions of the iso-

lated, far-driven soul, the soul which is now alone, without real human contact.

McCoy Tyner had been the first to leave the band, at the end of 1965. Then Jones left at the end of January 1966. They both gave the same reason, more or less. "He added another drummer," Jones told Whitney Balliett, "and I couldn't hear what I was doing any longer. There was too much going on, and it was ridiculous as far as I was concerned. I was getting into a whole area of frustration, and what I had to offer I felt I just couldn't contribute. I think Coltrane was upset, and I know in those last weeks I had a constant migraine headache."

So the quartet, such as it was, ended.

# 7 **best good**

Rashied Ali became the full-time drummer and Alice Coltrane the full-time pianist. Alice could sound like McCoy Tyner—the bass-clef fourths and fifths, the modal improvising—without the hard-driving rhythmic attack. She was a light and restful pianist, serenely moving chords up and down the entire keyboard, stretching out long, even improvisations without overexcitement; that was her style. She didn't come down hard on the "one" at the beginning of each measure, as Tyner had. With Rashied Ali—who didn't articulate a "one," either, and in fact largely did not play in any fixed time with Coltrane, but instead suggested the tides—she didn't need to.

The first significant concert of the new group was at the 2,600-seat Philharmonic Hall (now Avery Fisher Hall) at Lincoln Center, on February 19, 1966, in a show called "Titans of the Tenor." Dexter Gordon and Zoot Sims played in the first set, Sonny Rollins and Coltrane in the second. For many Coltrane fans of the generation who loved him at the Village Vanguard in 1961 and had believed in his process, his performance here was the final straw. Coltrane brought two drummers (Ali and J. C. Moses), Alice, Jimmy Garrison, Albert Ayler, Donald Ayler, Pharoah Sanders, and Carlos Ward. *Ascension* had not at all been absorbed into the jazz culture yet. It hadn't even been released yet.

This is what Amiri Baraka remembers about the concert:

> It was a Trane concert, armed to the teeth with some of the most impressive of the new musicians, who were now magnetized to the master . . . We arrived backstage, Norman's eyes shifting the shadows of the darkened staircase from which we checked and dug the fantastic out bad doom-a-doom whooah of the heavy jam. [Norman, a.k.a. "Black Norman," was a friend of Ayler's.]
>
> The whole of the *mise en scène* entered the playing, *as* the playing, danced and hugged everybody (alive)'s tender screamings or head casted to the rest of the audience like a transfusion, the blistering molten blood swishing through our hearing. Oh Yeh!
>
> At the top of that nuclear "My God!," that emotional convergence turned Albert into the horn he suddenly had in his hand. He began to stride out onto the stage. The horn raised high above his head, as if he wanted to take Pres *manqué* all the way out. The bell pointing as much as possible at the embroidered ceiling of the place. And then, Lord, with that pose as his heart's signature, he began to open a hole in the roof so his angels could descend, summoned by his exploding plaints.
>
> I mean (lovers of a graphic prose), that sound Albert created then was of an actual frightening nature. It had no older reference; it was like a thing born then, that we all witnessed, flying out of the womb of his horn, screaming, it seemed, in its suddenness, with a thousand times more force than all those assembled around him! It was like a thing that you could hear and feel and be made "other" by, because it swallowed you! . . .
>
> After the program ended, the first one back to the stairway was Trane (Albert had left the stage after his nuclear display, for the hallway where Norman and I waited). Trane came right up to Albert, his only words, "What kind of reed you using?"

This is what the saxophonist Dave Liebman remembers about the concert:

> Coltrane walked on with what looked like an army of guys he got off the street carrying shopping bags, two drummers, a bunch of saxophonists. He started chanting "Om Manee Padme Om," which was the Tibetan chant . . . Alice was doing a tremolo, and they all started "My Favorite Things," but not in the typical way. It was a much freer arrangement, and people started cheering. I mean this was a full house in a two-thousand-seat auditorium. Of course, after the melody, there was no semblance of anything at all approaching the tune "My Favorite Things"! This went on for the next hour plus, and I would say a good third or half of the audience left.

Some who saw this concert regarded it as the last straw, the last time they gave Coltrane a chance. They either thought it was too heavy for them, or they saw most of these extraneous players from outside of the band as barnacles, attaching themselves to the main chance—or, worse, thought that Coltrane needed all these younger musicians to validate himself in jazz's new era.

But Coltrane seemed not to be able to help it. Rashied Ali tells a story on this subject. He remembers playing at the Village Vanguard with Coltrane in 1966 and being asked by Coltrane, in the club's back room before the gig, what he thought about Frank Wright, the young free-jazz tenor player. He knew that Ali and Wright were friends, and Wright, who had come to the club that night, had independently approached Coltrane about the possibility of sitting in with Coltrane's band at the club. Ali reacted skeptically.

> I said, "Aw, man, he ain't playing shit."
>
> He looked at me. I said, "Man, he ain't playing shit."
>
> We go out on the bandstand, and the *first thing* he does is say [to Wright], "Hey, man, come on up."

In the dressing room, after it was over, he said something I never forgot. He said, "I don't care what a cat plays. If you're into music, there'll be something you hear [in that musician] that you might like. One note, one sound, that you might like."

How does one react to such a deeply impractical statement, coming from an artist at the top of his game? Do you laugh? Do you tell him that he's wrong? (No, some musicians really aren't worth wasting time on.) Do you argue with him? How can you do anything other than try to take his advice, even if you fail? As an addendum to that story, Ali added, "From that day to this, I've never put a musician down for anything."

And what of Frank Wright? Until his death in 1990, he distinguished himself as almost the last of a breed by his devotion to the principles of power, loudness, maximum nonmelodic screaming-through-the-horn. He adapted a small part of Coltrane's sound for himself, and that was enough for him. Later, he said: "No motherfucker can tell me what I have to play, and I know I'm right because what I do is countersigned by master John Coltrane who accepted me at his side by calling me 'little brother.' "

Coltrane made another live record, possibly from the week when Coltrane gave Frank Wright a chance. *Live at the Village Vanguard Again*, recorded May 28, 1966, gives the old fans a little bit to hold on to; the two long tunes are old favorites, "My Favorite Things" and "Naima." "My Favorite Things," by this point, had become dreary with use, a cosmic exercise that needed to be radically refreshed. But "Naima," with its drone and its consonant, melodious line, worked with wicked effectiveness.

Sanders's solo on this "Naima" begins with abrasive huffing and scrambling, not dissimilar from a sound Archie Shepp liked to get; it works through wild passages of fast and repetitive playing, terrifically ugly challenges of squelched and shrieking sounds, and hoarse, brawny tours through sections of the melody. The performance is full of personality, full of its own sound, not at all boring. Sanders uses almost purely metamusical logic—intuitive gestures of the emotions, of the nerves—to make the seven-minute solo cohere. With Coltrane, on the other hand, who plays two shorter, more driving and traditionally dramatic solos around Sanders, you always seem to be keeping your eye on the resolution about to come. All that he plays exists in relation to the harmony and melody of the song.

*Live in Japan*, recorded during Coltrane's two-and-a-half-week tour of Japan, with Pharoah Sanders and Jimmy Garrison still in the group, is a record of long-form stamina, closer than any other recording to what his performances had actually been like for about five years—a fifty-four-minute version of "Crescent," a forty-four-minute version of "Leo." It has its chaos, but in no way has Coltrane renounced grace: in "Peace on Earth," a new rubato ballad in the "Naima" style, he displays a technique that had never been more stunning, with rapid interrogations of harmony and extreme dynamics—from mild susurrations to a stretch before the end of his solo where he packs so much force into the horn that it sounds as if it might burst. Then, when he returns after Alice's solo, it's as if he's looking backward at his career; he seems to reference at various points the melodic cells of *A Love Supreme* and *Ascension*, the melody of "Naima," and the melody of "Body and Soul." But these are not in any way explicit references. He is working within his own improvisational language, a big pool, wide enough to accommodate all that music.

On July 9, 1966, Coltrane gave a press conference in the Tokyo Prince Hotel. The band played one piece for forty-five minutes and then Coltrane answered questions for a long time, in patient humor, answering questions he didn't want to answer by giggling and obfuscating. He said he would like to visit temples, travel to rural areas, and hear the koto played. Asked about his religious beliefs, he replied:

> I am [Christian] by birth, or my mother was and father was, and
> so forth. My early teachings were in the Christian faith. And now,

as I look out upon the world, and it's always been a thing with me to feel that all men know the truth, see? So therefore I have always felt that even though a man was not a Christian, he still has to know the truth in some way. Or if he was a Christian, he could know the truth, or he could *not* . . . The truth itself doesn't have any name on it. To me. Each man has to find this for himself, I think.

I believe that men are here to grow themselves into the best good that they can be. This is what I want to do, this is my belief: that I'm supposed to grow to the best good that I can get to. As I'm going there, becoming this, and if I ever become this, it will just come out of the horn. So whatever I will be, it will be. I'm not interested in trying to say what it will be, I don't know. But I believe that good will only bring good.

To the question "What would you like to be in ten years?" Coltrane answered: "I would like to be a saint."


The music from here through 1967 is generally seen as the rawest, most basic, wildest version of Coltrane, like the decadent stage of the Romantic movement. It takes a bit of attention to notice the order and theory, but it is there.

There is always a process with Coltrane, something thought through. Which makes the chest-beating situation so confusing. On more than one occasion in 1966 and 1967, during a performance, Coltrane took the saxophone out of his mouth, beat his chest, and sang into the microphone. Rashied Ali has described it as a kind of premature epilogue, the consequence of having played everything there was to play. "I'd say, 'Trane, man, why are you doing that, beating on your chest and howling in the microphone?' " Ali remembered in an interview. "He'd say, 'Man, I can't find nothing else to play on the horn.' He exhausted the saxophone. He couldn't find nothing else to play . . . he ran out of horn."

Tapes from this period do not suggest depletion or animalism.

During "Leo," on November 11, 1966 at Temple University in Philadelphia—an unreleased recording—the music reduced to a drum-saxophone duet between Ali and Coltrane. Ali solos alone for a while, with drumsticks, beating rapidly on snare and toms. Coltrane enters, first tapping bells, then singing while beating his chest; at first it is the I–II–V pattern, the same melodic cell that you hear at the beginning of the melody of "Wise One," and the "Acknowledgement" section of *A Love Supreme*, and then it builds methodically on that. The drumming on his chest mimics Ali's patterns. He is singing, not screaming. It couldn't be more logical. After forty-five seconds of this, he picks up his tenor and resumes where he had left off.

But this sort of thing has not passed down through history as an image of control—even to his friends, contemporaries, even learned musicians.

"I told him that he impressed me like somebody that was afraid," said Jimmy Oliver, the tenor player who was Coltrane's contemporary and one of his early colleagues on the late-1940s Philadelphia scene, about the music of this phase. "As if he was running scared . . . I pictured him running through alleys, knocking over cans, falling down. If you've ever seen anybody run scared, this is the picture he gave me, musically."

Coltrane didn't want to play forty-five-minute sets anymore. He was tired of playing clubs. Tired in general. After a club date at the Village Vanguard in November 1966, he stopped taking club bookings.

He helped support the Olatunji Center of African Culture, at 125th Street and Madison Avenue in Harlem, started by the drummer Babatunde Olatunji. He approached Olatunji in July 1966 and asked if he, Yusef Lateef, and Olatunji could form an organization to put on concerts, both at the Olatunji Center and at bigger venues—including Carnegie Hall and Lincoln Center. He wrote a number of checks, both while the Center was being built and later, to help cover its operating expenses.

•   •   •

Photographs of Coltrane during his Japanese tour in 1966 often show him with one hand on his chest. (Rashied Ali, with him through the tour, had no idea Coltrane might be ill.) He played the flute, which required less wind than the saxophone, during the studio sessions that would become *Expression*. He told Bob Thiele at Impulse that he wanted nothing on the album's jacket but the titles and the names of the musicians. No description or analysis: he was tired of words. He talked about wanting to travel to western Africa to explore the tonal properties of the Yoruban language, to find more fuel for his improvising, to give him new exercises.

The session of February 15, 1967, released as *Stellar Regions*, shows a potentially great band. There seems to be no question but that Coltrane did his best work in quartets, no matter how much a fifth member had to offer. This session, a quartet without Pharoah Sanders, not released until 1995, is the perfect representation of Coltrane at this stage. Alice Coltrane and Rashied Ali sound more connected and solidified; they are beginning to posit something concrete in place of the Tyner-Jones connection. At this point, Ali's concept of free-time drumming was sometimes shaped by Coltrane's suggestions: a chart in Coltrane's hand from early 1967 indicates varying phrase patterns for Ali, written out in numbers instead of musical notation. It indicates 1-2/1-2/1-2/1-2-3, repeated twice; then 1-2-3/1-2-3/1-2-3; then 1-2-3-4/1-2-3-4-5-6-7/1-2-3-4-5.

*Interstellar Space*, though, is unique. A set of duets with Rashied Ali alone, they capitalized on the strength of the saxophone-drum passages that had formed parts of *Crescent, Transition*, and the Half Note dates (as well, presumably, as many other gigs) but never as a complete concert or record. Yet this album wasn't club music; it was not built on the premise that the music is going to take you higher and higher. The music here is a mind-quieter.

It was minimally planned. Some have suggested that Coltrane kept convening his band in the studio in 1966 and 1967 because he didn't have the strength to tour much but still wanted to keep his sidemen paid. *Interstellar Space* happened on what seemed for Ali to be a routine visit to Rudy Van Gelder's studio. Ali arrived with his friend Jimmy Vass, expecting to find the other band members, and saw no one else there.

"Ain't nobody coming?" he said to Vass. Soon Coltrane arrived.

"Ain't nobody coming?" he said to Coltrane.

"No, it's just you and me."

"What are we playing? Is it fast? Is it slow?"

"Whatever you want it to be. Come on. I'm going to ring some bells. You can do an 8-bar intro."

They cut the record in one take. Ali says he wasn't completely at ease, that the whole thing brought him up short. He still feels he could have done better if he had been prepared.

Coltrane directs the music, beginning and ending at a place of calm, even though the music reaches frenetic states in between. It isn't show business, even hippie show business. It's an almost monastic record. Each piece begins and ends with bells, shaken by Coltrane. The pieces encompass a range of expression, from hard, fragmentary phrases to flowing, downward twelve-note scales, played so fast and articulated so clearly they give you the physical sensation of the floor dropping out from under you. This takes him back to 1958, when he started to become interested in the harp, expressing himself with fast arpeggios; it is sheets-of-sound done even better.

By the time of Coltrane's concert at the Olatunji Center of African Culture, a benefit for the Center's scholarship fund on April 23, 1967, he was quite sick, not that his playing would reveal it. He had liver cancer—possibly from damage to his liver done while addicted to alcohol and narcotics, though one can't be sure. At the final concert, he sat down in a chair to play, something he had not been known to do.

*The Olatunji Concert*, released in 2001, suffers from terrible unintended audio problems. Without a great amount of amplification, you can't make music as violent, scraping, tinnily climactic as this recording suggests. It is quite possible that no worse-sounding musical document has ever been issued in full by a major record label.

The acoustics in the room, a converted gym, were impossibly live, a giant echo chamber. This explains some of the extra boost in Coltrane's soprano saxophone solo in "My Favorite Things," and suggests how shattering Pharoah Sanders's performance in the same song might have been, though the sound is too distorted for one to know. Twenty minutes in, the taped noise becomes unbearable, a cloud of cymbals and overdriven screams. The recording can't be taken seriously; it can't be counted. But because it will be, and must be, it puts a question mark on the end of the story. Forget music with a social power, with a community function—that's all fine. This is almost impenetrable.

After the concert, Coltrane reimbursed the Olatunji Center for the money spent on promoting the concert, a sum of $425.

It was his last performance. Three months later, on Monday, July 17, 1967, at the age of forty, he died, in Huntington Hospital, in Long Island, New York.

# parttwo

# 8 the style of

John Coltrane tends to be understood in either one of two ways: as the one-man academy of jazz—the king student, the exhaustively precise teacher—or as the great psychic liberator of jazz who rendered the academy obsolete.

Indirectly, by example, Coltrane encouraged musicians to practice and study rudiments and scales and harmonic theory. He played the blues in unusual keys for the sheer challenge of it. He worked on himself until he became a great technical achievement, the complete jazz musician. Even more indirectly, he encouraged other musicians, in jazz and outside of jazz, to transcend their hang-ups and preconceptions and to play a pure intuitive expression, as opposed to learned figures. He helped people freak out; he gave them extramusical ideas.

Whether or not the ideas were his prime motivation—I think they were not—Coltrane played all his music with such commitment that he could seem as if he were selling intellectual ideas outside of music. Even Duke Ellington's later music pales by comparison in terms of its *commitment*: the *Afro-Eurasian Eclipse*, the *New Orleans Suite*, the *Sacred Concerts*—lovely works all, they are filled with niceties. Ellington never let you forget that music was his profession. On the other hand, the popular vision of Coltrane is that he seemed to ask you, repeatedly, to alter your life.

Here are some versions of Coltrane's story:

There is the coming-of-age of a tremendously gifted but tongue-tied student, learning to speak with assiduous practicing.

There is the story of an acolyte finding his way out of jazz's cheap and opportunistic operations—bad record-company dealings, hastily thrown-together sessions resulting in $41 for a day's work, bumping along week-to-week as a sideman—to a position of self-confidence, financial stability, and pride in one's own working band.

There is the story of a concentrated listener, opening jazz up to influences beyond its periphery, including Asian, African, and Spanish music. There is a principled man's resistance to—and, sometimes, his thoughtful compliance with—commercial directions that jazz musicians around him were following. There is a thoughtful musician's establishing of a new kind of intellectual seriousness in jazz, one that didn't need to rely on typically white middle-class or typically black street models of artistic coding and audience reception. There is a mystic's keen sensitivity for the sublime, which runs like a secret river under American culture—the meditative and semierotic aesthetic of endurance, of repetition, of ecstatic religion—which he first broached in 1960 and '61. And, to judge from his song titles alone, his playing suggested an explorer's mapping of some sort of terra incognita—meditative inside, astrological outside.

Coltrane's work gradually moved toward religious ideals until, at the end—as he indicated to Bob Thiele a week before his death, in a conversation about the packaging of *Expression*—he wanted no words, no explication. Love of God had emboldened him toward a position of silence about music and about politics. As the ambient noise of sixties culture grew louder around him, the more he desired to block it out and hear only himself; the more he went inward.

There is truth in all of these Coltrane stories, but in my view one of the most useful and overriding ways to comprehend the arc of Coltrane's work, one that contains significance for jazz now, is to notice how much he could *use* of what was going on around him in music. He was hawklike toward arrivals to his world, immediately curious about how they could serve his own ends, and how he could serve theirs. Every time a new jazz musician drifted into New York and began impressing people, every time he encountered a musician with a particular technique, system, or theory, every time a new kind of foreign music was being listened to by others in the scene, Coltrane wanted to know about it; he absorbed the foreign bodies, and tried to find a place for them in his own music. He learned as much as he could of the life around him and behind him, and retained only what best suited him, such that you usually couldn't tell what he had been drinking up. And his band afforded him a measure of protection, while he stayed in the vulnerable position of student—the men themselves, and their collective sound. They were his foundation, his grid for learning.

The decision to single out Coltrane at all, to focus on him, to see him as anybody worth forming a position about, came in 1957, his chrysalis year of quitting drugs and taking his graduate course in harmony with Thelonious Monk.

Through most of Coltrane's first tenure with Miles Davis, from 1955 to 1957, inasmuch as he was generally understood, he was understood as a question mark, a WATCH THIS SPACE. But many musicians, as soon as they heard Coltrane with Davis, heard a decidedly atypical tenor sound. Our ears are used to it now, but some of the novelty of it can be appreciated by listening to "On It," from an Elmo Hope date in May 1956 released as *Informal Jazz*, to hear the difference between Coltrane's sound and Hank Mobley's. Mobley is narrower and plummier, closer to Lester Young and to the norm of the time. Coltrane is broad and biting, almost braying.

The drummer Billy Hart and saxophonist Gary Bartz both turned sixteen in 1956, and each, independently, took notice of Coltrane's solo on "All of You," from the 1956 record *Milestones*, with Miles Davis—Coltrane's first recording of any commercial consequence. "I couldn't even figure out what kind of saxophone he was playing, a tenor or an alto," Hart remembers. It was the first suggestion of something Hart later became sure of: that in Coltrane's work there is a "clear representation" of American music, large and rhapsodic and lyrical.

The trumpet player Charles Tolliver was fourteen when '*Round About Midnight* was released, in March 1957. He had started playing jazz, and his parents had some records that he liked, particularly the Clifford Brown–Max Roach albums.

"Before Clifford Brown, I hadn't heard this advanced way of playing the music," he said. "When I heard Clifford Brown, I knew this was special. I ate and slept that for my teenage years, and then I wanted to hear everything that sounded like that, from Charlie Parker on. It didn't take me long. The next record I focused on in my uncle's collection was '*Round About Midnight*. When I heard Coltrane executing like Clifford Brown—this high, advanced execution on the record—Trane's executions were like Brownie's. So after that, my practice routines became looking at those solos, and examining them."

Andrew White, the saxophonist who has devoted much of his life to transcribing, studying, and playing Coltrane's work, had his ears opened by a track that lay a little deeper inside '*Round About Midnight*: the sixth track, "Dear Old Stockholm." "Up until that time in the record he sounded like any other tenor player at my first hearing," White wrote.

Still, it was something greater than notes and patterns that made people finally sit up and listen to Coltrane, even at this stage. Robert Levin's notes to *Blue Train* in 1957 set out the idea. "John Coltrane has often been called a 'searching' musician," he wrote.

"His literally *wailing* sound—spearing, sharp and resonant—creates what might be best described as an *ominous* atmosphere that seems to suggest . . . a kind of intense probing into things far off, unknown and mysterious."

When Cannonball Adderley joined the Miles Davis band in 1958, making it a sextet, the reception to Coltrane began to change. Adderley, an alto saxophonist and an unpretentiously brilliant, fast-thinking character, was immediately impressive to an audience; with him, you never waited for pleasure to arrive. Since Coltrane, on the tenor saxophone, spent a lot of time in his middle range, as opposed to the characteristic low, virile tenor style, he could sound alto-like, and together his sound and Adderley's superficially meshed. For Coltrane-doubters, this was vexing. It necessitated their taking a position.

At first that position was often one of skepticism. A review in *Down Beat* of the Miles Davis band at the Newport Jazz Festival in the summer of 1958 made the group at least sound impressively "confusing":

> Although Miles continues to play with delicacy and infinite grace, his group's solidarity is hampered by the angry tenor of Coltrane. Backing himself into rhythmic corners on flurries of notes, Coltrane sounded like the personification of motion-without-progress in jazz . . . With the exception of Miles's vital contribution, then, the group proved more confusing to listeners than educational.

One of the best Coltrane biographies, by C. O. Simpkins, published in 1975, called this "a very dumb-assed review."

This was the period when Coltrane occasioned two of jazz's most famous punch lines. They both amount to the same thing. One came from Cannonball Adderley: "Once in a while, Miles might say, 'Why did you play so long, man?' and John would say, 'It took that long to get it all in.' " The other seems to have no definite source. Coltrane says to Davis that he can't figure out a way to stop his solos. Davis retorts: "Why don't you try taking the horn out of your mouth?"

A few writers, particularly Nat Hentoff and Barbara Gardner, started to make great claims for Coltrane's influence, even while he was still with Miles Davis. Hentoff, in early 1958, wrote that Coltrane "has in the past year detonated more concentrated enthusiasm among eastern modern jazzmen than any tenor since Sonny Rollins." In 1959 Barbara Gardner mentioned the existence of a "Coltrane cult" in the liner notes for Wayne Shorter's first record.

Still, it would be hard to prove that Coltrane had any kind of wide effect yet, outside of a cadre of undeveloped musicians.

Jazz may not ever have gotten more alive and provocative than in the years when Coltrane played with Miles Davis. These were the harvest years from the rich past experiences of all the players who were coming of age at the time: all kinds of jobs, all kinds of music, from military band to rhythm-and-blues to big band to bebop. Only a few years earlier, before rock-and-roll arrived, jazz was still popular, and in the late 1940s, reputable touring bands had played dance gigs in cities like Gary, Indiana; Dayton, Ohio; Bogalusa, Lousiana; Sewickley, Pennsylvania; Beckley, West Virginia; Inkster, Michigan; and Pensacola, Florida.

Yet the late 1950s was also a confusing period for jazz. It was the dying end of the ten-year Fifty-second Street era, the pre–rock-and-roll, pre–Bay of Pigs, high-on-the-hog period of astounding triple-bills in jazz clubs. A John Coltrane, a Wayne Shorter, could get lost in the shuffle. By 1958, the action in New York had slid southward, to much smaller and more racially mixed places below Fourteenth Street. Now it was at the Five Spot Café, on the Bowery between Fourth and Fifth streets; the Half Note, at Hudson and Spring Streets; the Village Vanguard, on Seventh Avenue South.

The paradigms were shifting, too lumberingly to be documented as the process actually happened. There was a nearly complete media silence surrounding Coltrane's six-month gig with

Thelonious Monk at the Five Spot in the second half of 1957, and very little taped material survives of the band during that year; what does survive is of low fidelity.

But musicians and audiences noticed. The Monk quartet with Coltrane was one of the highs of the year in New York's live jazz scene, even if its reputation spread mostly by word of mouth. Near New York University, the Cooper Union, and the Lower East Side, the Five Spot was where artists and students went to buy a single beer for twenty-five cents and listen for a few hours, without the risk of being chased out between sets.

Newly opened, the Five Spot was a small and fairly nondescript bar, always crowded, its north wall behind the bandstand covered with flyers at odd angles, advertising jazz gigs and art exhibitions at the cooperative galleries five blocks north on East Tenth Street.

It was primarily an artists' hangout in 1957, for those who kept studios nearby or who were defecting eastward from the Cedar Bar, among them David Smith, Herman Cherry, Larry Rivers, Franz Kline, Joan Mitchell, Grace Hartigan, and Willem de Kooning; writers drank there, too, including Jack Kerouac, LeRoi Jones, Fielding Dawson, Robert Lax, and Frank O'Hara, who wrote his famous poem "The Day Lady Died" partially based on the memory of seeing Billie Holiday sing there one night with Mal Waldron. But it was also, at first, a neighborhood bar, and this created the possibility of the first nonmusician audiences in New York who would go to hear Coltrane play night after night, month after month, and come to understand him as a musician in perpetual development. He was developing in relation to himself, surely; he was also developing in relation to them. They wouldn't want to hear the same set every night.

Amiri Baraka—the former LeRoi Jones—and Steve Lacy have both spoken of Coltrane's awkwardness in his first summer nights at the Five Spot, and of his fluent raptures in the fall. They were tremendously lucky to accrue this knowledge, and it is precisely this knowledge—and their recounting of it—that helped fuel a later fascination with Coltrane.

A. J. Liebling once wrote that French food declined after World

War I with the rise of highway driving, since small restaurants suddenly weren't committed to satisfying the same clientele night after night. Now, they could serve the same dishes and not worry about improvement; regular waves of new diners would chew away, unaware of the stasis.

In a way, the same goes for jazz. Monk and Coltrane played as many as seventy-five nights within a six-month stretch at the Five Spot. That's enough time for a band to get good, and for a younger, attentive player to absorb some of the wisdom of the master he's standing next to.

Even before the group with Monk at the Five Spot, Coltrane was already one to watch; the Miles Davis job earned him recognition, and a blurb on the cover of his record *Soultrane* in 1957 advertised him as "the NEW tenor saxophonist STAR."

Ira Gitler, who had worked for Prestige Records in the early 1950s before becoming an important jazz journalist, had coined a memorable description of Coltrane's rapid arpeggio style in his liner notes to *Soultrane*, in 1957. It was in connection with his playing on "Russian Lullaby." The description was almost an idea in itself, the kind of thing a newspaper editor would call a "take-away." In "Trane on the Track," Gitler observed that Coltrane "has used long lines and multinoted figures within these lines, but in 1958 he started playing sections that might be termed 'sheets of sound.' "

"Sheets of sound" is one of the few phrases from jazz criticism that has more or less broken free of its origin; few know who coined it. Anyway, it is a suggestive description, a mellifluous phrase, and it has become the dominent cliché for describing Coltrane's sound. Coltrane even eventually used it himself to describe his own playing, citing Gitler. Perhaps he liked the image— suggestive as it was of flat surfaces that have no definitive length and width, or of music paper.

"You know 'Blue Train'?" asked Zita Carno, on the telephone with me from Tampa, Florida. "I don't know what got into me," she said, "but when that came out, I transcribed Coltrane's solo. I was doing a lot of that."

Carno is a concert pianist, formerly with the Los Angeles Symphony Orchestra, now retired. In 1959, she wrote "The Style of John Coltrane," an extensive two-part essay on Coltrane's strengths, for *The Jazz Review*.

"I got this notion," she remembered, "and I sent Coltrane a copy, anonymously, with a little note: *Does this look familiar?* I waited for three weeks, and I couldn't stand the suspense anymore, so I called him. He was in the phone book. He was living on West 103rd Street. I was in the Bronx. He answered the phone."

Carno was twenty-four and had just gotten her master's degree from the Manhattan School of Music. She was finding a little bit of concert work, and playing baseball in a Bronx sandlot league. She was about to give her first solo recital at Carnegie Hall, which would be favorably reviewed in *The New York Times*.

The trumpeter Donald Byrd, a student with her at the Manhattan School, had introduced her to jazz. She absorbed it quickly. Coltrane's organization of learned rhythmic and harmonic devices especially surprised her, and she wanted to use her gift for fast, accurate transcription to see how they worked. "When Trane was soloing," she said, "I'd notice the way he would start off kind of spare, like he did with 'Blue Train,' and he'd build up quickly, and I would just get carried away. I *knew* what he was doing, what he was driving at, and I'd just settle back and enjoy the ride."

Sonny Rollins remembers Carno as "one of the first people from the straight world who began to appreciate Coltrane." As a musician who had other standards—the standards of classical music—but appreciated his virtuosity, she was ahead of her time.

Not long after meeting and befriending Coltrane, Carno wrote an article about him, based on her transcriptions and what she heard in him that seemed unusual. She sent it to Nat Hentoff, then the editor at *The Jazz Review*.

Nobody can point to a performing artist and declare him better by measurable data. The greatest reputations in the arts often be-

gin with an excited pronouncement; somewhere inside it is a fool-
hardy challenge. The challenge is always the same: I defy you to
show me that I am overestimating X. Carno extended such a challenge. You may want to condescend to him or dismiss him, her essay implied, but you can't do so intelligently. The urgency of the
writing implied more: You will have to deal with him.

"The only thing you can, and should, expect from John
Coltrane is the unexpected," Carno's piece began. "That is what
makes listening to his tenor style hard for people who look for the
familiar and the conventional, for clichés."

"The Style of John Coltrane" was published across two issues of
the magazine, in October and November 1959. It was the first of its
kind—a piece backing up its large claims of his excellence and influence with transcribed examples of Coltrane's improvisational
style.

Carno isolated technical and structural particularities, down to
comparatively small strokes, rather than taking the generalist
critic's approach and talking about musical qualities in human
terms—power, intensity, patience, urgency. She wrote from the
point of view of an informed, objective outsider literate in music
theory, a musician fascinated by jazz but who was not of it.

She wrote about Coltrane's growing influence, giving examples
of other musicians who were absorbing his style: Benny Golson,
Hank Mobley, and Junior Cook. She may have read Ira Gitler's article in *Down Beat*, "Trane on the Track," published a year earlier,
which also mentioned Cook and Golson in a similar way.

Carno's essay, which never uses Gitler's name, is imbued with
the prescient awareness that "sheets of sound" would become a
cliché—and that other clichés, much more truth-obscuring ones,
would attach to Coltrane, too. Hers is a smoke-clearing essay, written when there was still not yet much smoke.

She considered "sheets of sound" to be a musician's argument
*against* Coltrane: that he just indiscriminately bombarded the area
with scales. Gitler was writing dispatches from the front for followers of jazz. Carno came upon the desire to prove a larger point

about Coltrane as a universal musician quite naturally. She even surveyed the issues about Coltrane that could possibly be damaging to his reputation, not just among older jazz enthusiasts but also in the legit world: that he didn't play in tune, that he was deliberately going outside of harmony, that he was wasting his breath.

She explicated him individually, as well as analyzing how he functioned within bands. The essay discussed his "hard-cooking" style, as well as blues and ballad playing. She cited his "frequently a-rhythmic phrasing"—meaning his use of odd-numbered groupings of notes for phrases that started and ended abruptly, in the middle of things—and his "unusual harmonic concept." She noticed his original "pet phrases," and transcribed several of them, such as the fast descending pattern based on the diminished scale that he plays toward the end of his second chorus on "Moment's Notice."

She mentioned his strength in all registers, and discussed how he got his sound. He had told her that his sound came from a combination of a hard reed, a very open-face mouthpiece with a larger chamber for streaming the air, and a tight embouchure.

She mentioned his rhythmic acuity at fast tempos. "His playing is very clean and accurate," she wrote, "and he almost never misses a note." She defied anyone to prove that Coltrane played out of tune. (He did play a touch sharp, but Carno defended that: it suited his drive, she said.) She managed to articulate, as nobody had before, that his style of blues went outside conventional blues playing, describing "Blue Train" as "a most powerful blues line, brooding, mysterious, almost like an eerie chant."

"Coltrane's kind of 'funk' drives, rather than swings," she wrote. "And it is less obvious. Listen carefully to his solos . . . But listen carefully, because it won't be as easy to spot as Horace Silver's kind. That solo on 'Blue Train' is such a revealing example of so many facets of his style and conception that I will transcribe it in its entirety, with accompanying explanatory notes." And in part two of the essay, she did: her transcription takes up the bottom half of two pages of the magazine.

She wrote about his harmonic choices, how he expressed chords and chordal relationships, and how he appeared to be "blowing out of the changes"—playing outside of tonal harmony—because of his fast, streamer-like phrases, which in fact remained within the moving harmony of the chord changes for each song. "Sometimes they do not come off the way he wants them to, and that is when the cry of 'just scales' arises," she wrote. "That may be, but I dare anyone to play scales like this, with that irregular, often a-rhythmic phrasing, those variations of dynamics, and that fantastic sense of timing."

When Leonard Feather was compiling his first jazz encyclopedia in 1959, the Coltrane entry was half as long as the Sonny Rollins entry. Elsewhere in the book appeared a list of the most important musicians in jazz history. A note explained that the judging process left out musicians who had risen to prominence after 1955, implying that the dust would have to settle a little more on the past few years. Still, a list of the greatest musicians, compiled by critics, included Rollins (who had become known in 1951) and five other tenor players. Coltrane did not make the list.

Wayne Shorter thought of Coltrane, Sonny Rollins, and Hank Mobley as the "adults" that he looked up to within his general style of playing. Shorter had been absorbing Coltrane's sound and adapting it to his own playing since 1955; he bore his traces, with his heavy long tones, from his first record date, in late 1959. You can hear just a little of Coltrane in Hank Mobley by late 1957, in a solo like "Gettin' into Something," on Mobley's album *Poppin'*—a darker seriousness, with fewer obvious bebop phrases, and the demonstration of his facility in all registers of the instrument. Others have pointed to Junior Cook and Clifford Jordan as part of the Coltrane cult, though Jordan was definitely still oriented toward Rollins's horizontal, melody-based improvisation in 1957 and '58.

Younger saxophone players wanted to emulate Coltrane's seriousness, and as a corollary, his shorthand ways of implying a lot of harmony: as a prime example, his frequent use of a type of diminished-scale pattern. (Diminished scales are the eight-note scales that alternate between whole steps and half steps, and Coltrane used them routinely in his sheets-of-sound phase—for example, as his means of turning around before the beginning of the second and third choruses on his "Straight, No Chaser" solo with Miles Davis from *Milestones*.) George Coleman, who also was watching Coltrane expectantly at the time, suggests that this wasn't new, that Dizzy Gillespie was improvising with double-diminished scales in the 1940s.

The "cult" of Coltrane perhaps only existed in relation to a more real cult of Rollins. Coltrane and Rollins were thought of in tandem: two distinct models of hard bop that weren't necessarily set against each other; two ambitious voices seeking to inhabit the void left by Charlie Parker's death.

Meanwhile, Coltrane was making his lines faster, more complex, drawing more from his early lessons in scales with Dennis Sandole, and possibly from his conversations with the Chicago saxophonist John Gilmore. And at the same time he was clarifying his sound, making it more romantic and lyrical no matter what he was playing. It is clear now that the post-Monk Coltrane was trying to *sing* no matter what he was doing, even in passages of the most breakneck speed.

But it was hard to argue against the charge that he was overdoing it. "Charlie Parker's playing is like an electric fan being switched on and off; Coltrane's playing is like an electric fan turned on and left on," wrote Mimi Clar in *The Jazz Review* in 1959. "There was a muchness about a lot of his work," the British writer Michael Gibson more sympathetically declared.

"From one point of view," Martin Williams reflected later in his book *The Jazz Tradition*, "the post-Monk Coltrane had pushed jazz harmonies as far as they could go. From another, such complex, sophisticated knowledge set its own trap, and Coltrane, still a vertical thinker, careened around like a laboratory hamster trapped in a three-dimensional harmonic maze of his own making."

. . .

*Giant Steps*, recorded in several sessions during 1959 and produced by Nesuhi Ertegun, was the most carefully made album of Coltrane's career, so careful that it suffered from the close attention. Here was, in essence, a menu of every type of piece which his name had become associated with, and his first major statement as a composer: every composed track was credited to John Coltrane, and published by Jowcol (short for John W. Coltrane), his own recently established music-publishing house. He was consolidating his reputation.

From H. A. Woodfin's review of *Giant Steps* (in *The Jazz Review*):

> The élan and aura of wonderful outrage [as exhibited on *Blue Train*, discussed in the same review] have been partially dissipated. A great deal of his playing seems rhythmically dull and disconcerting . . . Also, the feeling of freedom with the chords has vanished and he seems more bound by the changes. His solo on "Giant Steps" particularly shows a rhythmic stiffness and melodic tameness. He does not construct any real line with the arpeggios. The same is true of "Countdown," which seems to be only a very sophisticated exercise on the chords . . . Basically most of his work on the Atlantic LP seems to show a cautiousness that is alien to his art.

"Cautiousness" may not have been a bad choice of words given the dimensions of jazz then, but what critics like Woodfin couldn't see was that a new "cautiousness"—a new *studium*, the Latin term for a sense of devotion to form and discipline—would become normal in jazz about ten years later, and this wasn't alien to Coltrane's art: it came directly from inside it. Many musicians would later take up the challenge of "Giant Steps" as bliss through theory— and would keep the "Giant Steps" changes in their daily, active vocabulary as a platform for improvising.

"Giant Steps" is, unlike most standards, so associated with its creator, but it is also a challenge, on a basic level, and so dozens of versions of it have been recorded since Coltrane. The most interesting of these versions are by big bands, opening up the harmonic possibilities for a song whose chords change on every beat. They have included: the Woody Herman band, in a version arranged by saxophonist Frank Tiberi; Tito Puente and his large ensemble; Lionel Hampton and his orchestra; and Maria Schneider's orchestra. But as if to prove that it really *was* theory, Coltrane played the tune live for a little more than a year after recording it, then retired it completely from his repertoire.

Coltrane's trip to Europe with Miles Davis in the spring of 1960 set off another chapter of reception history: it was the moment when the general confusion over Coltrane turned toward hostility.

The Paris audience, in particular, reacted strongly to Coltrane's performance. What that means is that there was a handful of boos among the cheering (you can hear them on the bootleg, during Coltrane's solo in "Bye Bye Blackbird"), and that many column inches in French jazz journals were subsequently devoted to building the evening of March 21 into a *Rite of Spring* moment.

"I was very embarrassed," Coltrane said, when asked later how the European booing made him feel. "I don't see what they found so extraordinary in what I was playing; for me it absolutely wasn't."

"At that time," Wayne Shorter says, speaking of 1959 and 1960, "people were still hanging on to the words 'avant-garde.' 'Avant-garde' seemed to blot out something—the whole sound was lumped together in a group by that word, and nobody noticed the emergence of an individual who was bringing life to his music. It was a process, it was like a story, a work-in-progress kind of thing."

A Swedish radio disc jockey, Carl-Erik Lindgren, interviewed Coltrane during the intermission of the Stockholm concert. He mentioned that some audiences found Coltrane's playing angry.

"Maybe it sounds angry because I'm trying so many things at

one time," Coltrane answered. "I haven't sorted them out. I have a whole bag of things that I'm trying to work through and get the one essential one."

Coltrane said this—or a variation of this—so many times, whether the subject was stacking chords, or the length of a solo, or the number of drummers he wanted in his band, or his religious preferences. In time, that questing-without-end attitude became his signature, what people expected from him. Here it was, still early. On the 1960 tour with Miles, with his long, screaming split-tone solos, he could seem as if he were not just searching through his different devices but embarrassing himself. But it was a different order of embarrassment. He was open. He knew what he wanted to do, and felt strongly in doing it. The audiences weren't always up to his speed: either they hadn't been much exposed to jazz like his before, or the records, which he was now churning out, simply hadn't reached them yet.

In 1960, John S. Wilson, the jazz critic for *The New York Times*, wrote an article about the new trend of downtown jazz clubs—specifically the Five Spot and the Half Note.

The practice of presenting jazz was changing. The Canterino family, which owned the Half Note, didn't offer competitive money in late 1960: around $1,000 a week for the full band (the Village Vanguard offered $1,500 a year later). But they could offer bands long engagements without anyone else on the bill, twelve or fifteen weeks at the club per year. Even at the Five Spot, in 1957, for the Coltrane-and-Monk run—and in 1959, when Ornette Coleman's quartet became famous in New York City—those bands had been double-billed with others.

The Half Note occupied the southwest corner of Hudson and Spring Streets, in the southwest corner of the Village. Just a few blocks from the river, and Pier 40, the biggest shipping terminal in the country, the club was at the south end of an Italian and Irish longshoremen's neighborhood. Around the time Coltrane first brought his band in for an extended gig, in October 1960, Jane Jacobs was living thirteen blocks north on Hudson—the upper reaches of that neighborhood—and finishing her masterpiece on urban planning, *The Death and Life of Great American Cities*. In it, she writes of "the intricate sidewalk ballet" of Hudson Street, and its healthy mixed uses—small businesses, family dwellings, community areas.

The Half Note had a horseshoe bar; drinks were served across the round part of a letter D, and the bandstand was a raised platform atop its back panel. The entire club had a capacity of around 115. Patrons could sit at the bar, below the musicians, or in raised seating across from the bar so as to be at eye level with the musicians. It was deafening for the bartenders, but the Half Note was an extended-family business—presided over by Sonny Canterino and his son, Mike—and unusual in many ways. Among them all, the Canterinos parked four cars outside the bar, most nights. When crowds exceeded the club's limit, Mike Canterino would put new arrivals in one or another of the family's cars, serving drinks through the car window, until the crowd inside sufficiently dispersed.

Mike Canterino rarely booked bands more than two or three weeks in advance. He dealt with Coltrane's agent, Jack Whittemore, but more often with Coltrane himself. He paid the band below Coltrane's level; but he promised them, on a handshake, up to twelve or fifteen weeks at the club per year. This was the kind of consistency that Coltrane wanted, a family man running one of the strongest bands in jazz.

These were low-pressure gigs, and the band felt at home; they could do what they wanted, including playing a single song for half an hour or an hour. Audiences weren't turned over between sets, and the minimum was low: $1.50 at the bar. Scotch and soda cost a dollar, and a veal parmigiana sandwich, the house specialty, cost $2.50.

Most bands that played at the Half Note played six sets, from nine p.m. to three a.m.—forty minutes on, twenty minutes off. Coltrane's sets ran longer, and so there were fewer—three or four per night. Musicians descended on the Half Note en masse to check out Coltrane: Sonny Rollins, Roy Haynes, Freddie Hubbard, Miles Davis, and from that level on down.

Why did Coltrane's band, once Elvin Jones and McCoy Tyner were in place, become so widely noted? Why did the cream mysteriously rise to the top? First, it is the musicians, obviously. Coltrane had graduated from obsessive lick-playing; Jones, having had the benefit of growing up in a family of geniuses, was one himself. But beyond that, the answer may be in the band's itinerary.

Elvin Jones joined the band at the end of September 1960. For the first full year that Coltrane, Tyner, and Jones were together, they played eighteen full weeks at different American jazz clubs. In most of these engagements they were the only band on the bill. There were seven weeks in all at the Half Note, the club that became the band's home base when they were off the road; three in all at the Jazz Workshop in San Francisco; one at the Apollo in Manhattan; one at the Zebra Lounge in Los Angeles; six at the Village Gate in Manhattan; one at the Showboat in Philly. Except for the Apollo shows, Coltrane's quartet was always the only band on the bill.

One-band-on-the-bill had been the policy in some smaller jazz clubs around the country, but now it was becoming almost the norm in New York. In this way, as the sole extended-engagement act in a club, the quartet stayed in one place and settled in, concentrating its craft and slowly cultivating deep support. This may not have been fair to Coltrane and his band. They were paid for below what they were worth. The entire setup benefited the club owners above all. Still, it grew audiences, and it meant that the possibility of the band's internal growth, and the power of its external influence, was not being chopped up, diluted, stepped on. Most jazz musicians will tell you that this is the crucial element missing in jazz today; this is what is preventing bands from attaining a special coherence and preventing bandleaders from becoming properly seasoned role models and coaches. In jazz, experience is everything.

# 9 spiritual

Frank Tiberi's name has been associated with Coltrane forever, despite the fact that he met Coltrane only once. The association comes primarily from Tiberi's collection of tapes of Coltrane performances in the early 1960s, which have never been made public. He has also become known—though less so— for the arrangements of Coltrane's "Giant Steps" and "Central Park South," which he wrote for Woody Herman's band in the 1970s. Born in 1928, he was a saxophonist and arranger who led a band in Philadelphia in 1960 that briefly included McCoy Tyner.

Tiberi noticed a big difference in Coltrane in 1960. "I used to see him with the group with Miles, Cannonball Adderley, Bill Evans, and Philly Joe Jones," he remembered. "I really wasn't too impressed." Like most of his peers, he had become used to the sound of Lester Young and Coleman Hawkins; of the players who came up in the 1950s, he was impressed by Al Cohn in particular, for his adaptation of Young's lyrical playing. "Trane was a little too technical. He never impressed me as being that soulful. He was playing repeated patterns too much, even though they were all executed so very well."

Now he heard something new in Coltrane, and resolved to start taping him. "I saw the change. He became very melodic. He still had that anxiety, the aggressiveness. But he was able to play melodically on hard changes."

Not wanting to let this pass undocumented, Tiberi started bringing a portable reel-to-reel tape recorder into clubs to tape Coltrane's sets, most often at the Showboat Lounge, in Philadelphia. It was a small Transcorder model, using three-inch reels. His tapes are important evidence of what Coltrane was up to at the beginning of his bandleading—the period when he perfected and then moved away from his "Giant Steps" changes, which had obsessed him for two years; the period of finding an original group sound through unusually long performances (for that time) of single tunes, which encouraged Elvin Jones to create a new kind of jazz drumming that went beyond simple patterns. Jones responded by starting to play all over the kit, and layering rhythms.

Tiberi has, for instance, a version of "But Not for Me" that runs for thirty-six minutes, and a "Giant Steps" that runs for fifteen minutes. (Because there is no live version of "Giant Steps" in common circulation, this has become a particularly desired recording.) According to Tiberi, it's not just the length that's impressive, or the physical stamina involved. It is the purely melodic improvisations that are now replacing the old battery of original licks.

"At the Showboat he was performing alone," Tiberi said, meaning without another band on the bill. "So it didn't matter how long it took him to be satisfied to end the tune . . . It was amazing that he was able to play as much as he had in storage."

When Verve records made a digital transfer of Tiberi's tapes, in 2000, they amounted to eighty-six CDs. The sound quality, however, was deemed (by Tiberi as well as Verve) not to be good enough for release. And so an important part of Coltrane's story remains locked up, for now.

Nineteen sixty-one is one of those years, like 1959, with a staggering number of significant events in jazz—significant especially to critics.

It was the year Ornette Coleman's *Free Jazz* appeared, but a few years before top-to-bottom free jazz, with the rhythm sections abandoning regular pulse, would really gain traction. Bill Evans recorded *Live at the Village Vanguard*, and the idea of a piano trio with greater roles for the bassist and drummer became widely spread around. Sonny Rollins ended two years of self-imposed exile—an exile partly prompted by having to reconsider his role in jazz, after hearing Coltrane at the Five Spot and in his second tenure with Miles Davis. (Rollins had been practicing alone on the footpath above the roadway on the Williamsburg Bridge, where he could play as long and as loud as he liked, and the story of his solitary regimen, once it got in the newspapers, turned into a little fable about artistic purity; inevitably, he called his 1961 comeback record *The Bridge*.) Eric Dolphy formed a quartet with Booker Little that went on to make some extraordinary live records at the Five Spot. Abbey Lincoln recorded *Straight Ahead* with her husband, Max Roach, and gave a paint-peeling, consensus-building response—in an interview with Ira Gitler published in *Down Beat*—to the white critics' perception of the new black arts. Jimmy Giuffre assembled a new trio, with Paul Bley on piano and Steve Swallow on bass, introducing new music and a hushed style of interplay that threatened to dissolve the differences between jazz and classical music. Cecil Taylor brought the alto saxophonist Jimmy Lyons into his band and formed the Cecil Taylor Unit; they recorded "Bulbs," "Pots," and "Mixed," three extraordinary pieces of music, mixing the harmony and structural ideas of modern classical music with swing rhythm, the expressivity of free jazz, and some R&B licks, too; another rapprochement of the swing-to-bop jazz tradition and the newer, more chaotic forces, was rendered in Oliver Nelson's *Blues and the Abstract Truth*. In Chicago, Muhal Richard Abrams started his Experimental Band, a process of talent-shepherding that would later result in the Association for the Advancement of Creative Musicians, a musicians' cooperative and, in time, a brand name for new conceptual approaches to jazz.

American culture, of course, was being generally redefined with the noise of new voices in all the arts, but jazz was the only form of black art that repeatedly broke through to general audiences. Black theater, black film—apart from Lorraine Hansberry's play *A Raisin in the Sun*, there was hardly enough to make a dent; of black fiction, only Ralph Ellison, Richard Wright, and James Baldwin had pushed through to mainstream attention.

As a result, there are two versions of 1961 jazz: the one we see through a critical microscope, one in which gold stars are awarded for aesthetic transgression; and the one that a more general audience perceived—songs like Gloria Lynne's "I'm Glad There Is You," and Dinah Washington's "September in the Rain," albums like Nancy Wilson and George Shearing's *The Swingin's Mutual*, Nina Simone's *Forbidden Fruit* and her recorded performances at the Village Gate that spring, Count Basie's *Basie at Birdland*, and Dave Brubeck's *Time Further Out*. Coltrane meant the world to a restricted society of musicians and listeners, but his name was by no means synonymous with jazz. The record producer Joel Dorn, who went to work at Atlantic some months after the release of *My Favorite Things*, estimates that the album sold around 30,000 copies that year—a significant success in jazz, but still small compared to the 500,000-and-above sales level for later Atlantic jazz records like Herbie Mann's *Memphis Underground* and Les McCann and Eddie Harris's *Swiss Movement*.

But jazz does not exist in a vacuum, no matter how ingrown its rituals, no matter how specialized the knowledge of its interpreters, and one should try to see Coltrane in 1961 in relation to the arts in general at the time.

Between 1961 and 1964, the English literary critic A. Alvarez prepared a series of programs for BBC radio on the intellectual scene in America called "Under Pressure." In the broadcasts, various writers commented on the American character in art, especially the need for the American artist to create his own language. This is what Robert Lowell said to Alvarez:

We have some impatience with the sort of prosaic, everyday things of life, that sort of whimsical patience that other countries may have. That's really painful to endure: to be minor and so forth. We leap for the sublime. You might almost say that American literature and culture begin with *Paradise Lost*. I always think there are two great symbolic figures that stand behind American ambition and idealism and culture. One is Milton's Lucifer and the other is Captain Ahab. These two sublime ambitions that are doomed. I suppose this is too apocalyptic to put it this way, but it's the Ahab story of having to murder evil, and you may murder all the good with it if it gets desperate enough to struggle . . .

What one finds wrong with American culture is the monotony of the sublime. I've never lived anywhere else, but I feel maybe what is extreme and perhaps unique about America is that for the artist his existence becomes his art; he's reborn into it and he hardly exists without it . . .

I don't know enough about Englishmen or any other country to make a comparison, but I feel that we have a feeling the arts should be all out. If you're in it, you're all-out in it and you're not ashamed to talk about it endlessly and rather sheerly. That would seem embarrassing to an Englishman, and inhuman probably, to be that all-out about it . . .

Art is always done with both your hands in America. The artist finds new life in it and almost sheds his other life.

Whether one likes or dislikes Coltrane after, let's say, 1958, there is something in Lowell's formulation here that one must come to grips with, in order to understand the rap *against* Coltrane. It is "the monotony of the sublime."

As for monotony: Lowell was right to bring up Milton and Melville in relation to the obsession with the sublime shared by many American artists of the early sixties. Especially Melville: Coltrane's quest for a big, unified, transcendent group sound could seem Ahab-like. But there is another name to invoke in this short history of an idea. The standard work on the sublime, in Melville's time, was Edmund Burke's *A Philosophical Enquiry into the Origin of Our Ideas of the Sublime and Beautiful.* Melville owned a copy, and Melville scholars have traced his interest in the book, especially as it pertains to Ahab's conception of the whale.

Writing in the 1720s, Burke identified the differences between the sublime and the merely beautiful. He seemed to prefer the sublime, though implying that it was a doomed, self-destructive preference. The beautiful was soft, light, quiet, varied, charming. The sublime was large, repetitive, terrifying, dark. Solitude was sublime. The intimation of eternity and infinity was sublime. All that was sublime was also obscure.

Considered as part of Western music, Coltrane's music did approach monotony. "Sheets of sound" can be reduced to monotony. Drones can be reduced to monotony. Modes can be reduced to monotony. Coltrane was somehow referring to a way of making and receiving music that was almost ritualistic. Coltrane may have been reading about Sufism and Eastern religion, but he also seemed to be getting at the Native American and the African underneath the American character, qualities that have long separated the American from the European.

On December 10, 1961, a month after Coltrane's two-week run at the Village Vanguard and the recording of *Live at the Village Vanguard*, John S. Wilson considered Coltrane again in the *Times*. This time he addressed Coltrane specifically, based on several new recordings: *Thelonious Monk with John Coltrane*, *Olé Coltrane*, and *Africa/Brass.* Titled "One Man's Way," the piece lined out clearly—and probably about a year after the news could have been broken—that Coltrane was taking himself seriously as a bandleader, and was in fact ready to be taken seriously; that he still had a "tendency toward length," despite shaving down earlier excesses; that he was organizing what was previously incoherent power and

hunger into a real direction; that he had become the next important soprano saxophonist after Sidney Bechet. The praise was faint;
intellectually Wilson upheld Coltrane's importance, but never really warmed to the music. Still, the message was clear.

"The past year may be remembered in jazz annals as the year
when John Coltrane, a tenor saxophonist, achieved the top-rank
stature that his supporters had for some time felt was inevitable,"
the piece began.

> Mr. Coltrane is now 35 years old, relatively ancient for a newly ar-
> rived star by normal jazz standards. However, until about five
> years ago Mr. Coltrane appeared content to be a journeyman
> jazzman. Then, while he was a member of the Miles Davis Quin-
> tet, he began an exploration of the resources of his saxophone
> that led him to performances filled with long, hard-bitten, rapid,
> rising and falling runs that had the cumulative effective of an
> aural battering ram, described by one commentator as "sheets of
> sound."

But with this degree of status came many imprecise assump-
tions about what Coltrane wanted to do, what his intentions were.
He was moving a little too fast for most of his audience—lay listeners as well as critics. With "My Favorite Things," he had a hit
song that was actually played in jukeboxes and on the radio. (Jazz
radio, at first, and most strongly; it was released as a 45 RPM single, cutting up the tune into "part one" and "part two.") But what
he played in his performances later that year did not reflect a duty
toward public acceptance.

He bored some people to death, too. His fetishization of loud,
intense soloing on few chords could seem inelegant beyond reason.
Bob Brookmeyer, the trombonist and composer, was playing and
arranging in Gerry Mulligan's Concert Jazz Band at the time, a
marvelous group displaying wit, intricacy, and state-of-the-art improvisation; it is a group that has been washed over in subsequent
history partly because of the obsession with Coltrane and other pi-

oneers. Brookmeyer was intrigued by Miles's quintet with Coltrane, which he played opposite at the Café Bohemia when working with Jimmy Giuffre's trio. He was impressed by Coltrane's dedication and skill, and believes in appreciating Coltrane as an entirety, a process—"a study of defeating demons, and progressing toward an end."

"But by the time of John's own band," he remembered, "you could hear two people: Elvin and John. You saw Jimmy Garrison and McCoy Tyner, but you only heard two people." (This is a common complaint against Coltrane, though not demonstrably true in the recordings.) "And 'My Favorite Things'—a nice Broadway song, and then soprano for an hour? *Unnnh.*" Brookmeyer wasn't thrilled by "Giant Steps," either. He saw it as just a fussier version of conventional jazz changes. "It's ii–V–I!" he said, horrified. "It turned me off right away. I never learned it. I never played it. I never will."

In the lag time between the recording and the release of *My Favorite Things*, Coltrane had hired Eric Dolphy and expanded to a quintet; he had more work to do. The quintet's performances were received by some influential listeners not as a work-in-progress but as a faulty product.

"I heard a good rhythm section . . . go to waste behind the nihilistic excesses of the two horns," John Tynan wrote in *Down Beat*, after hearing the Coltrane Quintet at the Renaissance Club in October 1961. "Coltrane and Dolphy seem intent on deliberately destroying [swing] . . . They seem bent on pursuing an anarchistic course in their music that can but be termed anti-jazz."

Bob Dawbarn of the British magazine *Melody Maker* put it to Coltrane directly after hearing him live in November. "I found your quintet's music completely bewildering. Can you explain what it is you are trying to do?"

"I can't speak for Eric," Coltrane replied. "I don't know exactly what his theory is. I am playing on the regular changes, though

sometimes I extend them. I do follow the progressions. The sequences I build have a definite relationship to the chords. Can you
give me a particular example of something that puzzled you?"

Dawbarn suggested that his second solo in "My Favorite
Things" lost him. In response, Coltrane didn't address anything
but the structure: "That tune has a melody in the major key and a
short vamp in the minor. In the first solo I played straight through.
You could follow the melody in it. The second was more ad lib. It
was in the same form except that the vamp parts were stretched
out."

Later in the interview, Dawbarn tried to get Coltrane to remark
on what we have seen: that he sounded different now, compared to
all that he had recorded before. Coltrane went naïve, stalling him.
"So many people have told me that, it must be true. I've got to listen to those records again."

Publicly Coltrane remained stoic about these remarks, and in
conversation with Don DeMichael for a later *Down Beat* interview
("John Coltrane and Eric Dolphy Answer the Jazz Critics") he
talked about mutual understanding: he wanted to figure out why
people thought he represented anti-jazz, and he wanted the writers
to figure out the music by asking questions directly to the musicians. (As Dawbarn's example showed, however, they may have
come away from the encounter not having gotten what they
wanted, and still overreacted anyway. To a critic, a musician who
does not describe his music in terms of emotion and precise historical precedent can seem a blank slate.)

Mostly, it seemed, Coltrane felt guilty that the younger and less
established Dolphy took so much on the chin. "It hurt me to see
him get hurt in this thing," he told Frank Kofsky later.

*Down Beat* magazine, in 1961, was the reigning publication in jazz,
with an estimated reading audience of around 70,000. *The Jazz
Review* and *Metronome* had stopped publishing that year, leaving
the field clearer of competitors. It wasn't happily or gracefully

run—its publisher, James T. Maher, was convinced that black musicians should not be put on the cover, and it had a stodgy reputation. Yet there was a progressive element within the magazine. *Down Beat* published Ira Gitler, Martin Williams, Dan Morgenstern, Pete Welding, Gene Lees, Bill Mathieu, and Ralph Gleason, some of whom became editors there for a stretch. It also published Barbara Gardner, the first black critic in a national jazz magazine; her essay on Coltrane in 1962 was the most complete profile of him that had yet been written.

In the issue following the one that contained "John Coltrane and Eric Dolphy Answer the Jazz Critics," *Down Beat* published two reviews of *Live at the Village Vanguard.* Pete Welding's take was distantly complimentary: the record was "a torrential and anguished outpouring," he wrote, "delivered with unmistakable power, conviction, and near-demoniac ferocity." But, at the same time: "the very intensity of the feelings that prompt it militate against its effectiveness as a musical experience." Ira Gitler, on the other hand, drew a line: "Coltrane may be searching for new avenues of expression, but if it is going to take this form of yawps, squawks, and countless repetitive runs, then it should be confined to the woodshed."

Put it another way. It was late 1961. Coltrane finally had, as John S. Wilson wrote, "top-rank status." He came into the Village Vanguard to make a live record. The audience was with him; it had a standard to hold him to. His solo career so far rested on two recordings, pieces he had recorded not long before, within the last two and a half years: "Giant Steps" and "My Favorite Things." It is possible that he played them during the week, but none of them were recorded on the four nights when Bob Thiele set up his recording equipment at the club. Instead, the repertory Coltrane was now eager to play included a hectic blues long enough to take up nearly half a set ("Chasin' the Trane"), and a similarly long drone piece with dense, gestural, sometimes dissonant saxophone playing through it ("India"). He was also testing the integrity of his jewel of a group with Eric Dolphy, a saxophonist who would not engage popular interest. This is not business; from a commercial standpoint, these are almost perverse decisions.

But something else was happening. As Coltrane became a pop commodity, his interest went the other way, toward a kind of jazz-as-folk-music. And although he didn't keep those tunes in his live repertory forever—"India," for example, and "Africa" seemed to have left it shortly thereafter—he let the feel of those songs coalesce into an ongoing style of writing.

Some listeners knew exactly why they liked it. Steve Reich was living in New York from 1957 to 1961, studying for part of that time at Juilliard with the composer and arranger Hall Overton; then he moved to San Francisco to study with Luciano Berio at Mills College. In New York he had heard a lot about Coltrane, but once in San Francisco, he would see him perform every chance he could.

I saw the quartet around the time of *My Favorite Things*, and it made an enormous impression on me—so much music being made on so few harmonies . . . I admire "Giant Steps," but I'm not really interested in it, at all. While I was in San Francisco, he came out with "Africa/Brass," and that was by far the most influential on me. Because there you have an entire side of an LP in [the key of] E. "What's the changes, man?" "E." "Then what?" "E!" E, for half an hour! That was enormously impressive. What it showed was that you could maintain a harmony for a very long time. And through changes of timbre, you could play anything from any of the twelve notes of a scale on the piano to noise. They were all on that record. At that same time, I was listening to recordings of West African drumming, which doesn't move harmonically but has tremendous rhythmic complexity. And [later] I was also listening to Junior Walker's "Shotgun," which doesn't change in the sense of ABA—it's just A. All this stuff pointed out the possibility of harmonic stasis.

The composer and writer Allaudin Mathieu was known as Bill Mathieu in those days. He was a young musician who had worked as an arranger for Stan Kenton and Duke Ellington in the late fifties and early sixties, and he wrote a music-theory column in *Down Beat* during the early sixties that Coltrane was known to admire. This is what he says now about Coltrane:

> He understood something, maybe not first but certainly best. And that is, that his jazz solo doesn't have to tell the story chorus by chorus, which is what everybody was doing.
>
> A jazz solo for Coltrane was a kind of a psychological journey through his state of being at the present. It wasn't simple, and it wasn't short. He got to start at the beginning of his own self-discovery for that moment, that episode in time, and let the solo itself resonate with his deepest psychological state, and then develop it and amplify it. In that way the psychological plumb went deeper as the solo went higher. It took as long as it took.
>
> It wasn't about choruses. Modality was best suited for it, because you didn't want to be tied into a bunch of changes. You wanted kind of pan-modal harmonic changes. If you start nitpicking note choices in Coltrane, it's a dead end. Whereas you can nitpick note choices in Paul Desmond. [Desmond was the light-toned alto saxophonist in the Dave Brubeck Quartet.] Instead, you listen to the arc, the development of the feeling. In that respect, I think Coltrane is closer to blues shouters, who after all had the same modal strategy—five notes.

"Spiritual," from *Live at the Village Vanguard*, and "Africa," from *Africa/Brass*, embodied the sound a lot of people had been waiting for, something they didn't have to be introduced to: somehow they already knew it. These pieces resonated with cool-handed wisdom; at their most intense, they represented compulsion, too. They were the opposite of music played to fulfill a contractual obligation, and all that was obvious in their sound.

The young pianist Alice McLeod was still living with her family in Detroit in 1961.

I had heard about [Coltrane] from other musician friends, and they always spoke very highly of his music. But I heard a record by him and I remember upon listening that I felt something beyond the music realm . . . it was like an inner experience that I had listening to his music. And it was very memorable, very notable . . . I just seemed to identify with that person, just upon hearing, like I was hearing his heart speak or his soul speak, and I related to that.

The track she heard was "Africa," from the album *Africa/Brass*. Within a year, she heard Coltrane play in Detroit. In 1962, she moved to New York; in mid-1963, they met at Birdland, where Coltrane's quartet was double-billed with the vibraphonist Terry Gibbs's quartet, in which she was the pianist. Soon after, they moved in together, and she began traveling with the Coltrane band.

The Los Angeles pianist Horace Tapscott, an old friend of Eric Dolphy's, was in New York in November 1961, toward the end of two years of touring with Lionel Hampton. He and the trombonist Lester Robinson went to the Village Vanguard for a matinee performance during the recording of *Live at the Village Vanguard*. Later, he told an interviewer this:

That Sunday afternoon we went there and they recorded that and immediately after, all over the country, it started happening. I mean it happened a little before, naturally, but I mean after that, that sound got across, I imagine. It got all over the country and everybody thought "ah, music—the music."

Much later, thirty years after he saw Coltrane there, Tapscott explained how he was feeling when he returned to Los Angeles:

I was raised in music when music was respected, and the ones who gave it out were respected. It was, I guess, the religion they had for the music. The only way I felt like I could get satisfied was to make a move toward preserving the music that black musicians, through the years, have died unknown for, and have contributed so much to this country musically for, and not get that righteous recognition from their families.

After hearing Coltrane at the Vanguard, Tapscott returned to Los Angeles and redoubled his efforts as a community organizer, finally creating an organization called Union of God's Musicians and Artists Ascension, based in South Central Los Angeles. The idea behind UGMAA was to get Los Angeles youths off the street and into activities which benefited the community, chief among them being Tapscott's Pan-Afrikan People's Arkestra. At the same time—late 1961, early '62—the Association for the Advancement of Creative Musicians (AACM) started organizing in Chicago. Its plan was less community-service-oriented than UGMAA's; rather, the idea was to encourage modern-minded jazz musicians to produce their concerts on their own steam, to find work for the musicians in the absence of respect.

The drummer Billy Hart remembers seeing Coltrane in the early 1960s at the Showboat in Philadelphia, and remembers audiences *specifically* losing their cool for hymnlike, folklike pieces like "Spiritual." "As intellectual as some people can be when they get enamored with Coltrane," he said, "there's a natural folk music sound in there that people can relate to. I've seen audiences respond like they later would respond at rock concerts. It was more than just sitting there silent. Coltrane got through in a way that even Miles didn't get to people. I had never heard that many people screaming."

Coltrane was being associated with a feeling much greater than jazz.

# 10 you must die

A consensus was beginning to form around Coltrane: that since straightening out in 1957, he had done nearly everything there was to do on his instrument. "He could have just stopped after his explorations of Western harmonies with ii–V–I resolutions," says Charles Tolliver. "If anyone ever exhausted all the possibilities of running chord changes, he did. It just seemed that it was right for him to go cosmic, which he did. And he could *still* play a ballad with such beauty and such perfect execution, such tone, such romanticism. There's very few artists in history who could do that." Tolliver paused. "He was God."

We have already heard Miles Davis's and Coltrane's reasons for why they got into modal playing so heavily: the freedom of expression. And the ancient, folklike aspect of modal playing, as we have seen, also had a direct effect on audiences. But there was something else about modal playing—especially in the kind of modal playing that was based on the minor pentatonic scale. Lots of musicians could do it and sound good.

"The pentatonic scale is harmonically ambiguous," says John McNeil, the trumpeter and educator. "It doesn't have the harmonic direction that we use in Western music. [At first Coltrane] was a guy who wanted to add more changes, more changes, more changes—he wanted to put changes *in between* changes. Then, finally, he said, 'What if we have *static* harmony, and I superimpose these changes on it?' When Coltrane started using pentatonic scales, it became much easier to superimpose things on top of it, as opposed to the way it was with bebop."

Students like Tolliver, who was twenty-one in 1963, picked up on that quickly. *Live at Birdland*, recorded in 1963 and released in early 1964, was the first Coltrane album that McNeil took notice of. "I had no idea what I was listening to," McNeil said. "But I could sing it. As a trumpet player, it was hard to play that stuff. I didn't know what the changes were. But I knew it was great, even if I didn't know why."

There were others. Younger listeners had now been hearing Coltrane's name for about five years—long enough for him to be believed, to have some basic authority. *Live at Birdland* was also the first Coltrane album that the saxophonist Michael Brecker heard; later, in the 1970s, working for hire in pop and jazz fusion, he would fashion for himself a highly effective, focused version of Coltrane's tone and phrasing.

Dave Liebman, another saxophonist who has spent much of his life studying Coltrane's music, first heard Coltrane at Birdland in February 1962, not knowing much about him previously. The band played "My Favorite Things" and he was hooked.

Roscoe Mitchell, a saxophonist and founding member of the Art Ensemble of Chicago, first responded strongly to Coltrane in early 1963, through the album *Coltrane*. After understanding how Coltrane was moving away from chord changes and into modes and static harmony, Mitchell felt he could finally understand what Ornette Coleman and Eric Dolphy were up to. (A few years later, Mitchell's first album, *Sound*, was important because it was such a clear alternative to the dominating sound of the Coltrane group: it was quiet, ludic, pokey.)

Other admirers were anything but students. Art Pepper, a brilliant and original post-bebop alto saxophonist from Los Angeles, became subjugated to heroin by the late 1950s. Some prison terms took him off the live music scene and exposed him to younger players, and by 1964, he became a full-fledged Coltrane adherent for about four years, by his own admission. "More and more I found myself sounding like Coltrane," he wrote. "Never copied any of his licks consciously, but from my ear and my feeling and my sense of music . . . When I got out of the joint the last time, in '66, I had no horns. I could only afford one horn, and I got a tenor because, I told myself, to make a living I had to play rock. But what I really wanted to do was play like Coltrane."

Harold Land was another one, also from the West Coast. In the 1950s he had his own style: starting in rhythm and blues, he became a modern jazz musician through close studies of Sonny Rollins and John Coltrane. But by the mid-1960s, he turned more decisively to Coltrane, adopting Coltrane's strong, dark tone, and many of his late-fifties scale patterns (including the double-diminished pattern). And Frank Foster, too, the great saxophonist of the Count Basie band in the 1950s and sixties; he moved close to Coltrane's style, especially in a blues, as you can hear on his solo choruses in "Raunchy Rita" and the entirety of his playing in "Elvin's Guitar Blues," both from *Heavy Sounds*, the Elvin Jones–Richard Davis album from 1967.

Joe Henderson, who arrived in New York in 1962, received Coltrane's harmonic lessons hungrily. His language built on Coltrane's and Wayne Shorter's; a few weeks after Coltrane's death in 1967, he would arrange a version of "Without a Song" that interpolated Coltrane's "Giant Steps" changes for its A section.

And there was Wayne Shorter himself, who at first seemed to be absorbing Coltrane's ideas and reproducing them in concentrated, minimized form. In 1964 he recorded "Fee-Fi-Fo-Fum" (think giant, think "Giant Steps"), which also uses the "Giant Steps" major-thirds root movement briefly in its own A section. And perhaps more to the point, Shorter's album *Juju*, from the same year, reflected the generalized sound of Coltrane's band, with long modal parts in the tunes, and featured the actual members of

Coltrane's rhythm section—McCoy Tyner, Reggie Workman, and Elvin Jones—on the recording. (Someone who knew only a little about Coltrane and jazz might easily mistake it for a Coltrane quartet record.) Before long, of course, Shorter found an improvising style that was much more immediately personal, and it is bound up with his genius as a composer of runic, puzzle-like, beautiful small-group music—a gift that has very little to do with Coltrane.

The saxophonist Charles Lloyd got particularly close to the hardest-to-emulate, most free-expressive and also tightly controlled period of Coltrane. On "Bird Flight," from his 1966 album *Dream Weaver*, Lloyd takes charge of the babbling, short-phrase Coltrane, the full-strength incantatory style of "Chasin' the Trane."

With the British Invasion, the development and flowering of the East Coast folk scene, and the emergence of Stax/Volt and Motown, jazz was becoming a little more of an unusual choice for listeners. It wasn't much of a teenager's music anymore; that had stopped with the end of the big bands, in the early 1950s. (Inasmuch as they were still around—Quincy Jones led a fantastic big band in the early sixties—big bands were unwieldy bookings at the midtown clubs, costing too much to present even if they packed the houses. Birdland, the semiofficial perch for big bands among New York nightclubs, went bankrupt in 1964.) And if any American teenagers did still like it, the Beatles and the Stones were coming in hard to siphon them off.

Even in New York, the center of the jazz world, by 1964 musicians were starting to form bootstrap collectives in order to feed themselves.

The Jazz Composers Guild—founded by the trumpeter Bill Dixon, and with members including Sun Ra, Archie Shepp, Paul and Carla Bley, Cecil Taylor, Michael Mantler, and Roswell Rudd—put on concerts in December 1964 at Judson Hall. They continued at the Contemporary Center, a space two floors above the Village Vanguard. But the organization was short-lived. There were too many competing personalities in New York jazz; there were also still enough possibilities for work. In one sense, much of the organizing was encouraged by Coltrane's example: with the success of "My Favorite Things," and then with his autonomy at Impulse Records, he had shown that there was a window for challenging work to get through to audiences, jazz that wasn't so limited by definition. The work in New York would truly go away only later.

At the Half Note, during the band's peak in 1965, Coltrane grew into his shepherd role. He invited younger musicians to the stage—most famously Pharoah Sanders, Archie Shepp, and Rashied Ali. Some of the musicians had a hard time believing that Coltrane was interested in them. But his interest in them was enough for them, and his music encompassed theirs.

It gave Sonny Sharrock, the guitarist, the validation of his life to see Coltrane just *watching* him play with Byard Lancaster one afternoon in 1965 in Philadelphia. (Coltrane may have been there because Pharoah Sanders was joining the band as a guest that day.) Sharrock remembered Coltrane smiling at him. "That was quite a day, quite a day," Sharrock recalled in an interview twenty-five years later.

On the other hand. "At the zenith of his powers, he'd allow someone nondescript to come up on the bandstand," said Charles Tolliver. "Guys who were in the avant-garde scene, trying to emulate him."

As I sat in the audience, at the Half Note, I came there to hear him and his group, the four men. And at some point during the night, especially when he moved completely into free playing, a lot of guys who were wanting to be into that, they'd come because they knew he was allowing that to happen.

I felt an intrusion, at first. But it didn't dawn on me until later on that this great man was allowing babies—like, toddlers, crawling—to come onto his stage without feeling any problem about that at all. A lot of us were like, *why?*

Later it helped me to be more inclusive with everything. Really, bands with a set repertoire, they don't allow this. But when he allowed that, it was really great. It dawned on me later how inclusive that was. It made me open my ears to the possibility of not having to play ii–V–I all the time. This inclusiveness that he allowed was almost as important as the great execution.

"Coltrane was a *sound* player," says the trumpeter Charles Moore, and he says it vehemently.

In the early sixties, Charles Moore was a young trumpeter from the Shoals region of northwest Alabama who had moved to Detroit for college. He was friends with John Sinclair, the poet, organizer of the would-be revolutionary youth movement the White Panthers, and eventually the manager of the rock band the MC5. He first heard Coltrane play at the Minor Key, a storefront space in Detroit that had formerly been a furniture shop. Moore played in an experimental jazz group, the Detroit Contemporary Four, and later in the Contemporary Jazz Quintet, which made two records for Blue Note at the end of the sixties; at around the same time, he arranged the brass section on the MC5's album *High Time*.

Moore is now a teacher of Afro-American music at UCLA. He believes that Coltrane must be understood in a completely different framework—not just as a killer jazz musician with a killer band and a weakness for attracting strays.

"That is to say," Moore continued, nearly thundering, "like Miles before him and Dizzy before them and back to Monk, Coltrane studied sound *intensely*. And away from the horn, too: the sound of the horn was one thing, but the sound of the music was another. The importance of Coltrane was that he pursued it further than anybody; he went to the edge of it. In going to the edge of it, I mean the edge of harmonic sound. And so he hooked up with people who played from the edge-of-the-horn point of view."

Here Moore is referring to the idea that Western tonality is a construct, that ideas based in Western harmony are, similarly, constructs. Moore believes that sound is preeminent. Through quality of tone (which the term "sound" is often reduced to denote) and quality of motion (a phrase Moore prefers to the word "rhythm"), as well as through an individual harmonic framework, a musician can create a sound. And the sound spreads out to his band; it becomes a collective sound.

Moore's central thesis seems to me correct: that Coltrane had enlarged his musical concept—and "sound" probably is the better term—to become not just accommodating but *sticky*. So much so that players like Shepp and Ali (as well as Marion Brown, Albert Ayler, Donald Garrett, and Carlos Ward), who may not have been at the level of technical accomplishment of Coltrane and his band but who had their own strong and individual ways of playing, found a purpose in it, a footpath in it. They were not all at sea in his system, his sound. This is why Coltrane's changing music, during and after the dissolution of the quartet, always had a binding feeling, a coherent logic. The new members weren't being hired above their level of experience; they were allowed to flourish in it.

Within the individual group, the leader-with-sidemen idea seemed suddenly old; a freer and more simultaneous notion of group playing was moving in. Jazz had never been less hierarchical. The spirit of musicians' collectives was making obsolete the old story of band-versus-band competition, and this change reached all the way into the groups' names: the group that included Shepp and Don Cherry was called the New York Contemporary Five; Moore's ensemble took the name Detroit Contemporary Four. If there is any truth to the rumors that Coltrane was taking acid between '64 and '67, it would only amount to more similar evidence. LSD commonly encourages the user to see the ideal of life as cooperative and nonhierarchical.

Here is some of what Moore said.

Duke [Ellington] also had guys with different sounds. Clark Terry didn't sound like Snooky Young, but Duke made it all work. He had a sound in mind to include all of those different players. Coltrane, in the new music, had that same sense, and invited guys with a *sound* to play with him. The sound became important. That's how Rashied wound up playing with Elvin. It presented some problems, of course it did. Rashied didn't quite know how Elvin did his stuff, or how Elvin functioned in the group; Trane didn't quite know how to make the two drummers fit together, except let them work it out; and there were issues of respect that went down.

John Coltrane found that he could get up on stage with someone who didn't know how to play the first fucking thing about the tenor saxophone. Now, here comes Shepp. He didn't jump a level; he just made his way into it. Coltrane's level was so inclusive at that point that you could have put anything on stage at that time and he would have probably used it. Coltrane's wife was not another McCoy Tyner, but she came in and added a different thing. What he was hearing soundwise was so inclusive that he could have included a *goat* on stage.

Now we're looking at sound in a huge context. Huge, huge, huge. Coltrane was mixing sounds. He wasn't just playing blues. He played everything up through classical music, in the West. He went on into Indian raga.

African music says, "What you got? Come on and play." It's a philosophy that allows one to think that way—not, "Oh, man, you made a mistake—you played a B-flat!" In Africa they know sound, and sound has meaning. What the fuck do you know? Letters and numbers? They know *motion*!

The drummer Rashied Ali was one of the musicians Coltrane invited up on the stand, and Ali was representative of the kind of musician who seemed, to some, to be leading Coltrane away from his strengths. In retrospect, these were the greatest days of free jazz: between 1961 and 1965, the documents of free music are more thoughtful, better conceived, more intellectually jolting than they would be later. But the group of musicians playing free music was fairly small. "Trane was elected as the dean of free music, because he was the only person that we related to," Ali remembers. "He just took it upon himself to really explore this thing."

However, the force of Coltrane's imprimatur led many free-jazz musicians to shortchange themselves musically. They felt, in a sense, that they had inherited the mantle, that Coltrane's involvement in their music was all the evidence anyone needed of free music's absolute value, even its superiority. But eventually this led to the deepest internal crisis jazz has ever had. Sonny Sharrock remembered talking to Jimmy Garrison just after he had left the Coltrane band in 1965. Garrison told him to work on improvising over chord changes. "Get those changes together, man," he told him. But this was during the great proliferation of free jazz, where changes barely mattered. Sharrock, who felt validated by playing free, was enjoying himself. "Come on, man," Sharrock responded. "You played with Coltrane. You know what was happening in that band."

"Coltrane can play his changes," Garrison said.

He could do other things, too. His music was just about unmatchable in strength and breadth of tone, even by Pharoah Sanders; unmatchable in fury, even by Sharrock and Archie Shepp and Albert Ayler; and certainly unmatchable in fluency of technique, except maybe by Sonny Rollins, who was so psyched out by the whole Coltrane situation—for the second time, after his first retreat in 1959—that he made no new studio records between 1966 and 1972.

There are many ways to categorize Coltrane's late music—the term is itself a category—and this has led to general confusion and a forty-year critical breakdown. Many players of Coltrane's generation found free jazz just an excrescence—a growth on the main trunk that had developed freakishly and too fast, cultivated eagerly by those in a position to offer money and career advancement. Jimmy Heath is no fan of *Ascension*. He has jokingly called Coltrane's looser, bigger ensembles, as on *Ascension* and some of Coltrane's later concerts, the "antipoverty bands"; he saw them as charitable gestures for the benefit of musicians who might otherwise be struggling for work, even if the music's specialized character started to turn audiences away.

"The critics messed Trane up," said Johnny Griffin, a tenor saxophonist who left the United States, permanently, in 1962. He meant, of course, that Coltrane had adopted the transgressive romanticism of his white defenders, that he was perhaps acting out their desires for what they wanted him to be.

The writer Ralph Ellison would have agreed with Griffin. He didn't seem to like Coltrane much, anyway. In a letter he wrote to Albert Murray in 1958, after seeing the saxophonist play with Miles Davis at Newport, he complains about Coltrane's "badly executed velocity exercises" and protests that the new musicians were "fucking up the blues." But Ellison was more interested in talking about larger matters relating to the culture of jazz and the music's function in society. In a 1965 television program broadcast on the Network for Educational Television—the series was *Music U.S.A.*, the episode titled "The Experimenters"—Ellison appears in between filmed studio performances by the Cecil Taylor Unit and the Charles Mingus Octet. Standing in the back of the Village Gate, amid overturned chairs, his jacket casual-elegantly slung over his right shoulder, he delivers to the camera a three-minute lecture on "consciousness" and "false consciousness."

Any viewer who didn't know the context wouldn't know what he was talking about. What he was talking about was the manner in which he felt white writers had deformed the meaning of jazz, bending it toward some kind of European nihilism. "Any critic from outside this tradition," Ellison explains, "must of necessity fall back upon his own values, and thus may be unprepared to interpret what he has heard. It has been such outsiders, well-meaning to a man, who sponsored the false consciousness in jazz."

In the art criticism of this time, a certain Greek-derived term was enjoying some currency: "apodictic." The art critic Annette Michelson used it to describe a work of art that asserted itself beyond question, and brooked no "this could be," "this might be," "this represents." It meant art that completely resisted alternate interpretations, that had no guile, that didn't need historical context to flesh it out, that lived entirely within the truth of itself. For Michelson, Frank Stella's early-sixties symmetrical stripes of paint on canvas, and Robert Morris's sculptures like *Slab*, from 1962, a large, foot-thick rectangle of painted wood lying supine in the gallery, fit this description.

Modern critics borrowed the word from Kant's *Critique of Pure Reason*, where it refers to a judgment that, by the nature of the evidence, cannot be doubted as to its truth. The word probably doesn't belong in art criticism, describing a work of art: it refers to rational judgment, and not to a psychological state or an object. Still, however misused, it came to describe an idea that was in the air: that art could scale back on larger meaning, on the necessity of context, sometimes even on the necessity of content. The idea was that such stuff might be extraneous and unnecessary—that the real expressive work was the ready consciousness of the viewer, and that the work's single, potent gesture could be entirely understood by the most private soul and taken in as truth. That the tone or the texture or the rhombus or the word, delivered like a pill, like a judgment, could itself be enough. That interpretation was overrated.

"What is important now is to recover our senses," Susan Sontag wrote in *Against Interpretation* in 1964. "We must learn to *see* more, to *hear* more, to *feel* more. Our task is not to find the maximum amount of content in a work of art, much less to squeeze more content out of the work than is already there. Our task is to cut back content so that we can see the thing at all."

Jazz—and black music in general—was not one of Sontag's subjects. Her point is a general one about art: Sontag was beckoning her audience to attempt an intuitive understanding of art, to shut up and change from within. In that encounter, she found sex.

"In place of a hermeneutics we need an erotics of art," goes the end of the essay. Coltrane the Methodist might have argued instead, from his experience, for a gospel of art.

Or perhaps he would have argued, out of objective interest, for an African Practicum of Art. The period of 1964–65 in American culture wasn't only a time when secular guilelessness—John Cage and Andy Warhol and what would soon be called apodictic art—had reached the level of mass culture. It was also a time when black Americans were learning from the practical applications and social functions of African music and art, and applying it to their own reality—that this music had a function, brought a community together, preserved a culture. Or just energized individual agendas, better than any other music could. In the poem "AM/TRAK," Amiri Baraka wrote:

> . . . *last night I played* Meditations
> *& it told me what to do*
> *Live, you crazy mother*
> *Fucker!*
> *Live!*
> *& organize*
> *yr shit*
> *as rightly*
> *burning!*

A few years later, Baraka wrote "Nationalism Vs. PimpArt," an essay dealing, after the fact, with the mid-sixties in American culture. It contains a theme linking it to Sontag's essay: art exists so that you can change your consciousness in its presence. But Baraka insists that the best black art is crucially different from the Frank Stella–Robert Morris kind. It is, by definition, related to daily life, to culture, to public self-definition, and to self-realization, with regard to resisting racism. The extraneous stuff around a work of art, he proposed, similarly to Sontag, can be cut away. But what is left ought not just be neutral conceptual matter, shape or sound or thought. It ought to have social meaning for black Americans.

"New talk of Black Art reemerged in America around 1964," he wrote.

It was the Nationalist consciousness reawakened in Black people. The sense of identity, and with that opening, a real sense of purpose and direction. The Art is The National Spirit. That manifestation of it. Black Art must be the Nationalists' vision given more form and feeling, as a raiser to cut away what is not central to National Liberation. To show that which is. As a humanistic expression Black Art is a raiser, as a spiritual expression it is itself raised. And these are the poles, out of which we create, to raise, or as raised.

Coltrane was linked to Baraka (then LeRoi Jones) in the early 1960s, through Baraka's advocacy as a jazz critic. And Baraka was linked quite closely to Archie Shepp, whom Coltrane sponsored by helping him get a record contract with Impulse. But apart from playing at a benefit concert for Jones's Black Arts Repertory Theater/School in March 1965, Coltrane had no direct links to the Black Arts movement, which got off the ground that same year.

Gradually, after February 1965, with the assassination of Malcolm X, Baraka upshifted, growing more political. His hearing changed as well. As he tells it in his autobiography, "It was as if I had a new ear for black music at that point in the middle '60s. I was a jazz freak . . . but now the rhythm and blues took on special significance and meaning. Those artists, too, were reflecting the rising tide of the people's struggles. Martha and the Vandellas' 'Dancing in the Street' was like our national anthem." Baraka's notion of Black Art was super-dependent on words, on rhetoric. On the other hand, although Coltrane's music had some potent connotations in its titles—"Song of the Underground Railroad," "Africa," "Alabama"—it was moving toward ineffability.

Miriam Makeba, the South African singer, and the Nigerian drummer Babatunde Olatunji were major exponents of African culture in America at the time. Coltrane drifted toward Olatunji, who later told of Coltrane's specific fascination with the tonal languages of West African speech. Coltrane's obsession with language—the mechanical and signifying aspects of art—had taken him to this point, and perhaps here Coltrane saw signs of a much larger area to explore, one where the mechanics of music could liquefy and cross over into the mechanics of language. "It's obvious to me what Coltrane was about," the pianist Matthew Shipp, born in 1960, once told me.

> Once he got past jazz, he was trying to delve into some subconscious pool of language. When I was a teenager, there were times when I'd be totally into a certain Coltrane album for a while, and I'd listen to it over and over. Sometimes I'd be lying on my bed and falling asleep, and I remember hearing his playing, while I was in a semi-sleep state, decoded into some kind of words.

Late Coltrane music satisfies both ideals of culture. It can, for some, confirm the notion of art for art's sake, a sealed-off container that doesn't depend on a practical reason for being. (Believe this: there is a type of free-jazz record collector—in fact, after punk, part of an increasingly flourishing breed—who does not necessarily think of Africa when he hears a Coltrane album like *Expression*. Having come through punk, Japanese noise, and electro-acoustic improvisation, he may just like it because it sounds extreme and nonnegotiable.) And it can also reflect the notion of an art of religiosity and spiritual power, related by extension both to West African music and to American gospel.

"New talk of Black Art reemerged in America around 1964." That, roughly, was the moment when it became a much more common gesture for jazz critics to align Coltrane's musical truths with human truths, and the moment when it was a loaded gesture for a white man to criticize John Coltrane in public.

An example. The trumpeter Don Ellis, who was a white man—a blond white man, to be precise—reviewed Coltrane's album *The John Coltrane Quartet Plays Chim Chim Cheree* for *Jazz* magazine in 1965. Ellis was a technically astounding player with a big ego, and in his own groups he was biting off big chunks of jazz: big-band writing with complicated time signatures, fairly free-jazz quartet settings, ballads and standards. Ellis was always rhythmically precise and explicit about what he was doing; even his loosest experiments felt a little controlled. (In some ways, he foreshadowed Wynton Marsalis.) In his review, he soberly addressed technical issues: McCoy Tyner's overuse of fourth voicings in his left hand; the welcome sound of a new edge in Coltrane's tone. Then, some criticisms.

"Coltrane has never been a 'time' player," Ellis wrote.

That is, he never really gets "inside" the pulse, but rather plays over it. He now has his whole group playing with this same feeling! This is a good device, but it would be even more effective if balanced by strong "inside time" sections. In fact contrast in general is one of the weaknesses of this group.

It is a basic fact of life (psychologically and physiologically) that any one thing repeated for too long a time without variation becomes boring and/or dulling. It is the artist's job to be sensitive to the fine line to where a continued effect is building interest but if carried any further will lose its interest . . . In the great bulk of Coltrane's work we get a good deal of filigree or decoration (in the form of continuous scales and arpeggios performed at a rapid velocity) but very little "meat" or positive strong statements or ideas. It is like he is playing chorus after chorus, solo after solo on only one idea—that of continually varying scale patterns and arpeggios.

"Boring" is a politically charged word. By this point, there was a new, clean fracture in the audience for jazz. There were those few who recognized continuous root elements of black music, seeing the connection from West African drum choirs to Count Basie's vamping-till-ready in the 1930s, Horace Silver's call-and-response lines in early hard bop, the James Brown band's repeated riffs, Tito Rodriguez's and Tito Puente's *montunos*, Coltrane's static-harmony modal jazz—and those who did not. Ellis did not.

A response to the review, printed in the following issue, formed one of the most memorable dialogues in jazz-related literature.

"Don Ellis has finally shown himself for what he really is: a white," began the letter.

> His review of *The John Coltrane Quartet Plays* shows the white's utter contempt for black creativity. The white's ability to condescendingly dismiss black music as "filigree and decoration." . . . The white man always has to relate the black's music to the same old tired European standards & modes. I won't even bother to try to explain the music of the black to Ellis because he quite obviously cannot even understand the fundamental feelings from which this music was created. The white even in his most infinitesimal sexually-fantasized masochistic stages obviously cannot understand & feel pain and suffering . . . The white's mind still, even in '66, seeks to castrate the black's music and write it off in the form of European-based technical criticism and control—white control . . . The feeling of this music is more important to me than the technical matters; a feeling that you, Mr. Ellis, have insulted, thereby declaring yourself as another of my many white enemies. And for that, along with your ideals and artifacts from ancient history, you must die.

The letter was signed: "Charles Moore, Detroit, Mich."

Ellis responded, invoking what he felt was unimpeachable reason: "I hope the *rational* reader will take the trouble to listen to the record in question then read the review and judge for himself if the review is accurate. In your letter you imply you are mainly interested in 'feelings.' Well, there is one large difference between us then—I am interested in good ART!"

"Art," the word that Coltrane himself seldom used.

What was taking shape here was an ugly circle of irritation, based on reductive white-listener notions and reductive black notions of the white notions and reductive white notions of the black-listener notions. It was Aristotelian empiricism versus a more mystical (and more African) philosophy that didn't set store only in what could be scientifically proven. It was the supposed morality of variation versus the supposed corrupting influence of repetition. The faith that wider possibilities of tonality and rhythm could bring psychic liberation, versus the suspicion that such developments were diluting jazz. The perception that white people were making ugly, limiting inferences in their understanding of black achievement, versus the perception that the long, driving modal passages of Coltrane's group, or the famous twenty-seven-chorus solo played by Paul Gonsalves on Ellington's "Dimenuendo and Crescendo in Blue" at Newport in 1956, or, by extension, the 102 points scored by Wilt Chamberlain in a single basketball game in 1962, were all examples of instinctive gluttony.

And then, parallel to Ellis's position, there is the idea of the nonverbal Negro superman.

Eldridge Cleaver wrote about it in *Soul on Ice*, in the context of boxing. The white American (whatever enormous breadth of thought he meant that term to designate), wrote Cleaver, around the same time as the Don Ellis review, preferred Sonny Liston to Muhammad Ali, someone he can condescend to a lesser human over someone he really has to listen to.

Because, after all, it takes at least a birdbrain to run a loud mouth, and the white man despises even that much brain in a black man . . . The white man loves the Supermasculine Menial—John

Henry, the steel-driving man, all Body, driven to his knees by the Machine, which is the phallus symbol of the Brain and the ultimate ideal of the Omnipotent Administrator.

Clearly—though it was too embarrassing to make a point of it then—the writing about Coltrane, especially before it became tinged with social meanings, contained some element of worship of him as the primal masculine machine, emitting the "cry of jazz." Even the European journalists who dogged him in 1960 and 1961 for his long solos over static harmony and for what they felt was his seemingly foolish sponsorship of Eric Dolphy—their intense disapproval makes more sense as fascination.

Coltrane was above all of it. Like all great artists, he embodied multiple, often contradictory, aspects. He was Liston *and* Ali. He was, as some writers have pointed out, pretty country. He could look like a bumpkin; he had problem teeth, a wide waist, and was often photographed wearing ill-fitting, high-water pants. On the other hand, he owned a nice home in Dix Hills, Long Island, with a two-car garage and a wrought-iron railing at the end of a long driveway, and drove a white Jaguar XKE.

For the new world of jazz, for young musicians who hitched expression to protest or transcendence of the physical world, he was the motivating life force. And yet the great jazz musicians who came before him also admired him, even loved him, and vice versa. (A photograph taken in the early 1960s by Roy DeCarava shows Ben Webster, who was smaller than Coltrane, hugging Coltrane to his breast, as if he were his son, almost strangling him with affection.)

Forty years after he wrote it, I asked the trumpeter Charles Moore about his "you must die" letter to Ellis.

"Well, classical music did die," he said. "I wrote the letter because I thought, hey, in this game, you have no place. What you're calling 'repetition' is not just repetition. What you're calling 'filigree'—well, Buddy Rich would play all kinds of filigree, but there was no feeling to it."

* * *

A small slice of white music valued repetition and static harmony. In the mid-sixties, LaMonte Young and Terry Riley—both saxophonists, both quite serious Coltrane fans—were minority cases. The term "minimalism" had barely come into use. Steve Reich and Philip Glass had yet to make repetition safe, and even chic, for white audiences.

But static harmony more quickly infused rock-and-roll. "My Favorite Things," and then *A Love Supreme*, in particular, turned rock musicians on to Coltrane.

Phil Lesh and Jerry Garcia of the Grateful Dead had heard Coltrane with Miles Davis as far back as 1957. Lesh was cool on Davis but liked Coltrane intensely from the first. In his autobiography, he wrote enthusiastically about Coltrane's sound, evoking its physical characteristics in almost hallucinogenic terms. "His sound was so radical," he wrote, "not smooth and breathy, but solid and edgy, as if it were carved out of bronze—and his ideas! Chords stacked upon chords, phrases looping over the tiniest fraction of the beat, all with the most soulful inflections and passionate intensity."

David Crosby, of Buffalo Springfield and later Crosby, Stills & Nash, saw Coltrane with the classic quartet at the Jazz Workshop in San Francisco, as Lesh and many other rock musicians did. He has told an often-repeated story about seeing Coltrane finish a solo—or at least finish the part that was intended for the audience—then walk off the bandstand with the horn still in his mouth, playing all the way through the piano solo, but in an offstage room, before returning to the bandstand when McCoy had finished.

The story has been told many times, in many different variations; usually it involves Coltrane rehearsing backstage through his intermission break. But inasmuch as this story circulated in rock-and-roll circles, it suggested not only the enormity of Coltrane's inner drive but also the notion of a Coltrane performance as an ongoing happening, in which beginnings and ends weren't necessarily musically important.

Another story got around rock-and-roll musicians as well: that in 1964 Coltrane had supposedly begun to drop acid.

The beginnings of the recreational use of LSD in New York, Detroit, Chicago, and California, starting in the early 1960s, are anecdotally intertwined with Coltrane's biography. Much of this may have to do with the fact that Coltrane played in San Francisco at least once a year, and sometimes three times a year, between 1960 and 1963. The influential bohemian mafia of San Francisco—the crowd that included Ken Kesey, Neal Cassady, and the Grateful Dead—were all Coltrane followers. (Kesey had started taking LSD in a government research program at the Menlo Park Veterans Hospital in 1961; he incorporated references to Coltrane's music into his 1964 novel *Sometimes a Great Notion* as a kind of vector of truth for the character Leland Stamper.) The novelist Robert Stone has written about being on the periphery of this group. Along with the Kesey gang who lived on Perry Lane in Palo Alto in the early 1960s, Stone accompanied a crowd of people to see Coltrane; that night he took twelve gelatin capsules stuffed with peyote. "I was seeing Coltrane's music," he wrote. "I could see breath in those big jagged waves of frost; I could see the percussion."

In 1964, the Warlocks, Lesh and Garcia's electric blues band, started playing elongated jams in performance. Lesh urged the band members to listen closely to Coltrane's music to see how he took songs like "A Love Supreme," reduced them to a one-chord vamp for a long middle section, then exploded them into long-form performances.

That same year, Carlos Santana, only seventeen years old, heard *A Love Supreme*, and it altered his direction entirely. In October 1966, the Byrds played at the Village Gate in New York, using a new overdriven-amplifier sound instead of the chiming sound of their earlier, Bob Dylan–influenced recordings, in which the vocal harmonies were more prominent. The band had been listening to Coltrane in its tour bus for a year; that night, Jim (later Roger) McGuinn, the band's singer, guitarist, and principal songwriter, told Robert Shelton of *The New York Times* that he was interested in "the angry barking" of Coltrane's saxophone playing. (Clearly, Coltrane's displeasure with being understood as angry had not reached McGuinn.) "Eight Miles High," the song recorded twice by the Byrds, for two different record labels, in December 1965 and January 1966, intimated Coltrane's modalism—both in its intro-duction, a short twelve-string-guitar solo over a drone, and its frenetic middle-section solo. Later in 1966, the Doors extrapolated from Coltrane's "Olé" when they recorded "Light My Fire."

But the Byrds and the Doors were sixties generalists, and Coltrane was one of several different things in the air, along with the Beatles, Bob Dylan, and Ravi Shankar.

As we have seen, the quartet with Tyner, Garrison, and Jones broke up in 1965, and was very soon afterward referred to as his "classic quartet." (Michael Cuscuna, a young Philadelphia radio disc jockey and critic who would later be working for Atlantic and Impulse, remembers the term in circulation as soon as Coltrane started playing with Pharoah Sanders and Alice Coltrane.) That "classic" status made it approachable, comprehensible; the understanding was that post-classic-quartet Coltrane engaged other areas of the brain.

Bill Mathieu reviewed *Ascension* for *Down Beat* in the spring of 1966. His first sentence: "This is possibly the most powerful human sound ever recorded." Mathieu, a white critic, went on to explain that "this revolution, this black one, has a vested interest in 'now' as opposed to 'then.' " He set up *Ascension* as the most "now" recording ever made—not in terms of its catching a trend which would inevitably soon pass, but as the perfect musical apotheosis, essentially, of the most powerful moment in the social history of the world.

Good reviews of late Coltrane—from the middle of 1965 to the end of his life—often weren't just good reviews. They were across-the-board endorsements, fighting-words defenses, reflections of a profound change of life that was caused *directly by* Coltrane's music.

In a 1965 review of *Meditations* for *Down Beat*, Coltrane's friend Don DeMichael—who had cowritten the excellent piece "Coltrane on Coltrane" with him several years earlier—focused on his own inner conversion. (Rarely before had jazz criticism gotten so Augustinian.) He wrote of hearing Coltrane's group earlier in the year, a group with Pharoah Sanders and two drummers. He had read someone else's negative review of the band, he explained, and he went into the concert prepared not to like it. Indeed, at first he didn't.

> The blast of sound almost bowled me over. It repelled me. I hated what they were playing—those drums and maracas and bells and tambourines . . . with all the clatter I couldn't hear Jimmy Garrison's bass and sometimes couldn't hear Coltrane or Sanders, even though I was seated six feet away.
>
> I decided to go home but had a couple beers instead. Intermission. John came over and sat down. What was he trying to do in the music? Just trying to get *it* out, he said, making a scooping motion with his hands away from his chest. But what was all this, I said, pointing at the bandstand? He didn't know for sure; things were not right with the music yet, he said; but he wants to get into rhythm more, and this is what might lead him to it.
>
> The next set I heard it. Experienced it. Not what John talked about so much as what I was grappling with . . . *why* I was repelled, *why* I wanted to run . . .
>
> I do not pretend to understand this music. I doubt if anyone, including those playing it, really *understands* it, in the sense that one understands, say, the music of Bach or Billie Holiday. I *feel* this music, or rather, as I said, it opens up a part of my self that normally is tightly closed, and seldom-recognized feelings, emotions, thoughts well up from the opened door and sear my consciousness.

Frank Kofsky was the most aggressive of the Coltrane-backers. Of *Live at the Village Vanguard Again!* he wrote in late 1966: "This recording just might be the greatest work of art ever produced in this country—not to mention the greatest selection of jazz music to get set down on wax."

Then Kofsky wonders about the total futility of his own labors for a moment—but only a moment. Clarity returns.

> I sometimes suspect that criticism of the conventional type has been obsolesced by the new music, which is why I have become so reluctant to write "reviews" in a strictly musical frame of reference . . .
>
> It seems to me that what these men and women are showing us is the heights to which the human spirit can soar when selfish egotism is subordinated to the goal of a common good. Hence by implication, their statements pose a critique of capitalist society, which puts supreme emphasis on acquisitiveness and disregard for the welfare of one's fellow man (witness our indifference to American genocide in Vietnam). The music is in effect telling us about a future existence in which love and cooperation have replaced strife and oppression. Once we have achieved a glimpse of that future state, our present mode of life becomes increasingly intolerable: who could be satisfied with prison after having breathed the sweet air of true freedom?

Kofsky is a special case: he was a Marxist. He published with Pathfinder Press, funded by the Socialist Workers' Party, the unofficial American arm of the Fourth International. He had a grid for understanding culture.

Let's put these ideas in concentrated form. This is their essence: Coltrane's loud and dense late-period music cannot be separated from the path toward racial tolerance and absolute worldwide human equality. It is not really meant to be recorded—such enormities can't be frozen and sold in measured units—yet the recordings are transcendent in spite of themselves. Resistance or intolerance toward this music is a kind of sclerosis; to open oneself to it is to admit honesty and greater feeling. "Understanding it" is empirical Western foolishness; the will to understand is just more sclerosis.

Bach and Billie Holiday may enter our emotions at prescripted levels, but this music requires new inventions of selfhood. Understanding yourself is important, but to try to use explanatory language about how the music achieves such power is churlish. The music separates itself from jazz of the past (if it is relevant at all to reduce it to "jazz") by its call for freedom from oppression; by extension, to pine for the jazz of the past is to pine for oppression.

No art can hold up under the weight of these hopes. They mystify and sanctify the art beyond possibility, and do damage to all that lies in propinquity to it. Giving Coltrane such thunderous credence, too, automatically minimized the work of others around him. Coltrane was connected in so many ways with nearly all the greatest jazz of the period: with elder figures like Duke Ellington and Johnny Hartman; with bright and brilliant hard-bop like Cannonball Adderley's and Horace Silver's; with a line of compositionally ambitious music for standard jazz ensembles, neither "inside" and mainstream nor "outside" and abstract, represented by Andrew Hill and Booker Little. But it seemed that the really titanic claims of importance could only be attached to one person.

In claiming the music was beyond language and understanding, writing like this used a specific language. It is the language of nineteenth-century Romanticism, and it tended to be used vestigially, mostly about three things: deities, psychedelic drugs, and music.

Some believe that Coltrane may have seen the end of his life approaching, even from some distance. This is what Wayne Shorter thinks. He believes that anyone who practiced as obsessively as Coltrane did (when Shorter spent time around him in the late 1950s) must have had a premonition that he wasn't long for the world. "He must have known something about his condition," he said. "Like, I gotta do this *fast*." But in the late fifties, by most accounts, Coltrane appeared to be in the prime of his life. Couldn't he have been merely obsessive? "He had to let people *think* he was obsessive," Shorter maintained. "He didn't just all of a sudden arrive at a love supreme, glory to the creator, glory to this and that. He was working, purifying himself."

Even if you disagree with Shorter (whose ideas are influenced by the Buddhist philosophy which holds that everything you accomplish in life, you take with you after death and into your next life, like a report card) you may be unknowingly subscribing to the Romantic theory, deeply embedded in secular Western culture, that an artist's late works are his most important, that they are the artist's most transcendent summations, that they contain the artist's deepest sentiments. This was a very nineteenth-century notion, and its implications for music were grasped, partially, by music publishers and biographers who were eager to promote a view of late Chopin, late Schubert, and late Beethoven as mystical utterances. This notion had a philosophical agenda as well, serving as a reply to the eighteenth-century artistic theory of the Enlightenment, which held that an artist's greatest achievement is to uphold his formal excellence as long as possible without letting it decay or mutate.

But let's suppose that for reasons of health or otherwise, Coltrane, in 1965, was entering his "late style." One would expect nothing less of humble, mindful Coltrane than a music that somehow reflects the mute cataclysm of death, the feeling of a body that has seen a preview of the end, yet can no longer be reached. Intensely animated from within, facing the gravest challenges, the music on the outside becomes more and more unscalable, unhearable, unintelligible.

"The maturity of the late works," Theodor Adorno wrote of the late Beethoven, "does not resemble the kind one finds in fruit. They are . . . not round, but furrowed, even ravaged. Devoid of sweetness, bitter and spiny, they do not surrender themselves to mere delectation."

That sounds right for Coltrane, too, and it has the weight of a universally applicable theory. Except that it *doesn't* apply universally: Willem de Kooning's paintings, for example, grew simpler and more aerated as he aged.

It would be tidy if Coltrane progressed in a straight line from lightness to dark, with no doubling back. But that's not quite the case. Even a late-period piece like "Ogunde," the three-and-a-half-minute track from *Expression*, had the ring of one of his earlier ballads; it was a composition, beyond just a short motif; it had that romantic-contemplative affect, the surface of control, strength, and tenderness. (The saxophonist Roland Alexander, who had known Coltrane since the mid-fifties, recalled the last time he saw Coltrane play, one afternoon at Olatunji's studio in Harlem, and his description runs counter to what most of us have heard from Coltrane's last days. "Coltrane sounded like he was playing a *velvet saxophone*," he said. "When he was playing a ballad, man, the sound was like velvet.")

By comparison, the live "Ogunde," from *The Olatunji Concert*, Coltrane's last recorded statement, quickly grew wild and scuffed, and went on for twenty-five minutes. There were echoes of his old harmonic motion in his playing, but that was mechanical, a part of his brain.

No one ought to accuse *The Olatunji Concert* of being "honest"; that makes it seem pathetic, as if a great artist's final resource was the truth. It's art, so the picture is more complicated. It glows from within; it rotates furiously; it is a blur. Come close to it and it throws you off. You can read it as an act of resistance (though this would contradict most of what Coltrane talked about, when he took the opportunity to speak to the media); or you can get in line and read it as an act of inclusion, of drawing everything closer to him. (Those huge, repeated, sweeping downward scales in "Offering," from *Expression*, and again in "Jupiter," from *Interstellar Space*—one of the most remarkable gestures of his final year— can sound like someone frantically, powerfully gathering something, scooping it up, bringing it closer.) Either interpretation is, finally, reductive, and probably faulty. Mainly, an artist's final work won't objectively sum up anything. It is, however, likely to be fuller of subjectivity than ever before. It's full of the life force: that's all, that's enough, that's what it needs to be. If it's truly good and powerful, it deserves to engender a thousand misunderstandings. The idea of a last work acting as a summary or a capstone is a sweet and hopeful construct. But life doesn't add up for the living.

## 11 dark days

Coltrane's funeral took place on July 21, 1967, at St. Peter's Lutheran Church, at Lexington Avenue and Fifty-fourth Street in Manhattan. Reporters estimated the crowd at nearly a thousand people; it included Dizzy Gillespie, Max Roach, James Moody, Sonny Stitt, Gerry Mulligan, Jackie McLean, Archie Shepp, Milt Jackson, Elvin Jones, and Nina Simone. The Albert Ayler Quartet played. The Reverend Dale R. Lind read passages from the Bible. Coltrane's friend from Philadelphia, Calvin Massey, read Coltrane's poem "A Love Supreme." The Reverend John G. Gensel read next; and the Ornette Coleman Quartet followed, with the bassists Charlie Haden and David Izenzon and drummer Charles Moffett, before the final benediction was read.

Afterward, Coleman drove out to the cemetery—Pinelawn Memorial Park, in Farmingdale, Long Island—with the drummers Billy Higgins and Harold Avent, and the trumpeter and saxophonist Joe McPhee. He spent a while alone at Coltrane's gravesite. That night he played "Naima" with his quartet at the Village Vanguard.

*   *   *

Musicians first filled the vacuum with literal tributes. Albert Ayler had recorded a free piece with strings live at the Village Theater in February 1967, later included on *Albert Ayler in Greenwich Village*; recorded while Coltrane was still alive, it was released after his death, and given the title "For John Coltrane." (Ayler claimed to have knowledge that, toward the end of his illness, Coltrane was trying to heal himself by chanting with an Indian spiritual healer.) Beyond that, roughly the first year after Coltrane's death, there was "John's Children," written by Sonny Sharrock, on Byard Lancaster's *It's Not Up to Us*; Calvin Massey's "Message from Trane," on McLean's *Demon's Dance*; Nathan Davis's "Blues for Trane," on *The Nathan Davis Quartet*; "A Tribute to John Coltrane," by Rahsaan Roland Kirk, on *Volunteered Slavery*; McCoy Tyner's "Mode to John," on *Tender Moments*; "Gospel Trane," on Alice Coltrane's *A Monastic Trio*. None were mawkish; if anything, they were grim. They all suggested resilience, and they all referred to different parts of Coltrane, modes or "Giant Steps" changes, or the Elvin Jones–Jimmy Garrison groove, or particular themes he had recorded.

Some dark days of American jazz began here. There was room in New York clubs like Slugs and Boomer's for the hard and searching post-bop mainstream, a sound in line with the kind of music McCoy Tyner was making on his own records, like *The Real McCoy*, toward the end of Coltrane's life. But in general, jazz went off track in the late 1960s, and it could all be reduced to matters of scale: of audience size, room size, ego size, ambition size. Miles Davis, once the consummate straight-ahead jazz musician, was making piles of money playing near-rock music to rock audiences. The sense of almost tribal unity that the Coltrane Quartet experienced swiftly became anachronistic: more and more jazz musicians—bassists and drummers, too—realized that they could compose and lead bands themselves. They had to, in order to find local work, to receive commissions from arts organizations, to gig overseas.

Jazz musicians had to become more opportunistic. Jazz in performance was losing its basic, night-after-night, mixed local constituency. Now its economy depended much more on single encounters: tourists dropping in to experience "jazz," as an abstraction, in a certain club, or bands playing one-nighters across Japan and Europe, then moving on. Meanwhile, jazz as an organic part of small-scale, local daily life in America—like the social interactions on small urban blocks that Jane Jacobs had identified as part of daily life in Manhattan—was going away.

Meanwhile, the younger musicians who had changed their lives from top to bottom because of Coltrane—who accepted late Coltrane as a philosophical proposition and were modeling their music on records like *Expression*—weren't feeling provided for. Gene Ammons, an elder, in a *Down Beat* blindfold test from August 1970, said: "Before John died, he had gone into a very advanced thing, and had quite a few cats like Pharoah and Archie in the middle of this thing, and leaving the scene as suddenly as he did—he sort of left their minds in a turmoil, to the effect that they weren't quite sure in what direction they wanted to go."

Albert Ayler decided to stop playing in nightclubs after the fall of 1968. One night too many at Slugs, playing till three a.m., and he was done. He said his music just wasn't right anymore for the old ways of jazz—the usual drinking and small commerce. "Coltrane, Pharoah, Archie, they play space bebop," he explained. "We play energy music." He was dead two years later, found drowned in New York's East River. It remains unknown whether or not it was a suicide.

A new paranoia wafted up. Repetition, remorse, anger, new paradigms. "The new music seems like it died," Sonny Sharrock suggested in an interview in 1971. At the time Sharrock was in a position of almost absurd luck: a hard-core free-jazz musician who had a steady job working with the flutist and bandleader Herbie Mann. (Mann's record *Memphis Underground*, which Sharrock plays on, sold nearly a million copies at the time.)

"Something happened, man," Sharrock claimed.

Guys aren't playing like they used to. I remember the first time I came to New York and was playing on the East Side and the music was so *strong*. And then Trane died. And it seems like a lot of the cats just sort of backed up. I know this is gonna be a weird thing to say and I don't know if you're going to understand this, but Trane *had* to die, man. Musically, anyway, to release everybody else. Because everybody was just sitting down waiting to see what Trane did . . . Trane had tambourines and [then] everybody else had tambourines and bells and all that. And then Trane dies, and most of the cats just said, "Well . . ." That's *why* he's gone, man. It's time to start again.

It was already hard to say anything bad about Coltrane, or to hear anything bad about Coltrane, but after he died, it became harder. There did exist a feeling that he had disrupted jazz, knocked the pleasure out of it, especially after the quartet broke up. This feeling became characterized, of course, as a white phenomenon, even though plenty of black people felt it, too.

And there also existed a suspicion, now that he wasn't around to disprove it, that he might have actually been saintly—that one oughtn't question what he did, because his righteousness had nothing to do with the usual scale of aesthetic accomplishment. He wasn't to be compared to anyone else. He offered the sublime a chance in jazz, and he might even have died for it. His death seemed so mysterious. Nobody had known of his illness until so late in the game. Certainly he had lived a healthy life, once into his thirties; perhaps he had practiced himself to the limit, exploded himself until his body shut down.

The poet Philip Larkin, who at the time was also a sometime jazz critic for London's *Daily Telegraph*, wrote a brutal essay about Coltrane after his death. "I still can't imagine how anyone can listen to a Coltrane record for pleasure," he wrote.

> That reedy, catarrhal tone, sawing backwards and forwards for ten minutes between a couple of chords . . . that insolent egotism, leading to forty-five-minute versions of "My Favorite Things"

until, at any rate in Britain, the audience walked out, no doubt wondering why they had ever walked in; that latter day religiosity, exemplified in turgid suites such as "A Love Supreme" and "Ascension" that set up pretention as a way of life; that willful and hideous distortion of tone that offered squeals, squeaks, Bronx cheers and throttled slate-pencil noises for serious consideration—all this, and more, ensure that, for me at any rate, when Coltrane's records go back on the shelf they will stay there.

Coltrane's aesthetic problem, Larkin argued in the essay's meanest stroke, was that he was an American Negro. "He did not want to entertain his audience: he wanted to lecture them, even to annoy them. His ten-minute solos, in which he lashes himself up to dervish-like heights of hysteria, are the musical equivalent of Mr. Stokely Carmichael."

For whatever reason, *The Daily Telegraph* rejected the piece.

From Coltrane's death until about 1975, his sound was like a dust cloud: it spread out through jazz and finely infiltrated it.

There were several different levels of Coltrane-ism.

First, there was the trajectory of Alice Coltrane, who may be understood as Coltrane's most committed disciple. Until 1971, she worked with Jimmy Garrison and Rashied Ali, among others, making records that sounded very Coltrane-like, often reflective, minor, and modal, with flowing and harplike phrases over mid-tempo swing. But as she went deeper into Indian religion—she met her guru, Swami Satchidananda, in 1970—she wanted to play a music more conducive to meditation, which didn't contain so much pausing for breath.

"The instruments which require breathing are more in line with what's happening on an earthly level," she explained in 1971. "But the instruments that can produce a sound that's *continuous*, to me, express the eternal, the infinite." She meant, particularly, the organ, and the flowing sound of string orchestras. On *Universal*

*Consciousness,* released in 1972, she used both, playing a Wurlitzer organ with a buzzing, ribbonlike tone not unlike John's sound on soprano, amid Ornette Coleman's tossing, unruly arrangements for strings. Thereafter, she went further toward pure meditation music, and away from anything resembling jazz.

There were the established players of Coltrane's own age who had formed their own styles perfectly well but then became fascinated by his. They included Harold Land and Art Pepper, the ever-popular Stan Getz, and Frank Foster.

Then, among the younger musicians who passed through the bands of Tyner, Jones, Sanders, and Alice Coltrane, there was an entire school, an entire generation of players born in the 1940s: Sonny Fortune, Cecil McBee, Billy Hart, Steve Grossman, Dave Liebman, Billy Harper, Hannibal Marvin Peterson, James Spaulding, Calvin Hill, Juini Booth, Joe Ford, Gary Bartz, Charles Tolliver, Gene Perla, Azar Lawrence, Woody Shaw, Herbie Lewis, George Cables. With hindsight, it was as though they were trying to prove themselves to an absent father. Their common bond was Coltrane, and he was gone.

America was being ground down by the battles of the civil rights movement and the philosophical and physical tortures of its involvement in the Vietnam War. Around the turn of the decade, pop lyrics had begun to progress from idealism to postidealism: instead of songs valorizing liberal idealists, there were now songs criticizing liberal hypocrites, like John Lennon's "Revolution," from *The Beatles,* and George Clinton's "If You Don't Like the Effects, Don't Produce the Cause," from Funkadelic's *America Eats Its Young,* and "Won't Get Fooled Again," from the Who's *Who's Next.* In their frustration, the cynical anti-Nixonites of pop reached the self-hatred stage. But jazz musicians only became more credulous, more spiritually humble, more proud and indignant; they focused on forces that nourished their own culture, rather than stripping it.

•   •   •

You couldn't not be a part of the movement, some part of the movement. Hipness, in the illicit underworld sense, was suddenly meaningless, a sham, another way of buying into the system. By the early 1970s it wasn't cool to be a junkie anymore; Lee Morgan's "Speedball," recorded in 1965, was one of the last examples in the long tradition of hard-drug song titles.

Rock had started to eclipse jazz as young thinking people's music. But within jazz, Coltrane's jazz took monolithic precedence as the model for what noncommercial jazz should be. It had a bully pulpit of morality—virtue was so scant in popular music. So few children grew up with a piano in the house anymore. The jazz record business had reached a pathetic, fleabitten stage. Only Coltrane had momentum: the possible authority to lead listeners back to jazz as music, rather than as meaningless cultural mystique, and the force of character to generate some kind of generalized, internal revolution.

Charles Tolliver said: "One of the reasons the music of that era sounds the way it does is because there was at that time a oneness of purpose among black people in general and musicians in particular. The whole push toward equality, along with John Coltrane's music, permeated everything we did for about five to eight years." One of his tunes, a burning piece for quartet on *Charles Tolliver Music Inc. Live at Slugs*, was called "Our Second Father (Dedicated to the Memory of John Coltrane)." It doesn't borrow specific things from Coltrane so much as one big, general thing: a style of group projection, a force.

Coltrane had taught musicians a new flat, high plane of delivery; the playing wasn't as dynamically varied as jazz used to be. Now the pieces of music began strong and stayed strong. Coltrane alone made this musical demeanor applicable to learned, harmony-rich jazz improvisations like the kind played by Tolliver and the pianist Stanley Cowell, as well as fully raging, static-harmony tornadoes. His influence narrowed the distance between the two, for a time.

Frank Lowe's *Black Beings*, from 1973, is one of the ragers.

Recorded with a quintet including saxophonist Joseph Jarman, violinist Raymond Cheung, bassist William Parker, and drummer Rashid Sinan, it includes a piece called *In Trane's Name*. It lasts twenty-five minutes and takes up all of the record's side A.

First there is a solemn unison theme, built on a mode. Then the piece opens up to Lowe playing tenor saxophone with scabrous, runaway energy, like a giant screaming teakettle, against the drummer Sinan in free time. The reference, clearly, is to Coltrane and Rashied Ali. (A little earlier that year, Lowe had made his own duet record with Ali, *Duo Exchange*.) But unlike Coltrane and Ali's *Interstellar Space*, which contained deep harmonic ideas, Lowe doesn't really build the performance. It is, in its way, another landmark: perhaps the furthest iteration of frustration, anger, ecstasy, stubbornness, in New York free jazz.

As time passed, Coltrane was becoming less specific, more nebulous. Musicians began to emulate him in a more generalized way: a big sound, an ocean of empathy.

In 1971 Frank Lowe was a musician in his late twenties, originally from Memphis, who naturally drifted into Coltrane's sphere after the master's death. He was moved by the sound of late Coltrane. Not Coltrane's technique in particular. The sound in general. "I used to listen to Trane and Pharoah as one horn," he said. "I didn't try to play like Trane or Pharoah, I tried to get the record's *sound*." He met Ornette Coleman in San Francisco, where he had been living and studying with three Coltrane-inspired saxophonists: Bert Wilson, Sonny Simmons, and Donald Rafael Garrett. Coleman suggested that Lowe move to New York, and that was all he needed: he moved immediately. Weeks after he moved to New York, he was offered a gig playing with Alice Coltrane at the Berkeley Jazz Festival in San Francisco. It was like a fantasy: he was in a band with Alice Coltrane, Jimmy Garrison, and Rashied Ali. Suddenly he was in John Coltrane's position. And he didn't get there the old way, by hard apprenticeship, by passing tests and trying to measure up against a Sonny Rollins or a Wayne Shorter. He was chosen because he had a sound, and because he was part of the new era. He recorded with the band on the record *World Galaxy*.

"There were two tenors," he remembered. "Archie Shepp was in the band . . . [He] stayed in the band until I learned the book. I felt real privileged, because I just went from listening to records, and the next thing I knew I was on stage. Sometimes, I'd look around, and it was Coltrane's rhythm section—and me! You know what I'm saying? So then I really knew that some kind of way I could play Coltrane licks naturally."

The idea of beginnings or endings being contrivances went hand in hand with meditation, and with the breath line or natural phrase line. Allen Ginsberg, who practiced meditation, had talked about it in the 1950s. Coltrane, who also practiced meditation, by 1960 and '61 was confirming the idea for an even larger audience with his half-hour tunes.

In 1970 the poet Michael Harper published a volume called *Dear John, Dear Coltrane*. His poem "Brother John" attempted to replicate the babbling, short-phrase repetitions of Coltrane's early-sixties "Chasin' the Trane" improvisational style:

> *Black man:*
> *I'm a black man;*
> *I'm black; I am—*
> *A black man; black—*
> *I'm a black man;*
> *I'm a black man;*
> *I'm a man; black—*
> *I am—*

The point seemed to be that phrasing, basically, is breath, and breath is unending, until the body gives out.

There is a modern classical-music analogue here, a history of expanded patience and a belief in the infinity within reduced materials. The composer LaMonte Young started writing tones that lasted for minutes at a time into his pieces in 1958; by 1962 he was writing for a band, the Theater of Eternal Music, which would improvise around drones for long stretches; his *The Well-Tuned Piano*, written for a piano tuned to just intonation, has had performances of up to six hours. In 1975 the composer Arthur Russell, a cellist whose performances bridged the worlds of avant-garde classical music and pop, envisioned a single piece called *Instrumentals* whose performance would be forty-eight hours long. In 1976 the composer Morton Feldman—who had no discernible interest in jazz—bought his first of many oriental rugs, and the hours he spent gazing into them would influence his music; shortly after this, he began to compose longer and longer pieces, ceasing to worry about the music as prepackaged entertainment, but thinking more about an ongoing environment full of small delectations of timbre and interval for the listener. His unbroken pieces began to last longer than an hour, and finally his *String Quartet No. 2*, from 1983, stretched to five.

In the early 1960s, Steve Reich had played a kind of free jazz in a group with Phil Lesh, who would later become the bassist of the Grateful Dead. Later he studied drumming in Ghana, Balinese gamelan music on the United States' West Coast, and cantoral chanting of Hebrew scriptures in New York. In the mid 1970s, he wrote *Music for 18 Musicians*. Finished in 1976, it was his first extended-work masterpiece. Its fourteen sections, growing into each other without rests, took over an hour but created an elastic sensation of time. It is, essentially, a work about the continual repetition of short melodic patterns, and set in single chords for long periods of time, not unlike some things Coltrane was working with—in "Chasin' the Trane," *Crescent*, and other works.

When the market for contemporary jazz collapsed in the late 1960s under the onslaught of rock and economic recession, many jazz musicians of the sixties generation went into academia, and jazz promoters and producers started investing in the music's more distant past. The avant-garde had bottomed out as a commercial proposition. There was jazz fusion, but it appealed to a different, more rock-leaning audience. It was time to look at jazz either as an academic or a repertory music.

There were albums of musicians revisiting Duke Ellington and Thelonious Monk compositions, a ragtime revival that had the odd effect of making Scott Joplin popular, and the establishment of repertory orchestras—among them the National Jazz Ensemble, founded by Chuck Israels; the New York Jazz Repertory Company, founded by George Wein, the festival impresario; and, at times, the New England Conservatory Orchestra, directed by Gunther Schuller. Coltrane figured into this reexamining-the-family-tree business very little. He was too recent, too mystifying, and too symptomatic of what had gone wrong, business-wise, in jazz.

Many of the jazz musicians whom Coltrane had directly inspired—Marion Brown, Bill Dixon, Archie Shepp, Milford Graves, Roswell Rudd—began teaching in recently established Black Studies programs at colleges like Bowdoin, Brandeis, Wesleyan, Bennington, and Antioch. Many others in one way or another set themselves loose into the wilds, setting up their own places to play, creating their own opportunities to record. It was a period of "beating our own drum," as Julius Hemphill said. "It was lean, but a fairly vigorous time." In the early seventies, when you saw an advertisement in *Down Beat* for a free-jazz record—like Clifford Thornton's *Freedom & Unity*, or LeRoi Jones's *Black and Beautiful . . . Soul & Madness*—often it listed the artist's own post-office box at the bottom, for direct ordering.

Because so little of this music was created on a company clock, because there were few professional outside producers on the job, a lot of shortcuts were taken; internal arrangements were initially loose for reasons of lack of time and money, and then that became a style, a sound in itself. Working bands became scarcer in new, modern-sounding jazz, because there was so little work to commit to.

It was also a time when jazz musicians were suddenly more

likely to be funded not by audiences but by government agencies or private foundations. It has been supposed that Richard Nixon, embattled by Vietnam, wanted to aid projects that didn't divide so easily along lines of the political left and right; the arts were one such project. The budget of the National Endowment for the Arts, created in 1965, exploded starting in 1969: money given to jazz increased tenfold in two years (from the tiny sum of $5,500 to $50,325), and then by more than tenfold again, by 1975 (to $671,208), then doubled again by 1980. Most of the major free-jazz musicians received individual NEA fellowships during these years, but so did musicians working in straight-ahead jazz—usually under the umbrella of some kind of cooperative organization.

A good jazz musician needs to play jazz; doing anything else is a waste of his time. And when audience support falls off—especially because musicians have no control over the business of clubs—there should be some mechanism, some service, to help. But this money didn't produce much jazz of lasting value. Typically it would be funneled toward a concert based on an extramusical concept or someone else's repertory, often with a band convened for a one-off occasion rather than an ongoing concern, in a place not conducive to the social rituals of jazz: a community center, a park, a university auditorium.

Suddenly there were fewer jazz clubs in New York, with more restricted bookings. Studio work, for skilled musicians—especially for skilled black musicians—was drying up as well. Jimmy Owens, the trumpeter, remembered that in 1967 he would be the only black musician out of forty at midtown studio sessions. It was a systematic problem in the studios: the jazz pianist Hank Jones and the trumpeter Joe Wilder found themselves among the few black musicians to find steady work at CBS and ABC in the 1960s and seventies. Old-boy systems and white-dominated unions ruled, and they seemed to favor white players.

In 1969, Owens was one of the founders of the Collective Black Artists, a cooperative association of players who paid regular dues and eventually set up concerts at the Apollo Theater and at Town

Hall. (Coltrane's old bass player, Reggie Workman, was another cofounder.) Through the 1970s, the CBA commissioned new work, putting on repertory concerts honoring musicians of great stature—Max Roach, Ahmad Jamal, Randy Weston, and, inevitably, Coltrane.

The program from a Coltrane-themed CBA concert in April 1975 at Town Hall (Andrew White conducting the eighteen-piece CBA Orchestra) included a biographical sketch of Coltrane which neatly encapsulates the rhetoric of that period vis-à-vis Coltrane, with its righteous, uncompromising tone, its trenchant anger toward critics, its capitalization of the word "Black."

John Coltrane has been the towering influence of the '60s and '70s much like Charlie Parker was in the decades before. His music spoke to Black audiences and other Black musicians like no one else has. Yet critics' comments throughout his career were, for the most part, years behind in understanding what he was about and how important he was. His use of modes and scales, the influence of African and Eastern music and philosophy, the beautiful ballad style of earlier days, the misnamed "sheets of sound," his revival of the soprano saxophone, his building and sustaining of moods, his dedication to God and his music—all these have been written about and analyzed to death. But beyond the technical explorations is the soul. It was the soul of the man and his music that came through then and will continue to reach out forever.

The members of the CBA were looking out for themselves, but the whole endeavor was also an extension of the civil rights movement. "The seventies was an intense period," said Don Moore, one of the CBA's founders. "People would come up to you in the street and say, 'What are you *doing?*' You had to be doing *something*. It would be embarrassing to say you weren't."

But black jazz musicians were not just one thing or another, not a monolithic whole. The only thing that most performing jazz musicians under fifty had in common, during the 1970s, was that they identified with John Coltrane; yet suddenly the division between free-jazz-oriented musicians and more mainstream ones was becoming plain. At a panel discussion on the history of the CBA, held at the New School in 2006, Rashied Ali got up to address the panelists and scratched open the old wound.

"Coltrane was talking about change, organization, owning your own stuff," Ali said, addressing the panelists, who included Owens, Moore, and Workman. "And I was here in New York when the CBA started—it was about trying to get black musicians work, because all the white musicians had work. It all circled out of that." Then he got down to what he had come to say:

> I can dig education. But I didn't come to New York to *learn* how to play, I came here to play. I never got no gigs from [the CBA]. We were the avant-garde cats, and the avant-garde cats were frowned upon by the beboppers. "Outside" musicians were not represented in the CBA to a great extent. There was a deep dichotomy between the so-called avant-garde and the mainstream.

As a consequence of their philosophical isolation—and the general decline of jazz audiences after the late sixties—musicians like Ali, Sam Rivers, Joe Lee Wilson, and Charles Tyler opened their own loft spaces in commercial buildings on the Lower East Side, in Chelsea, and in pre-gentrified SoHo, to present jazz in the 1970s. More and more jazz in New York went this way; much of jazz became specific actions by specific guerrilla operations, sometimes funded by specific private financial sources.

Horace Tapscott's Los Angeles–based UGMAA—the organization he set about founding not long after he saw Coltrane play at the Village Vanguard—made such a connection with the Watts and greater Los Angeles community, which was hungry for homegrown culture, that it ran for decades. Coltrane's music was the lingua franca of UGMAA. (The Union of God's Musicians and Artists Ascension borrowed part of its name from Coltrane's *Ascension*.)

In Steven L. Isoardi's history of Tapscott and UGMAA, *The*

*Dark Tree*, a story is told by Sylvia Jarrico, the wife of the actor William Marshall, who often collaborated with Tapscott and his various bands. Tapscott and some of his crew came by one day, Jarrico told Isoardi. "As I sat down, I moved over to the radio, which was on the jazz station, and turned off the radio. Horace walked out of the group, came past where I was still standing by the radio panel, and as he passed me, he leaned over very tactfully, so that you could hardly see he was leaning toward me, and he said, 'We don't turn off Coltrane.' "

At this point, Coltrane almost ceases to be real. A church in his name—first called the One Mind Temple Evolutionary Transitional Church of Christ, then called the St. John Will-I-Am African Orthodox Church, but now better known as the Church of St. John Coltrane—was established in San Francisco in 1971 by the Bishop Franzo King. Though financially strapped, it still exists. Church members have baked bread with Coltrane's image on it and called it their "daily bread"; King plays saxophone through Coltrane numbers in services. Alice Coltrane sued the church in 1981 for $7.5 million, claiming it infringed on copyright laws and exploited Coltrane's name. As an actual church, it limps along. As a metaphor, it is robust, astounding.


*A Love Supreme* may have become magic words—and Coltrane's record may have spread widely into the consciousness of popular culture—but the jazz record industry would not underwrite all the serious-minded suites that musicians composed as a consequence. Again, self-determination was the answer, and hand-in-hand with small musician-run labels, self-financed artists' collectives, and unpretentious ways to bring jazz performance to ordinary citizens as grassroots, handmade, noncommercial family entertainment (a notion advanced by the Black Arts Movement) was the sudden proliferation of the long-form work in jazz.

One example was by the trumpeter Hannibal Marvin Peterson. Peterson was a 1960s-generation Coltrane-ist who moved in the

master's circles: he arrived in New York in 1970, played with the
bands of Elvin Jones and Pharoah Sanders.

Peterson's album *Children of the Fire*, released in 1974 on the
tiny label Sunrise Records, with a modest orchestra conducted by
David Amram, started with the small-band modal sound of *A Love
Supreme* and worked outward with symphonic writing and songs.
It is separated into five movements: "Forest Sunrise," "Bombing,"
"Prayer," "Aftermath," and "Finale." Note the similarity to *A Love
Supreme*'s four movements: "Acknowledgement," whose opening
gong and saxophone phrase is so redolent of sunrise, "Resolution,"
"Pursuance," and "Psalm." But unlike *A Love Supreme*, it had very
definite political implications. "Dedicated to the children of Vietnam," it read, and in its second movement, Barbara Burton
whomped on detuned tympani drums to approximate the sound of
bombs.

In 1972, Carlos Santana and John McLaughlin, both devoted to
Coltrane as an improviser, composer, and sage, collaborated on
*Love Devotion Surrender*, a record interpolating the "Acknowledgement" theme from *A Love Supreme*, as well as "Naima," from
*Giant Steps*. The music was big-boned, pneumatic, athletic jazz-
rock, a direct aorta to later fusion guitarists like Allan Holdsworth
and, by extension, to a heavy-metal aesthetic that persists today.
(Its grandiosity, its superpowered phrasing, was doubly bolstered
by a kind of divine inspiration. Both guitarists at the time were in
thrall to the same guru, Sri Chinmoy, an Indian holy man whose
acolytes proved their fealty by performing acts of great physical
strength or stress, including swimming the English Channel and
running sixty-mile endurance races.)

Consequently Coltrane became recognized as a hero to electric-
guitar "shredder" heroes: the heavily technical-minded players
who descended from musicians like McLaughlin, Duane Allman,
Frank Zappa, and Steve Morse. Certain qualities of Coltrane's
playing spoke to the intensity of rock music—the force of his playing in long, legato lines could be more easily approximated with an
electric guitar and amplifier on a high-gain setting.

. . .

What did Coltrane's heavy blanket of influence show for itself in American jazz during the 1970s? A flood of self-produced records, a lot of mechanical imitation of his technique, and very few masterpieces. Other things were indeed happening in jazz: among them, Keith Jarrett's quartets and solo concepts, in which the length of a rapturous melody created its own form; the imposing entrance of the young Pat Metheny, who brought in an entirely new style of hypermelodic, nearly bucolic (in the Aaron Copland sense) jazz composition; the evolution of Ornette Coleman's sound, as played by groups led by Coleman's old sidemen Charlie Haden and Dewey Redman and Don Cherry; Miles Davis's dark and gnashing electric ensembles. But Coltrane was still the major figure, and he didn't seem to be providing much in absentia.

His sound spread into other disciplines, though. Rock, for sure. But Latin jazz, after the sixties, was also deeply affected by Coltrane.

Much of *Olé Coltrane*, in fact, bore traces of Latin rhythm, and later, "Africa" had a clear clave rhythm in it—the African-derived mother-pulse of Afro-Caribbean music. The Latin bandleader Eddie Palmieri began to check out Coltrane in 1963—his trombonist, Barry Rogers, took him to hear Trane at Birdland—and several years later, after the great mambo dance palaces had shut down, the Coltrane modal sound stole into Palmieri's music, in records like *Vámonos Pa'l Monte*, from 1971.

But the Coltranizing of Latin jazz wasn't just a case of artistic influence: it was part of a natural process of creolization. Afro-Latin music lent itself to Coltrane: as he headed deeper into modal music, where he and the band would play for long stretches within the setting of a single mode, he naturally evoked the single-chord *montuno* vamps of mambo. And Coltrane's music, conversely, lent itself to Afro-Latin bands.

The trombonist Conrad Herwig has spent long stretches working with Eddie Palmieri. Of his own records, he is best known for one made in 1996 called *The Latin Side of John Coltrane.* Here, working on Coltrane tunes with Latin jazz musicians (mostly members of Palmieri's band, including Palmieri himself), he began to understand on a more technical level why Coltrane's music is so dear to Latin-jazz players. It has to do with the similarities between soloing in a mode and in a *montuno,* yes, but also there is a particular rhythmic issue.

Coltrane's phrasing, Herwig explains, was asymmetrical within an even number of bars: this is why it sounds so different from the neater, 8-bar phrases of bebop and swing, where the on-the-beat notes and the off-the-beat notes are clearly demarcated. (Herwig describes this sort of phrasing—the phrasing of Ben Webster, for example—"hoo-va, hoo-va, hoo-va"; the jazz critic Martin Williams called it "heavy/light/heavy/light.") But Coltrane played uneven-bar phrases and made his phrasing sound smooth and flowing.

What this has to do with Latin music is that the clave, too, is asymmetrical: it is a 2-bar phrase expressed in five strokes. "Jazz musicians sometimes have a problem with clave because of the asymmetry of it," Herwig said. "Ornette, and cats after that, were playing asymmetrical, 9-bar or 11-bar or 13-bar phrases. The problem with clave is that it's got to be an *even* number of bars. If there's an odd number, you turn the clave around." Herwig was a jazz player who immersed himself in Latin music, instead of the other way around; when he made *The Latin Side of John Coltrane,* he was uncovering the latent Latinness of Coltrane tunes like "Blessing," "Impressions," "India," and parts of *A Love Supreme,* which he had previously known only as jazz. "Sometimes I feel that when you do jazz in a Latin way, you have to change the arrangement so much," he said. "With Coltrane, it was kind of homogeneous. It's as if there was a Latin arrangement there to begin with."

This is likely why Palmieri and the Latin-jazz bandleaders who followed him—Papo Vasquez, Jerry Gonzalez, Herwig himself— have been drawn to Coltrane; and this is why, when you hear a good Latin-jazz tenor saxophonist take a solo today—say, David Sanchez, or Mario Rivera—that there's a good chance it will sound like Coltrane.

Several features prominent in Coltrane's work were perfect for the do-it-yourself, artist-owned jazz of the 1970s: modality and vamps, which could be slotted into all kinds of simple pieces, particularly those with Eastern connotations; the idea of "multidirectional" rhythm sections, the Rashied Ali–Jimmy Garrison way of late Coltrane; the idea of meditative music; and the idea of instant momentum through a hot, purposeful, improvised music that surges from the first note, as "Chasin' the Trane" or "Transition" did.

Chicago had a jazz identity appreciably different from any other place. Unlike the musicians revolving around Horace Tapscott in Los Angeles, the Chicago players didn't mention Coltrane that much in interviews, and didn't evince an obsession with his playing in their own. Roscoe Mitchell's imaginative album *Sound*, from 1966, which gave rise to the Art Ensemble of Chicago, had operated on different imperatives from the start. In the 1970s and eighties, these groups broke up the density of free jazz, and felt no necessity to have it be truly "free," either. Mitchell, Anthony Braxton, Henry Threadgill, Leroy Jenkins, Muhal Richard Abrams—these people composed piles of music, far more than Coltrane ever did. And they let music breathe more than Coltrane had. The musical lines were shorter, more scabrous and humorous, just as committed to free improvisation, but they were more everyday, less heroic.

# 12 syllabus

Coltrane naturally shifted from being the last great man in jazz to being just another precursor. When you heard the Coltrane sound in mainstream jazz, from the late 1970s to the nineties, you were hearing a choice, not a reflexive motion. Jazz became a question of strategy, and suddenly there were numerous available strategies—partly because they were now being codified and taught, by teachers like George Garzone and Frank Tiberi at the Berklee College of Music (Boston), and Reggie Workman at the New School of Social Research (New York).

Coltrane was eventually seized upon as a perfect academic subject: he was, after all, the most accomplished autodidact in the history of jazz. But the problem was how to teach his music—should it be done by analyzing his use of scales and modes, his harmonic patterns, his blues lines, his rhythmic patterns, his "Giant Steps" changes? (These were obviously just tools to get him where he wanted to go; in the end, they were unimportant in themselves.) Or should it be done by feeling, by emotion, by allegory? The image of Coltrane as a space traveler, rocketing off the surface of the earth toward more specialized, little-explored, and potentially dangerous atmospheres has been used in the teaching of Coltrane courses both by Workman at the New School and Ran Blake at the New England Conservatory.

George Garzone went to study at Berklee in 1968, when higher education in jazz was still in its primitive phase. His teacher, Joe Viola, supplied him with a few transcriptions made by the Coltrane scholar Andrew White; they included "Giant Steps." Other than that, he was on his own, fanatically transcribing Coltrane solos from records, just as young musicians had done with Charlie Parker records twenty years before. The mechanical part, the notes, was the beginning of his studies; the rest of his life, he has been studying how to get at Coltrane's sound.

Jamey Aebersold, the author and marketer of teach-yourself-improvisation books and records, produced his first jazz play-along record in 1967; it was called *How to Play Jazz and Improvise*, and on it, a pianist played basic forms with a bassist and drummer: the blues in two common keys, ii–V changes, and so on. Though it was about ten years before Aebersold secured rights from the Coltrane Estate to make a Coltrane play-along record, it is not a coincidence that the pragmatic study of solo technique started to spread at the same time that Coltrane died. It was an emergency response. Something had to take his place.

Looking to Coltrane's late period as a starting point, or as a kind of revelation, wasn't much of a guarantee of an artistic career. "Of course, Trane just kind of drowned everybody," said Von Freeman, the wise elder of Chicago tenor players. "Because he had all that stuff together." He was talking about Coltrane's early time spent playing with Earl Bostic.

"He left a lot of wounded soldiers along the way," Freeman continued. "See, cats are still trying to recover from the Trane explosion. And, of course, they shouldn't look at it that way . . . Trane assimilated everything; they've got to assimilate everything up to Trane and move on."

After Coltrane, jazz students who hadn't even gigged could be in on the aesthetic choices that previously only professional players considered; the jazz-education movement organized the music into easily digested repertory and improvisational devices, making the whole proposition more businesslike. If you wanted to play a modal tune, the most effective way to do that was to use McCoy Tyner's stacked-fourth chords: it would produce the colors you wanted. If you wanted to use substitutions to modernize an old tune, you could use the "Giant Steps" device. If you wanted to play hard and fast from the start of the tune and not let up, there was the example of "Chasin' the Trane." And if you wanted to study the inner structure of the solos themselves, you now had the proper resources. Starting in 1973, the saxophonist and independent scholar Andrew White began privately publishing his own transcriptions of Coltrane solos; the first volume contained 209 of them, and through subsequent volumes he has gone past 700.

These were now specifically isolated elements; they could be extracted from the greater body of work. You didn't need to take the whole thing on anymore.

In 1979, Branford Marsalis was studying at the Berklee College of Music, thinking he wanted to be a music producer. (Michael Jackson's *Off the Wall* had just come out, produced by Quincy Jones, and Marsalis had it in his head that he wanted to be a younger Quincy Jones; Jones himself, similarly brash and catholic in taste, had attended Berklee in the early 1950s.) He was also a tenor saxophonist who had played in New Orleans R&B and pop bands, and was studying sax with Bill Pierce, a member of Art Blakey's Jazz Messengers who was on the Berklee faculty. Pierce urged him to start studying Coltrane.

Marsalis, as it turned out, was avoiding Coltrane. "I don't want to listen to that stuff," he told Pierce. "Listen to the way these guys sound."

By "these guys" he meant players who absorbed Coltrane's hard, focused tone and harmonic technique. What had happened during the 1970s was that among younger players, Coltrane's legacy had neatly split in two. There was the spiritual Coltrane and the technique Coltrane. "These guys" meant those on the technique side, including some of the players who had passed through McCoy Tyner's and Woody Shaw's bands, like Carter Jefferson and Azar Lawrence, but also Michael Brecker, Dave Liebman, Jerry Bergonzi, Bob Berg, Steve Grossman, Gary Bartz, John Stubblefield, Billy Harper. They were all excellent players, but there was a certain soldiering determination in their sound. And below them—also practicing that focused tone and miles and miles of sophisticated scale patterns, but less appealingly—were the leagues of players labeled "Coltrane clones."

"Don't blame all that on Coltrane," said Pierce. His advice was to ignore Coltrane's Atlantic period—all the paradigm-building of the "Giant Steps" chord changes. So Marsalis went straight to the Impulse records, and found what he liked.

Both Branford and his brother Wynton spent the 1980s fascinated with an ideal set by Coltrane's early Impulse recordings, like "Chasin' the Trane"; they talked about a style that they called "burnout," meaning playing hard and fast in time and in a particular key but without prearranged chord changes. But this is the difference between them and some of the players who had come before them: they were fascinated by the communicative workings of the entire Coltrane Quartet, not just Coltrane himself. Finally, it was Coltrane's rhythm section, even more than Coltrane the saxophonist, that influenced mainstream jazz in the 1980s.

With the Marsalises, two big new concepts entered the jazz business. They were: youth and empiricism.

Wynton Marsalis was especially responsible for this change. He arrived in New York in 1979, released his first albums in 1983, and won his first Grammy award in 1984. Accepting his award on television, he gave a speech about jazz as a force "that cannot be limited by enforced trends or bad taste." (He was probably responding to the fact that Herbie Hancock, one of his idols, received an award that night for his hip-hop song "Rockit"—and was criticizing

Hancock, hip-hop, and the song itself.) Nobody knew it yet, but he was bringing back Enlightenment thinking to jazz. He wasn't opposed to expression per se, and said repeatedly that he liked his Marvin Gaye, he liked his Stevie Wonder. He just thought that things were getting to the point where the word "jazz" had no meaning anymore—where, if the most gifted jazz pianist since Bud Powell was making hits with Fairlight synthesizers, pop-funk drums, and vinyl-scratching DJs, then all the other incoming talent in jazz would be going that way, too, unless someone spoke up. He believed that there were concrete verities of good jazz playing that had started to be overlooked, forgotten, since Coltrane's time. Glossy pop music was what irritated him most, inasmuch as it took away the audience for jazz.

His outspokenness about pop delighted journalists: finally someone was arguing on behalf of jazz without using abstractions. They couldn't get enough of him. Soon enough, they started asking Marsalis about free jazz. He would say he loved Don Cherry, Ornette Coleman's trumpet-playing foil, despite the fact that he thought Cherry couldn't technically play the trumpet very well. (Cherry was alive then, and this kind of sentiment was seen in some jazz circles as viciously uncool.) That was about as far as his endorsements went for jazz that prized expression over strict tonality and rhythm. He loved the Coltrane of *Africa/Brass* and *A Love Supreme*, and didn't talk much about late Coltrane. But everyone who cared enough to have an opinion on the subject began to improvise a narrative about what he thought: that Coltrane was a casualty of the sixties, that radical chic had importuned Coltrane to let go of his carefully organized working principles, such that he began to accommodate non-jazz and the extramusical; that Coltrane broke his contract with his audience. Marsalis's thoughts on jazz history were deeply influenced at the time by the writer Albert Murray, who talked and wrote eloquently about how the best jazz subdued the chaos of life. Late Coltrane, by this logic, didn't subdue anything; rather, it promoted chaos.

As soon as Marsalis began his role as an arts administrator at Lincoln Center in 1987—a part-time activity that grew into a full-time one with the establishment of Jazz at Lincoln Center in 1991—his programming omissions became understood as opinions. Lincoln Center is an institution dedicated by definition to repertory, and late Coltrane isn't about repertory, isn't about compositions; it is about sound. There wasn't much late-Coltrane repertory that would have worked on Jazz at Lincoln Center's stage. Naturally, the first concert that the institution devoted to Coltrane, in 1991, stressed Coltrane the composer; naturally, it leaned heavily on polished pieces of writing like "Countdown," "Giant Steps," "Alabama," and "Miles's Mode," and did not present any of Coltrane's music from after the classic-quartet years. The concert was criticized for being insufficiently "spiritual," but that aspect of it, in a sense, was intentional.

If Marsalis's opinions on a particular matter weren't yet fully fledged, he was cornered into making them so. If he didn't make them so, his colleagues Stanley Crouch, the critic who became an artistic consultant for Jazz at Lincoln Center, and Rob Gibson, the operation's executive director, made them, on behalf of the institution. In the meantime, Marsalis indulged in the sport of baiting those who believed in the avant-garde, partially because it was so easy to upset them. In 1994 he arrived at the New York jazz club Sweet Basil with his trumpet and challenged Lester Bowie, the trumpeter of the Art Ensemble of Chicago, to a playing contest. It was Bowie's stage that night, and he declined, but he got to address Marsalis as "boy" in a crowded room. Jazz appreciation was entering a weird, decadent phase, a time when the notions of "straight-ahead" and "free" playing stood in pure opposition to each other, and each one was grossly distorted for the purposes of argument.

The common criticism against the whole group of musicians who were, by the late eighties, called "young lions"—Wynton and Branford Marsalis, Terence Blanchard, Donald Harrison, Marcus Roberts—was that they were a trend; that they represented a feat of marketing more than of music; that young black men, confident-looking in well-tailored suits and confident-sounding on their instruments, had become irritatingly easy to advertise.

This is only true inasmuch as one concedes that late Coltrane, and the ideas of musical freedom surrounding him, was a triumph of advertising as well. Late Coltrane is, one supposes, honesty, playing without boundaries, the banning of cuteness. But it also fits neatly within more than ten years of post-Beat and hippie piety that had almost completely settled into American culture—let the sun shine in, let your freak flag fly, to live outside the law you must be honest, if it feels good do it. The Marsalises, especially, were sick to death of this kind of posturing.

One of the kinks in the reception of Coltrane's music is that while it has become synonymous with technical expertise, it has also become synonymous with rebellion, and self-conscious rebellion is always suspect: it matters deeply who's doing it, what they think they're rebelling against, and what might be the goals of the next wave of impressionable young musicians who respect rebellion tout court.

Coltrane was always concerned with blazing ahead, one popular line of reasoning goes; he didn't place much value in what he left behind him. And in jazz, it is the self-conscious trailblazers, always, who give listeners extramusical matter for guide ropes, so that they might progress with him more easily. Coltrane gave them *A Love Supreme* complete with text. He gave them some astronomy, some Africa, some Spain, some not-so-subtle civil rights messages; he seemed to be encouraging you to receive ideas about history as well as his sound.

The pianist Mulgrew Miller has said some fascinating things on this topic. A pianist who became recognized in the early 1980s, McCoy Tyner being one of his greatest influences, Miller is widely seen by jazz musicians as a master, and outside of musicians, as a bit of a bore. There is no identifiable element of extramusical transgression inside or outside his playing; he is not combining languages; he is not giving bourgeois culture the finger; he is not straining credulity. He is not asking you to alter your life. He plays jazz as black music, and there is a deep sense of propriety to it, but it's not also history and politics and musicology and philosophy: it is music alone.

In an interview for *Down Beat* in 2005, he talked about moderation and refinement, about a standard of language for jazz piano, about jazz as folk music, and the idea that "folk music is not concerned with evolving."

> A lot of people do what a friend of mine calls "interview music," [Miller said]. You do something that's obviously different, and you get the interviews and a certain amount of attention. Jazz is part progressive art and part folk art, and I've observed it to be heavily critiqued by people who attribute progressivity to music that lacks a folk element. When Charlie Parker developed his great conception, the folk element was the same as Lester Young and the blues shouters before him. Even when Ornette Coleman and John Coltrane played their conceptions, the folk element was intact. But now, people almost get applauded if they don't include that in their expression. If I reflected a heavy involvement in Arnold Schoenberg or some other ultra-modern composers, then I would be viewed differently than I am. Guys who do what I am doing are viewed as passé.

Miller is not wrong to say that jazz as a quietly evolving folk music, rather than as some metamusical statement, or something that illustrates a particular well-known narrative about its own evolution, tends to be slept on. In Oscar Wilde's dialogue-essay "The Critic as Artist," the Wilde character, Gilbert, says:

> It is sometimes said by those who understand neither the nature of the highest Criticism nor the charm of the highest Art, that the pictures that the critic loves most to write about are those that

belong to the anecdotage of painting, and that deal with scenes taken out of literature or history. But this is not so. Indeed, pictures of this kind are far too intelligible. As a class, they rank with illustrations, and even considered from this point of view are failures, as they do not stir the imagination, but set definite bounds to it.

If only Wilde were correct, as far as jazz is concerned. In fact, jazz critics love most to write about music as anecdotage—about records that propose a canon, or pose a counterintuitive theory about the jazz tradition, or pay props to a neglected musician, or suggest the obscured importance of painters, filmmakers, writers in a musician's life. Writing about such records, one doesn't have to talk to a musician to find out what's going on in the band; one can just read liner notes and make an analysis. There is a direct connection between coming up with extramusical concepts and making more records. And jazz critics tend to respect discographies as much as, if not more than, live performances.

"Interview music" is a perfect way to put it. Coltrane's music became heavily conceptual even without his talking about it much. He was hopelessly modest in interviews; he didn't offer up directives about how to interpret his music unless called upon to disentangle misinterpretations imposed upon it by others. But nearly everything he ever put his hand to has become part of the anecdotage of jazz: understood from a certain point of view, any given piece of Coltrane music is either from *before* he artistically rebelled and broke into a new social consciousness, or *after*.

All of his music slots into this mythology, which he—amazingly—seemed uninterested in building or furthering while he was alive. To most people, it is much less interesting to consider Coltrane as a slow but unstoppable process than as someone who had a clear modernist agenda, who discarded "the past" and rode blindfolded into "the future." Coltrane was reluctant to talk to liner-note writers about his music, believing that if it were any good it would speak for itself. Nevertheless, the favoring of the Big

Statement in jazz, a suite or an homage or a cross-discipline work, as a measure of artistic value—particularly as practiced by grant committees like the MacArthur Foundation—is entirely due to the influence of John Coltrane.

Coltrane has become an ongoing metaphor for different kinds of rebellion, different modes of resistance. Kamau Daaood's poem "Liberator of the Spirit" says: "John Coltrane was a freedom fighter / Liberator of the spirit from the shackles of form."

The poet, playwright, and activist Kalamu Ya Salaam wrote as recently as 2002 that "both Malcolm X and John Coltrane represented the combination of an innovative articulation of a blues-people sensibility with an avowedly anti-western/pro-Africa stance, inherent not only in the meaning of their message/music but in the aesthetics they employed."

The singer Iggy Pop, who became famous in the late-sixties Detroit rock band the Stooges—a band that for a time found its own profound center of gravity *despite* a will to be the wildest, loudest, even dumbest band going—was a Coltrane-head; he internalized his music through one sensibility and fed it back to the audience through another. "What I heard John Coltrane do with his horn, I tried to do physically," he has said. "And the simplicity of the compositions was—how should I put it?—encouraging to me, because I did not have more than an extremely rudimentary sense of chordings and song structure."

The post-punk band the Minutemen, touring the United States in 1985, played a tape of *Ascension*—the entire thirty-eight-minute piece—for their audiences before the set. Mike Watt, the band's bass player, still idolizes Coltrane as a man prepared to live by his convictions, and one who made a gigantically strong art while remaining personally humble. This, for him, is similar to the logic of punk rock at its best. "I think he wanted to stay in the realm of possibility," Watt says. "He didn't want to get fuckin' nailed down. That's that anarchistic spirit. He had an autonomy, but he was taking in all kinds of things. Life deals you hands. Things aren't fixed and static."

These statements can be confusing. You can't make too rigid a parallel between the art of Coltrane and the extended range of his following. The freaking out, the liberation of the spirit, the construction of a new ideal of post-hippie humility—all this was happening anyway. A non-Western stance from such a profoundly Western artist—culture was opening up; this was inevitable. Coltrane made a respectable action of going to extremes when black culture—in fact, all culture—needed that; he gave freaking out a noble purpose, and in fact, more or less, a nonprogrammatic one. (He didn't have an end goal. He was always unsatisfied. He didn't specify *the* religion or *the* style of jazz playing.) He presided over the opening up of culture, not the pinpoint-sharpening of it.

On the other hand, the perception of his rebellion has guaranteed his inclusion in the jazz curriculum, the postwar black-studies curriculum, and the punk-rock curriculum. Merely putting him on a postage stamp wouldn't have achieved that.


It became widely acknowledged by the mid-1980s that all the goodwill in the world didn't make a difference: the point of jazz, at least to some degree, is being yourself. And you'd better not fall too deeply into Coltrane if you want to be yourself.

Even the freest players discovered this. "I found out . . . that playing like Coltrane is a *lock*," said Frank Lowe. "Like, you can't get out of it. It's not open enough for me. I can play Sonny Rollins, and it's more in the bebop or hard-bop vein. But when you take Trane's stuff, his tone is so personal . . ."

Coltrane's influence was still overwhelming, but in a different way now. Mature, performing musicians weren't sweating to sound like him, not at the risk of losing work opportunities or losing respect from their peers. But Coltrane's ideas became necessary to *understand*, off the bandstand, as a basis for practice and development.

Sonny Rollins's example proved more fruitful in the pluralistic 1980s and nineties—partially because it didn't engender an orthodoxy. It was and is, in essence, playful: slightly weird, naturally and gently ironic and knowing. It connected with modern sensibilities. David Murray considered himself aligned with Rollins, as opposed to Coltrane. So did David S. Ware, perhaps the most popular of the second-wave free-music musicians in the mid-1990s, when music like his began to be called "ecstatic jazz."

By the mid-nineties, some of the interest had waned in the circle around Wynton Marsalis. His first several serious, long-form works, commissioned by Lincoln Center, had the curious effect of pushing him both further into high-culture approval (culminating with his Pulitzer Prize in 1997 for the oratorio *Blood on the Fields*) and lower in the estimation of average jazz listeners (and critics, who tended to be bored by the long works).

But something else happened. The declarations on jazz he regularly delivered on public television, on public radio, and in newspaper articles—which were often the only current opinions on jazz heard by great swaths of the country—ceased so much to matter. Suddenly, as Internet-based scholarship took shape, anyone interested in jazz could look online and find acres of research on all eras and styles of jazz; this raised the possibility that no one era or style could take precedence over another.

And since the young-lions movement, the only hope for the major-label jazz industry, had effectively gone bust, record labels began to pay closer attention to remarketing their back catalogues. Suddenly there was a new Impulse Records—first owned by GRP, then Universal—and it would lose no time promoting every one of the thirty-odd Coltrane records on the label, both the classic-quartet period and the late work.

For the early-sixties Coltrane quartet, they based their Coltrane catalogue sales on a steadily growing consensus that there had been no greater group since. For the later works, they had the growing audience for second-wave free jazz, as well as its more chilled-out cousin, the music known in some quarters since 1997 as "kozmigroov." What is kozmigroov? "Kozmigroov," says the definition at www.freeform.org, "is a transgressive improvisational music which combines elements of psychedelia, spirituality, jazz, rock, soul, funk, and African, Latin, Brazilian, Indian and Asian influences culminating into an all-encompassing cosmic groove." Some of late Coltrane fits within it, including the album *Expressions*, and the posthumous *Cosmic Music* and *Infinity*, released after Coltrane's death with Alice Coltrane's overdubbed string sections. As a subgenre, probably its most useful purpose has been to provide a framework for anyone outside of Hindu religious circles to appreciate the work of Alice Coltrane, who gave up reaching jazz audiences in the late 1970s to become a full-time spiritualist. In 1983 she founded the Sai Anantam ashram in Agoura, California, where until her death in 2007 she was known as Swamini A. C. Turiyasangitananda; worshipers at the ashram study the Vedic scriptures of ancient India, as well as Buddhist and Islamic texts.

But the limitation of kozmigroov is that it is ultimately a record-collector pursuit: it reflexively points toward the 1960s and early seventies, when there were a creditable number of people who believed that music was capable of broadening and altering Western consciousness toward more empathetic and peaceful ends. (Such people form a tiny minority now.)

Likewise, if one wants to believe in Coltrane's late music for its political implications, one must approach it with an entirely theoretical framework. The American scholar Mike Heffley has recently characterized *Ascension* as an example of "panarchy"— reflecting "Marx's vision of the socialist utopia following the transitional dictatorship of the proletariat." It may indeed suggest that notion—and yet such an interpretation would make the music even more difficult to embrace.

As for middle-period Coltrane—that group of LPs whose CD reissues were being marketed as the "classic quartet"—there were Branford Marsalis, and Kenny Garrett, among others, publicly working out their extensions of Coltrane's broad, attacking sound and intensity, and serving as models for music students. Garrett's record *Pursuance*, from 1996, drew from Coltrane repertory of the six years between *Giant Steps* and *Transition*; live, he routinely demonstrated something of the quiet, reserved, stored-up intensity and slightly pious feeling that one associates with Coltrane records. Marsalis was another matter: a more earthbound and joking presence, he evoked the athleticism of Coltrane playing with his quartet. (Two of his best rhythm-section players during the 1990s, Robert Hurst and Jeff "Tain" Watts, also played in his brother Wynton Marsalis's small groups; with Wynton, they often went after grooves that approximated the slow, heavy swing of the Coltrane quartet's rhythm section.)

Branford Marsalis was always careful not to dip too much into Coltrane's language: he made room for Sonny Rollins and Wayne Shorter and eventually Ben Webster as well. He was committed to the idea of using the past to enliven current jazz, without being overly studious about it, and his public fascination with Coltrane crested with the 2001 record *Footsteps of Our Fathers*, which included his quartet's version of the entire *Love Supreme* suite.

This *Love Supreme* was a reputable piece of work: the band pressed itself up closely against the original structure of the work, and then circulated its own sense of groove and dynamics through it. But what may have been most useful about Marsalis's version was his nonchalant boldness about covering *A Love Supreme* from start to finish, rather than just piously touching on one of its motifs. It seemed to be saying: Forget the worship, the aura, the sanctimony. This is *music*; it is our nuts and bolts. The weird paradox of the gesture was that it took Marsalis's playing of the entire work to make the act of covering the music at all less worshipful.

Mid-period Coltrane was widely approved since the 1980s—Impulse sold roughly 500,000 CD copies of *A Love Supreme* in the years 1986 to 2006, averaging around 600 each month. Late-period, less so, as one might expect: 38,000 sold of *Interstellar Space* during the same period. And there were still some rather bitter dogmatic reactions to late Coltrane.

Albert Murray, in lectures and on the Ken Burns television series *Jazz*, referred to free jazz as "entropy." He wasn't specifically referring to late Coltrane; he meant a generalized notion—which included Coltrane—of what he considered the unswinging avant-garde. Stanley Crouch has written about a time at which "Coltrane jumped off the cliff into hysteria," and about "Coltrane's naive submission to actual noise and incompetence." Interviewed on camera for the Burns series, Crouch presented a vision of Coltrane as a great man muddled by current history, a man who made a terrible choice—who became convinced that he should expose himself to the "ants" of the avant-garde, who eventually nibbled away at his body.

Today there is no center in jazz, no steady voice in the back of the head. Information is so much easier to come by now. The people running Jazz at Lincoln Center used to be derided as "gatekeepers"; there is no such thing as a gatekeeper anymore. More and more, musicians are doing what they want—within the tiny specificity of their particular cohort of musicians—and with high standards. It is not just that they have become academic, or rejected academia: they have done both, figuring out a way to thoroughly learn (at least) the long sliver of postwar jazz history that interests them, then push beyond it, toward something that makes contemporary sense.

In New York City, at this point, I tend to hear something played in a club that strongly suggests Coltrane about every two weeks. Fifteen years ago—in New York, especially, where Coltrane's deepest audience lay—his sound (or, by extension, the Coltrane-Tyner-Garrison-Jones sound) seemed almost thick on the ground. But, for that matter, the standard jazz quartet—lead instrument with piano, bass, and drums—was much more widespread. In the last ten years, jazz has been in the beginning stages of new formal changes.

The most obvious change is instrumentation. Piano-led trios and saxophone-led quartets are as abundant as ever, but it has become more normal now to hear two tenor saxophones in front of a rhythm section, or a band without a bassist, or a band with no drummer or two drummers, with a kora or *pipa* or *balafon* or harmonica, or a small group with a saxophone or brass choir. Established musicians—Roy Hargrove, Nicholas Payton, Stefon Harris, Joshua Redman, Christian McBride, the kind of musicians who in the late eighties were described as part of a "neotraditionalist" movement—have gone through periods of touring with their own funk bands, and trying to play funk with some of the detail and mystery with which they would play jazz. Musicians like the saxophonist Mark Turner—who went through a hard Coltrane phrase himself, as a jazz student in the late eighties—are suggesting a change of rhythm, composing toward more of an even eighth-note language, as opposed to, say, the behind-the-beat, syncopated, deep-swing feel of the classic-quartet Coltrane. Others, in a long line that seems to begin with Steve Coleman in the mid-1980s, are busy writing funk in odd meters with stresses on the upbeats.

In the cases of Michael Brecker and the once R&B, later smooth-jazz musician Grover Washington, Jr.—who in terms of purely guessed numbers might have been the two most influential jazz saxophonists since Coltrane—here were talented musicians who found a way to extend jazz into a commercial proposition. They played on jazz and pop records that the average person knew—Brecker, in particular, on records by Jackson Browne, Joni Mitchell, Steely Dan, and dozens more. Outside of artistic messiah figures, like Coltrane, jazz advances according to what information is available in a given time and place. The Brecker and Washington albums were widely distributed—and so there is a concrete reason why, for example, so many saxophone students in Cuba since the 1980s sound like Michael Brecker. But the most popular jazz-fusion music has not aged especially well; that particular version of "popular art" now feels grasping and fussy.

And yet among younger musicians, the Coltrane influence can still be stifling. At the Thelonious Monk International Jazz Competition in 2002, in Washington, D.C.—jazz's equivalent of the Van Cliburn International Piano Competition—fifteen saxophonists took part. (The proceedings were filmed for partial broadcast on Black Entertainment Television network.)

Each saxophonist could play three songs each, and was advised to show different sides in his playing. Most musicians took this to mean slow, medium, and fast. The most authoritative modern ballads are Coltrane ballads; the medium-tempo tune could be a harmonic exercise with "Giant Steps"–related changes, showing the ability to improvise over fast-changing chords; a fast tune could be a quicker version of the same thing, or something freer with some Coltrane speed and intensity.

Some of the young saxophonists seemed to have a future. (A third of them, in the four years since, have already set themselves up as bandleaders in New York and proven it.) Some of them surely played in that way knowing that it would ring important bells for the judges that year, who included Wayne Shorter, Joshua Redman, George Coleman, James Spaulding, and Don Braden, whose styles are all related, in various degrees of directness, to Coltrane.

Three out of the four semifinalists were particularly steeped in Coltrane, and one of them, Marcus Strickland, made the fatal mistake of playing, in his fifteen-minute performance slot, two Coltrane pieces from the same album. (*Oh no, you didn't*, some of us were thinking in the audience, as it happened.)

One was the blues called "Equinox," and the other was "Satellite," a tune written in the "Giant Steps" cadence of thirds, both from *Coltrane's Sound.* It was primarily because of this that he didn't win the contest; his focus was judged to be too narrow. He took third place.

Why did he do this?

"I felt that although both were Coltrane tunes, they showed different sides of playing," Strickland told me four years later, when the memory of the competition had ceased to matter, and when his own career had gone further than those of his fellow contestants that day. "The 'Satellite' tune, of course, being the more harmonically involved tune. We were very limited in what we could do. I could have brought in some originals, but we had one day to rehearse with the rhythm section . . . And I didn't want to bring standards that the judges had been listening to all day."

Strickland was born in 1979. He is small, polite, handsome, and animated, with medium-length braided hair. His twin brother, E.J., is a jazz drummer, and they have played in many of the same bands together. He has properly diversified to meet the splintered jazz audience, with two different bands of his own—one relatively straight-ahead and swinging, another playing his own tunes with odd time signatures and smaller solo spaces. He has also been playing with some of the better bandleaders in American jazz—Roy Haynes, Jeff Watts, and Dave Douglas. He is emblematic of how serious young musicians think about Coltrane, after a generation and a half of distant, self-limiting worship: time and ambient skepticism have allowed him to see the past more clearly.

Marcus Strickland continued:

My dad used to put my mom's [pregnant] womb up to the speaker and play "My Favorite Things." I grew up in Miami, Florida. My dad's a lawyer now, but when he was in college, he played percussion, classical percussion. He also played drum set, and he was kind of like a DJ for parties. He had a lot of music on vinyl.

When I was eleven, I started playing. Both me and my brother were eleven. We were trying to pick some elective classes, and I was looking at the choices: dance, I definitely didn't want to do that. Singing, no. But I wanted to do music, and naturally I gravitated toward instrumental music. My dad started playing this stuff and explaining it for us. The first record was John Coltrane's "My Favorite Things." He said, "This song is written by Rodgers and Hammerstein, and it was from this movie, *The Sound of Music*." He said, "The original version is nothing compared to what

Coltrane did to it." He talked about how Coltrane did the melody differently every single time he came to it. He was describing the quartet and how they interacted with each other—Elvin's snare-drum triplets and everything. But overall, the power of the music, it was just really reaching out to us.

So, okay. We went to a performance high school, and we started doing gigs of our own and started composing. We realized by sophomore year of high school that this was what we were gonna do for the rest of our lives. At this point we were fully engulfed in music, always listening. Trading music with our friends. Jazz in particular. Our basic schedule throughout high school was, we'd go to academic classes from seven-thirty to noon, then at one we'd continue with the arts classes until three, then we had a rehearsal in the jazz combo afterwards, from three to five, and sometimes a gig after that. [For college] both of us went to the New School. We definitely wanted to go to New York. We got here in '97. And as you notice, it's hard for me to not say "we," because he's been there all the way.

At the New School, I didn't encounter anybody who didn't know about Coltrane or who didn't admire Coltrane. Everybody was deep into it. That really states something about the significance of his presence. If you're a saxophonist in this day and age, you gotta know about Coltrane and what he did. I feel that his endeavors were based on both spirituality and the pursuit of getting better. He was never satisfied. He wasn't really consciously saying, "I want to be in the history books, I want to innovate." He was always searching.

*What do you think about the theory that he led musicians the wrong way?*

I hear that sometimes. Mostly from rhythm-section players who are tired of playing behind saxophonists who play twenty-eight choruses each! But I don't see him as being necessarily a negative

influence on horn players, in terms of stretching with the choruses, and everything. I think it's really just the responsibility of
each person to be tasteful with his solo. I mean, that's the reason
Coltrane's music cuts people even though it could be, like, an hour
long. He was always reaching for something different. He was always inventing. A lot of people, when I hear them playing long solos these days, it's a lot of ranting. It's not really shaped, it's very
repetitious. It seems like they're trying to fit everything they know
into one solo. The fact that he played so long was, like, a channel.

*What do you mean, a channel?*

It was like something grander than just him. A channel of expression, I think. It was very spiritual. It's almost like getting a
sermon from a preacher, a long sermon that keeps you interested,
that motivates you because it has depth.

If there's anything negative about his influence, it would be
that he made a lot of people insecure about their work—that if
they don't practice as much as he did, they're not worth anything.
I don't really think of that myself. That was him. That was who
he was. I didn't necessarily hear this from people in the same
grade as me, but when I graduated college, and started touring
with Jeff "Tain" Watts, I would come across college students, and
we'd start talking about Coltrane, and they'd say, "Man, how long
should I practice? Should I practice as long as Coltrane did?" I
would try to encourage them to think of their own journey, not
necessarily compare it to Coltrane's. I don't think Coltrane was
comparing his journey to anyone else. I get feedback from saxophonists that there's nothing else to be done. I think that's totally
ridiculous, but I understand where they're coming from. There's
so many changes that he went through in his playing. In the academic realm of the music, you hear a lot about "Giant Steps," but
that was just at the beginning. He was just working out some
numbers there. He got to so much other stuff later on.

*Do you find stuff you can use in his late work?*

Yeah, I can get some things out of that. As he went on, his music became more and more organic. Bar lines started disappearing; time wasn't as pronounced; phrasing was more lucid; it was more fluid than before. Even though the quartet was breaking down walls within the structure, when that quartet vanished, and he started doing stuff with Rashied, it became something intangible. It came from more than one direction at the same time. It was hard to really pinpoint what was going on. It shows me that it would be scary if he was still alive.

I compare the compositions he has to the compositions that I hear now, even mine, and I'm, like, *man* . . . People now, they write *toward* something. So much so that you're not necessarily gonna hear so much of the personality of the rest of the group. It's kind of like the leader's personality and interpretation. Whereas with Coltrane, the compositions allowed the other members to breathe *so much*, that the music got to a place that most musicians during that time have not been able to get to. Some people write their group into a box. He didn't.

*When you were learning, was his influence in any way oppressive? Did you get to a point at which you said, I have to get away from this guy?*

There were points where it was, like, Okay, I admire this guy, but man, I gotta look at other things. Naturally I started listening to other ways of playing the saxophone. I got into a long Joe Henderson binge for a while, and that brought me out of it. I've never really spoken to a saxophonist from John Coltrane's era about this, but I would love to ask somebody: *How did you do it?* The answer is obvious with Sonny Rollins—he just walked away. But, I mean, how did they avoid getting sucked into such a powerful force? Coltrane's presence was so powerful that people couldn't escape getting compared to him. You're playing like yourself, but

Coltrane had this thing that was so powerful that it's sucking up the attention.

These days, I notice that the minute Roy [Haynes] starts talking about Coltrane, it's almost like he takes a deep breath—and then talks. It's funny how people act like that whenever his name is mentioned.

*Do you get a sense that fewer saxophone players are locking into Coltrane's sound? Or fewer groups, even?*

Yeah, definitely. When I was in high school and college, I felt more like the beat, especially from the drummer, was coming out of that Coltrane quartet. But I feel the beat is changing, the overall rhythm of the groups are changing. I hear a lot of straight eighth notes going on. I think musicians like Mark Turner have a profound effect, and you probably won't know now how profound it is. I feel things are definitely changing. Whenever there's a change, a very big change, I've noticed that it's mostly been with the overall rhythm of the group.

A lot of musicians say jazz is dead, there's nothing to be done after Coltrane. It's probably because after Coltrane, people started getting very eager. It seems like the process is sped up by expectations. People want something deep right away. Record companies don't allow a group to develop a sound. It's kind of tough to develop a sound these days. The gigs are for a much shorter amount of time. The process has been sped up to a point where it doesn't really allow things to happen. It kind of stimulated a few things through gimmicks. A lot of people are saying, "I want to do this because it's different." It's such a conscious decision. In the old days, musicians had much more time to develop a sound.

Jazz life continues and proliferates, infinitely less cowed by Coltrane these days, but whenever his name is proposed again with any muscle, people listen again. It happened in 2005, with two of the greatest jazz records of the year. One was a 1957 Monk quartet concert with Coltrane in the band, from a tape discovered at the Library of Congress. It was important as a historical discovery, but so much better than most historical discoveries in jazz: a lush, creamy performance, thick with the beauty of the late-fifties swing, an album that bears repeated listening. In one year, Blue Note sold 370,000 copies of *Thelonious Monk Quartet with John Coltrane at Carnegie Hall* around the world. (A fine and reputable new jazz record that year, like, for example, Ravi Coltrane's *In Flux*, sold about a hundredth as much.)

Soon after came *One Down, One Up,* which was, in old Marsalis parlance, the ultimate "burnout" recording: at its peak, on the title track, it came down for fifteen minutes to just tenor saxophone and drums, Coltrane and Elvin, no chordal instrument. For a stretch within that, Jones's bass-drum pedal breaks. For a few minutes, there's no low end. Suddenly it's not like a regular jazz recording at all. It starts to sound rudimentary, like a basement-practice recording. Yet it is the most extraordinary connection between Coltrane and Jones that exists anywhere on record.

Who will be the next Coltrane? Which is to say: Which single musician will construct a style that a plurality of his colleagues want to emulate—not just out of reflexive following-the-current, but because that single musician represents the lifting up of an entire sensibility, some form of light and truth, achieved not just through devices and ideas, but through tone and sound, and represents the apotheosis of core ideals in jazz that are larger than just one generation's gathering wail?

My answer to the question is this: It is the wrong question for jazz—hostile to it, or basically uninterested in it. In some ways, after all, Coltrane was lucky. His greatness wasn't all his own making. There were circumstances.

He found his way when Miles Davis took a chance on him. He found it comparatively late in life, as an adult of newly organized habits who had his own physical weaknesses to defend. He found it when thousands of intelligent listeners in America were waking up to music from other cultures. He found it just when audiences were ready to place their trust in a popular musician as a kind of divine messenger. He found it precisely when club owners were more willing to countenance a bandleader who felt like playing the same song for half an hour.

Above all, Coltrane created possibilities for good things to happen in *bands*. He had a knack for benign direction.

The workings of a band, whether the band is one with an unvarying hierarchical structure of leader and sidemen, or whether it keeps shifting around to accommodate the surgings of different players, like Canada geese in flight, taking turns at the point of their V-formation—this is what defines jazz.

It is an art that thrives on what it *can* do, not so much on what it does. It is a possibility, only as good as what it is now, and then a minute from now, and then an hour from now. Great records can be made from it. But nearly every great record in jazz is only a partial picture of an ongoing process, on a good day at a certain time in a certain place, and it will take the creation of many more clubs and spaces to hire musicians and let them play, and play, and play some more—not the creation of many more record companies to document them—to conjure the next Coltrane.

The truth of jazz is in its bands.

# notes and sources

# notes

Sources not given here are given in text.

## part**one**

4 **"John just sat there, taking it all in":** J. C. Thomas, "Chasin' the Trane," p. 36.

6 **"I used to practice a lot with Trane":** Jimmy Heath, interview with author.

7 **"We were extracting the cadenzas":** Jimmy Heath, interview with Howard Mandel for documentary film *The World According to John Coltrane*, early 1980s.

7 **"Who's Willie Mays, Jim?":** Jimmy Heath, interview with author.

8 **Johnny Griffin saw that band:** Johnny Griffin, interview with Jim Standifer, October 30, 1982, oral-history interview from University of Michigan African-American Music Collection.

9 **"Yeah, little ol' Coltrane":** Coltrane, interview with Gardner.

12 **"peculiar hypnotic pattern not met with before":** from Steven Watson, *Prepare for Saints: Gertrude Stein, Virgil Thomson, and the Mainstreaming of American Modernism* (New York: Random House, 1998), p. 42.

12 **"What I didn't know with Diz":** Coltrane, interview with Gitler.

13 **"I found that by using":** Nat Shapiro and Nat Hentoff, *Hear Me Talkin' to Ya* (New York: Dover, 1966), p. 354.

14 **Von Freeman, the tenor saxophonist:** Von Freeman, interview with Ted Panken, WKCR, June 17, 1987.

16 **In a landmark sociological study:** Charles Winick, "The Use of Drugs by Jazz Musicians," *Social Problems* 7, 1959.

17 **Briefly in 1952 he played with Gay Crosse:** Coltrane is known to have played with Gay Crosse and possibly recorded with him. Lewis Porter suggested that Coltrane was the airy-toned alto soloist on "Bittersweet," a ballad recorded by Gay Crosse & The Good Humor Six in 1952. In the capacity of researcher and adviser, he passed on the track to Atlantic Records for its Coltrane box set *The Last Giant* in 1993, and suggested in his 1998 biography that among the Crosse recordings it was "a likely candidate" as a Coltrane item. He has since changed his mind, on the grounds that it just doesn't sound convincingly like Coltrane on alto.

19 **"a style that had no name":** Benny Golson, interview with author.

19 **"I really enjoyed that job":** Coltrane, interview with DeMichael, "Coltrane on Coltrane."

19 **"those chords screaming at me":** Coltrane, interview with Blume.

20 **Columbia Records signed Davis:** George Avakian, interview with author.

23 **The Prestige sessions proceeded without rehearsal:** Ira Gitler, interview with author.

25 **"A bassist of Paul Chambers's stature":** Coltrane, interview with Postif (translation mine).

25 **"I've always been struck":** Red Garland quoted in Nat Hentoff's liner notes to Garland's *Soul Junction* (Prestige/Fantasy).

26 **"He said, 'How are you?' ":** David Amram, interview with author.

28 **"Miles eventually cursed Trane out":** John Gilmore quoted in Robert Palmer, "Exploring the Jazz Legacy of John Coltrane," *New York Times*, September 29, 1974.

30 **Coltrane told Rollins that he wanted to record with him again:** Sonny Rollins, interview with author.

31 **"Sonny Rollins, you heard him recently?":** Coltrane, interview with Blume.

31 **He believed in jam-session recordings:** Ira Gitler, interview with author.

32 **"There is too much echo on the soloists":** Bill Coss, *Metronome*, July 1956.

34 **The contract, dated April 9, 1957:** Contract was reproduced in the auction catalogue for Guernsey's Jazz Auction, held February 20, 2005, at Rose Theater in New York City.

34 **An article came out . . . in a Cleveland newspaper:** From Simpkins, p. 83.

34 **He later made reference to drinking late-night scotches:** Coltrane, interview with Postif.

36 **"Monk was just another iron in the fire for John":** Benny Golson, interview with author.

36 **"I always had to be alert with Monk":** Joe Goldberg, *Jazz Masters of the Fifties*, p. 199.

37 **letting the band play for twenty minutes at a time:** Coltrane, interview with Postif.

40 **Orrin Keepnews, who ran Riverside:** Peter Keepnews, e-mail to author, December 2005.

42 **"I was trying for a sweeping sound":** Coltrane, interview with DeMichael, "Coltrane on Coltrane."

42 **"I thought in groups of notes, not one note at a time":** Ibid.

42 **"I was beginning to apply":** Ibid.

43 **"I got interested in [the harp] around 1958":** Coltrane, interview with Wilmer.

43 **". . . due to the direct and free-flowing lines":** DeMichael, "Coltrane on Coltrane."

45 **Russell had already talked with Miles about modes:** Kahn, *Kind of Blue*, p. 69.

46 **"When you go this way, you can go on forever":** Nat Hentoff, "An Afternoon with Miles Davis," *The Jazz Review*, December 1958, pp. 11–12.

47 **"making substitutions on my substitutions":** George Russell, interview with Ashley Kahn, in *Kind of Blue*, p. 69.

48 **In a review of the Newport concert:** Don Gold, review of Miles Davis Sextet at Newport Jazz Festival, *Down Beat*, August 7, 1958.

48 **at home Coltrane was listening hard to contemporary symphonic music:** Zita Carno, interview with author.

48 **Coltrane was thirty-two:** Wayne Shorter, interview with author.

48 **Coltrane had already told a journalist:** *Oakland Tribune*, June 14, 1959, quoted in Simpkins, p. 90.

49 **"The way Miles used these modes":** George Russell, interview for "Tell Me How Long Trane's Been Gone."

49 **Davis revealed two extramusical inspirations:** Davis and Troupe, p. 234.

52 **Tommy Flanagan, the pianist on "Giant Steps":** Porter, p. 155.

53 **"*Giant Steps*, everything I did on that":** Coltrane, interview with Grant.

55 **"He didn't really want to make the gig":** Thomas, pp. 108–109.

58 **"I have never tired of his complex . . . playing":** Bobby Jaspar, "Elvin Jones and Philly Joe Jones," *The Jazz Review*, February 1959.

58 **including, Tyner remembers, the "Giant Steps" changes:** McCoy Tyner, interview with author.

58 **Steve Kuhn, the pianist he worked with:** Porter, p. 176.

58 **he himself has used the word "metronomic":** McCoy Tyner, interview with François Postif, quoted in Porter, p. 178.

58 **He told the French critic François Postif:** Coltrane to Postif, "John Coltrane: Une Interview," *Jazz Hot*, January 1962.

61 **one need not be within earshot:** Scott, p. 116.

61 **"closely resembled the music of primitive savages":** Scott, p. 142.

62 **"If you repeat: flower, flower, flower":** Khan, p. 21. The writer Eric Nisenson has said that Sonny Rollins thought he remembered Coltrane recommending Hazrat Inayat Khan's book to him.

62 **Unlike Cyril Scott, Khan had no problem with jazz:** Khan, p. 51.

62 **"I dunno, I may be wrong on this":** Coltrane, from Tokyo Prince Hotel press conference, 1966.

63 **"The playbacks haven't sounded right":** Coltrane to Wilmer.

64 **In 1960, during a stint:** Roy Haynes, interview with author.

64 **He asked Paul Motian in 1965:** Paul Motian, interview with author.

64 **"The person with whom I would have the most pleasure":** Coltrane to Postif.

64 **"When [Ornette] came along":** Coltrane to Benoît Quersin, *Jazz*, January 1963.

65 **"Here's how I play":** Coltrane to Postif.

66 **"My real pianist":** Ibid.

68 **Roy Haynes remembers going by Dolphy's house:** Roy Haynes, interview with author.

68 **Coltrane would travel with Dolphy's picture:** Randi Hultin, "I Remember Trane," *Down Beat Music Handbook 13*, pp. 104–105.

69 **Leisure time became a higher priority:** Information on the New York art world comes from issues of *The New York Times* from the fall and winter of 1961–62, as well as from Jed Perl's *New Art City*.

73 **As he put it in a conversation with Frank Kofsky:** Coltrane to Frank Kofsky, from *Black Nationalism and the Revolution in Music*, 1970.

74 **"Coltrane had his own drummer in here":** Roy Haynes, interview with author.

76 **"that certain fast thing I was reaching for":** Coltrane to Kofsky.

76 **"I don't think it was something that plagued him":** Ravi Coltrane, interview with author.

80 **Thiele said that Johnny Hodges later told him:** Frank Kofsky, "The

New Wave: Bob Thiele Talks to Frank Kofsky about John Coltrane," *Coda*, May 1968.

80 **Bob Thiele described Coltrane's difficulty:** Ibid.

81 **"I was a Coltrane fan":** Johnny Hartman interview, from Will Friedwald's liner notes to *The Johnny Hartman Collection 1947–1972* (Hip-O/Universal).

82 **"Many thanks":** Coltrane, letter to Don DeMichael, reprinted in *John Coltrane Speaks* (San Francisco: Sunship Publishing Company, 1981).

84 **Coltrane told Haynes that with him he could hear Tyner:** Roy Haynes, interview with author.

85 **It was the rare situation:** Ibid.

85 **"For a drummer":** Ibid.

86 **"I'm not actually progressing right now":** Coltrane to Karl-Erik Lindgren, interview from the album *Miles Davis in Stockholm 1960 Complete* (Dragon DRCD 228).

88 **Coltrane would later intimate that his melodic lines:** Coltrane, interview with Michel Delorme.

88 **The implication was clearly that the texts were his own poems:** Ravi Coltrane, interview with author.

89 **he had even found ways to derive song from the shape of a cathedral:** Alice Coltrane, interview with Fred Seibert, WKCR, c. 1971.

90 **"He was the type of person, he didn't care for socializing":** Alice Coltrane, interview with Robert Palmer, transcript from early-1980s interviews for documentary film *The World According to John Coltrane*.

90 **Alice Coltrane has said:** Alice Coltrane, interview with Branford Marsalis, *Coltrane's A Love Supreme Live* DVD (Marsalis Music).

90 **A manuscript showing this preliminary musical arrangement for *A Love Supreme*:** Reproduced in the auction catalogue for Guernsey's Jazz Auction, held February 20, 2005, at Rose Theater in New York City.

91 **"Thank you, God" is the refrain in between lines:** Lewis Porter has written a thorough analysis of *A Love Supreme*, connecting it to Coltrane's text, in *John Coltrane: His Life and Music*, pp. 231–49.

92 **The saxophonist Joe McPhee saw him in 1965 at the Village Gate:** Joe McPhee, interview with author.

93 **"The intensity":** Morgenstern quoted in Porter, p. 217.

93 **"What is called good is perfect":** Walt Whitman, from "To Think of Time."

94 **the drummer Rashied Ali:** Rashied Ali, interview with author.

95 **Ali remembers Coltrane pulling out a chair:** Ibid.

95 **Coltrane is said to have given money to Ayler:** Valerie Wilmer, "Spiritual Unity," essay from liner notes to Albert Ayler, *Holy Ghost* (Reverant, 2004).

95 **At some point in early 1965:** Rashied Ali, interview with author.

99 **He called Bob Thiele after the release of** *Ascension*: Thiele, to Kofsky, *Coda*, May 1968.

99 **"There was a thing I wanted to do in music, see":** Coltrane, to Kofsky.

100 **Jimmy Garrison said he had to learn "to phrase, rather than to walk":** Jimmy Garrison interviewed by Ed Michael, WKCR, c. 1971.

101 **"He was a deep, great artist":** D. H. Lawrence, *Studies in Classic American Literature*, p. 154.

102 **"He was a real American":** Ibid., pp. 154–55.

103 **"He added another drummer":** Elvin Jones, to Whitney Balliett, *American Musicians II*, p. 464.

105 **"It was a Trane concert":** Amiri Baraka, "You Think This Is about You?" essay from liner notes to Albert Ayler, *Holy Ghost*, 2004.

106 **"Coltrane walked on":** Dave Liebman, interview with Vic Schermer from Allaboutjazz.com, www.allaboutjazz.com/iviews/liebman_on_trane.

106 **"I said, 'Aw, man, he ain't playing shit' ":** Rashied Ali, from panel discussion entitled "Did John Coltrane Lose His Way?" Jazz at Lincoln Center, September 20, 2006.

107 **"No motherfucker can tell me":** from CD liner notes to Frank Wright's album *Uhuru Na Umoja* (Universal France, 2004).

109 **"I'd say, 'Trane, man, why are you doing that' ":** Rashied Ali, interview from "Tell Me How Long Trane's Been Gone."

110 **"I told him that he impressed me like somebody that was afraid":** Jimmy Oliver, interview from "Tell Me How Long Trane's Been Gone."

110 **He helped support the Olatunji Center:** Olatunji, *The Beat of My Drum*, pp. 155–57.

111 **He talked about wanting to travel to western Africa:** Olatunji, interview from "Tell Me How Long Trane's Been Gone."

111 **Ali's concept of free-time drumming:** Sheet in Coltrane's hand reproduced in Simpkins.

112 **"Ain't nobody coming?":** Rashied Ali, interview with Carlos Kase, WKCR, March 23, 2004.

113 **After the concert, Coltrane reimbursed:** From Olatunji's essay "John Coltrane: My Impressions and Recollections," *Cosmic Colors: A Black Music Magazine*, issue 1, 1974.

## part**two**

120 **"I couldn't even figure out what kind of saxophone"**: Billy Hart, interview with author.

120 **"Before Clifford Brown, I hadn't heard"**: Charles Tolliver, interview with author.

120 **"Up until that time in the record"**: Andrew White, from *Trane 'n Me*.

120 **"John Coltrane has often been called a 'searching' musician"**: Robert Levin, liner notes for *Blue Train* (Blue Note).

121 **"Although Miles continues"**: Don Gold, *Down Beat*, August 7, 1958.

121 **"a very dumb-assed review"**: Simpkins, p. 81.

121 **"Once in a while, Miles might say"**: Jack Chambers, *Milestones*, p. 272.

122 Coltrane **"has in the past year detonated more concentrated enthusiasm"**: Hentoff, review of *Coltrane, HiFi & Music Review*, February 1958.

124 **Coltrane even eventually used it himself**: Coltrane, from DeMichael, "Coltrane on Coltrane." Since DeMichael was the amanuensis, it is possible that he could have inserted the reference to Gitler's phrase.

124 **"You know 'Blue Train'?"**: Zita Carno, interview with author.

128 **Wayne Shorter thought**: Wayne Shorter, interview with author.

128 **Shorter had been absorbing**: David Amram, interview with author.

129 **"Charlie Parker's playing"**: Mimi Clar, review of *Soultrane*, *The Jazz Review*, April 1959.

129 **"There was a muchness"**: Michael Gibson, "John Coltrane: The Formative Years," *Jazz Journal*, June 1960.

129 **"From one point of view"**: Martin Williams, *The Jazz Tradition*, p. 230.

130 **"The élan and aura of wonderful outrage"**: H. A. Woodfin, *The Jazz Review*, September/October 1960.

131 **"I was very embarrassed"**: Coltrane, to Dargenpierre.

131 **"At that time"**: Wayne Shorter, interview with author.

132 **The Canterino family, which owned the Half Note**: Information on the pay rates of the Half Note and the Village Vanguard comes from Mike Canterino and Lorraine Gordon.

133 **When crowds exceeded the club's limit**: Mike Canterino, interview with author.

135 **"I used to see him with the group with Miles"**: Frank Tiberi, interview with author.

138 **The record producer Joel Dorn**: Joel Dorn, interview with author.

139 **"We have some impatience"**: Robert Lowell, from A. Alvarez, *Under Pressure*, pp. 163–64.

142 **"a study of defeating demons"**: Bob Brookmeyer, interview with author.

142 **"But by the time of John's own band":** Ibid.

142 **"I heard a good rhythm section":** John Tynan, *Down Beat*, November 23, 1961.

142 **"I found your quintet's music completely bewildering":** Bob Dawbarn, *Melody Maker*, November 25, 1961.

143 **"It hurt me to see him get hurt":** Coltrane to Kofsky.

143 **an estimated reading audience of around 70,000:** John Gennari, *Blowin' Hot and Cool*, p. 144.

144 **"a torrential and anguished outpouring":** Pete Welding, *Down Beat*, April 26, 1962.

144 **"Coltrane may be searching":** Ira Gitler, *Down Beat*, April 26, 1962.

145 **"I saw the quartet around the time of *My Favorite Things*":** Steve Reich, interview with author.

146 **a music-theory column in *Down Beat* . . . that Coltrane was known to admire:** Coltrane to J. C. Dargenpierre, "John Coltrane, un Faust Moderne," *Jazz* 78, 1962.

146 **"He understood something":** Allaudin Mathieu, interview with author.

147 **"I had heard about [Coltrane] from other musician friends":** Alice Coltrane, from transcript of early 1980s interview with Robert Palmer for the film documentary *The World According to John Coltrane*.

147 **"That Sunday afternoon we went there":** Kofsky, interview with Horace Tapscott, *Jazz & Pop*, December 1969.

148 **"I was raised in music when music was respected":** Horace Tapscott, interview with author.

148 **"As intellectual as some people can be":** Billy Hart, interview with author.

149 **"He could have just stopped":** Charles Tolliver, interview with author.

149 **"The pentatonic scale is harmonically ambiguous":** John McNeil, interview with author.

151 **"More and more I found myself sounding like Coltrane":** Art and Laurie Pepper, *Straight Life*, p. 375.

153 **"That was quite a day":** Sonny Sharrock, interview with author.

153 **"At the zenith of his powers":** Charles Tolliver, interview with author.

154 **"Coltrane was a *sound* player":** Charles Moore, interview with author.

157 **"Trane was elected as the dean":** Rashied Ali, interview with author.

157 **Sonny Sharrock remembered talking to Jimmy Garrison:** Sonny Sharrock, interview with author.

158 **the "antipoverty bands":** Jimmy Heath, interview with author.

159 **In the art criticism . . . "apodictic":** Annette Michelson used the word in 1969, writing about Robert Morris's *Slab*, from 1962; Carter Ratcliff ex-

panded on the subject with an essay, "Apodicticity," in his book *Out of the Box: The Reinvention of Art, 1966–1975.* Thanks to Arthur Danto for an elucidation of this term's meaning and origin.

159 **"What is important now is to recover our senses":** Sontag, *Against Interpretation,* p. 14.

160 **the poem "AM/TRAK":** *Selected Poetry of Amiri Baraka,* p. 332.

161 **"New talk of Black Art reemerged in America":** LeRoi Jones, "Nationalism Vs. PimpArt," from Barksdale and Kinnamon, eds., *Black Writers of America* (originally published, in slightly different form, in *The New York Times,* November 19, 1969).

161 **"It was as if I had a new ear for black music":** Baraka, *The Autobiography of LeRoi Jones,* p. 210.

162 **"Once he got past jazz":** Matthew Shipp, interview with author.

163 **"Coltrane has never been a 'time' player":** Don Ellis, *Jazz,* December 1965.

164 **"Don Ellis has finally shown himself for what he really is":** Charles Moore, *Jazz,* April 1966.

165 **"Because, after all, it takes at least a birdbrain":** Eldridge Cleaver, *Soul on Ice* (New York: Delta Publishing Company, 1968), p. 164.

167 **The term "minimalism" had barely come into use:** I am going by Henry Flynt's idiosyncratic, but very well-documented, essay "LaMonte Young in New York, 1960–1962," in Duckworth and Fleming, eds., *Sound and Light,* p. 67. Flynt writes that the term was first used to describe visual art around 1966. The *Village Voice* music critic Tom Johnson may have been the first to apply the term to music, in a review of an Alvin Lucier concert in 1972.

167 **"His sound was so radical":** Ibid., p. 10.

167 **He has told an often-repeated story:** Ibid., p. 27.

168 **"I was seeing Coltrane's music":** Robert Stone, quoted in Perry, Schwartz, Ortenberg, p. 28.

169 **"This is possibly the most powerful human sound ever recorded":** Bill Mathieu, *Down Beat,* June 23, 1965.

170 **"The blast of sound almost bowled me over":** Don DeMichael, *Down Beat,* December 1, 1966.

170 **"This recording just might be the greatest work of art":** Frank Kofsky, *Jazz,* January 1967.

172 **"He must have known something about his condition":** Wayne Shorter, interview with author.

173 **This was a very nineteenth-century notion:** More on this topic can be found in *Late Thoughts,* edited by Karen Painter and Thomas Crow, par-

ticularly in Painter's essay "On Creativity and Lateness." It should be noted that Painter was brave enough a scholar to commission essays by serious writers on the topic of "late style" in music, art, and architecture, and then write in her own essay that lateness is really a construct of art criticism rather than the creation of art.

173 **"The maturity of the late works":** Theodor W. Adorno, ed. Richard Leppert, *Essays on Music* (Berkeley, Los Angeles, and London: University of California Press, 2002), p. 564.

174 **"Coltrane sounded like he was playing a *velvet saxophone*":** Roland Alexander, interview with Phil Schaap.

175 **Afterward, Coleman drove out to the cemetery:** Joe McPhee, interview with author.

177 **"Coltrane, Pharoah, Archie, they play space bebop":** Ayler, interview with Kiyoshi Koyama for *Swing Journal*, July 25, 1970, from the *Holy Ghost* CD box set.

177 **"The new music seems like it died":** Sonny Sharrock, interview with Michael Bourne, *Down Beat*, June 1971.

178 **"I still can't imagine":** Larkin, pp. 187–88.

181 **"One of the reasons the music of that era":** Charles Tolliver, CD liner notes to *Live in Tokyo* (Strata-East, 1998).

182 **"I used to listen to Trane and Pharoah as one horn":** Frank Lowe, interview with author.

183 ***"Black man: / I'm a black man"*:** Michael Harper, "Brother John," *Dear John, Dear Coltrane*, p. 3.

185 **"beating our own drum":** Julius Hemphill, interview with author.

186 **The budget of the National Endowment for the Arts:** information from Anderson, pp. 168–71.

188 **At a panel discussion:** Quotes from Jimmy Owens, Don Moore, and Rashied Ali in this section come from a panel discussion at the New School in New York City, February 22, 2006.

189 **"As I sat down, I moved over to the radio":** Sylvia Jarrico, interviewed in Isoardi, *The Dark Tree*, p. 129.

192 **Martin Williams called it "heavy/light/heavy/light":** Martin Williams, *The Jazz Tradition*, p. 73. Williams here is using the phrase in relation to Coleman Hawkins.

192 **"Jazz musicians sometimes have a problem with clave":** Conrad Herwig, interview with author.

195 **"Of course, Trane just kind of drowned everybody":** Von Freeman, interview with Ted Panken, WKCR, June 17, 1987.

196 **"I don't want to listen to that stuff"**: Branford Marsalis, interview with author.

201 **"A lot of people do what a friend of mine calls 'interview music'"**: Mulgrew Miller, interview with Ted Panken, *Down Beat*, March 1, 2005.

201 **"It is sometimes said"**: Oscar Wilde, p. 30.

203 **"both Malcolm X and John Coltrane"**: Kalamu Ya Salaam, "A Primer of the Black Arts Movement, *Black Renaissance* no. 4, Summer 2002.

203 **"What I heard John Coltrane do with his horn"**: Iggy Pop to George Varga, from "The Survivalist," *San Diego Union-Tribune*, April 26, 2001.

203 **The post-punk band the Minutemen:** Mike Watt, interview with author.

204 **"I found out"**: Frank Lowe, interview with author.

208 **"Coltrane jumped off the cliff into hysteria"**: Stanley Crouch, "John Coltrane's Finest Hour," *Slate*, March 10, 2006.

210 **"I felt that"**: Marcus Strickland, interview with author.

# sources and acknowledgments

Two books were of great help through the entire writing of this one. They are *John Coltrane: His Life and Music*, by Lewis Porter (Ann Arbor: University of Michigan Press, 1998), and *John Coltrane: A Discography and Musical Biography*, by Yasuhiro Fujioka with Lewis Porter and Yoh-Ichi Hamada (Lanham, Maryland, and London: The Scarecrow Press, 1995).

Porter and Fujioka, among others, are in the middle of creating a new reference book which promises to be even more authoritative about Coltrane's discography and chronology: *The John Coltrane Reference Work* (New York: Routledge, 2007), by Chris DeVito, Yasuhiro Fujioka, Wolf Schmaler, David Wild, and general editor Lewis Porter.

*Coltrane: The Story of a Sound* draws on my interviews with the following musicians; portions of those conversations appear in the text.

| | |
|---|---|
| Rashied Ali | February 2006 |
| David Amram | January 2007 |
| Michael Brecker | January 2002 |
| Bob Brookmeyer | April 2006 |
| Zita Carno | November 2005 |
| Nels Cline | March 2006 |
| George Coleman | January 2005 |
| Ornette Coleman | August 2006 |
| Steve Coleman | August 2002 |
| Ravi Coltrane | April 2005; May 2006 |

| | |
|---|---|
| Sonny Fortune | January 2006 |
| George Garzone | May 2006 |
| Benny Golson | January 2006 |
| Billy Hart | January 2005 |
| Roy Haynes | January 2002; February 2006 |
| Jimmy Heath | March 2004 |
| Conrad Herwig | October 2006 |
| Yusef Lateef | April 2006 |
| Eddie Locke | May 2003 |
| Frank Lowe | January 1992 |
| Branford Marsalis | August 2006 |
| John McNeil | February 2006 |
| Joe McPhee | September 1995 |
| Charles Moore | March 2006 |
| Paul Motian | October 2005 |
| Greg Osby | January 2002 |
| Danilo Perez | January 2005 |
| Joshua Redman | April 2004; March 2005 |
| Sonny Rollins | July 2006; January 2006 |
| Sonny Sharrock | July 1991 |
| Matthew Shipp | April 1994 |
| Wayne Shorter | January 2005 |
| Marcus Strickland | April 2006 |
| Horace Tapscott | November 1991 |
| Frank Tiberi | March 2006 |
| McCoy Tyner | January 2005 |
| David S. Ware | December 1991 |
| Mike Watt | March 2006 |
| Miguel Zenon | April 2006 |

Thanks to Wolfram Knauer of the Jazz-Institut Darmstadt for his comprehensive Coltrane bibliography.

I have depended heavily on Coltrane's interviews at various points in this book: Coltrane with August Blume (*The Jazz Review*, January 1959); Jean-Claude Dargenpierre (*Jazz* [magazine], January 1962); Bob Dawbarn (*Melody Maker*, November 25, 1961); Michel Delorme (*Jazz Hot*, September 1965); Don DeMichael ("Coltrane on Coltrane," *Down Beat*, September 29, 1960, and "John Coltrane and Eric Dolphy Answer the Jazz Critics," *Down Beat*, April 12, 1962); Barbara Gardner (*Down Beat Music*, 1962); Ira Gitler (*Down Beat*, October 16, 1958); Frank Kofsky, in *Black Nationalism and the Revolution in Music*

(New York: Pathfinder Press, 1970); Carl-Erik Lindgren (audio interview from the album *Miles Davis in Stockholm 1960*, Dragon Records); François Postif (*Jazz Hot*, January 1962); Benoit Quersin (*Jazz* [magazine], January 1963); Valerie Wilmer (*Jazz Journal*, January 1962); a series of interviews with Coltrane, McCoy Tyner, and Elvin Jones that Alan Grant aired on his radio show on WABC–New York in 1967; and the tape of Coltrane's press conference at the Tokyo Prince Hotel in July 1966. References in the notes refer to each interview by the name of the interviewer.

Quotes from Coltrane's letter to Don DeMichael come from *John Coltrane Speaks* (San Francisco: Sunship Publishing Company, 1981).

Other information comes from Zita Carno ("The Style of Coltrane," *The Jazz Review*, October and November 1959); David Baker ("Profile of a Giant," *Jazz Spotlite News*, February/March 1980); John S. Wilson ("'Village' Becomes Focal Center for Modern Jazz," *The New York Times*, October 27, 1960); an unpublished interview with the drummer Vernell Fournier by Charles Keil; Ted Panken's interview with Von Freeman on WKCR-FM (New York) on June 17, 1987; Will Friedwald's notes to *The Johnny Hartman Collection 1947–72* (Hip-O/Universal); Nat Hentoff ("Challenges Without End," *International Musician*, March 1962); the book, edited by Ben Young, that accompanies the Albert Ayler CD box set *Holy Ghost* (Revenant Records); the collected run (1958–61) of *The Jazz Review*, the greatest periodical in jazz journalism; K. Leander Williams's interview with Charles Gayle and David S. Ware ("Tenor Madness," *Down Beat*, January 1995); Frank Kofsky's interview with Horace Tapscott (*Jazz & Pop*, December 1969); Michael Bourne's interview with Sonny Sharrock (*Down Beat*, June 1971); Branford Marsalis's interview with Alice Coltrane (*Coltrane's A Love Supreme: Live in Amsterdam* DVD, Marsalis Music, 2004); Ted Panken's interviews on WKCR-FM with Von Freeman (June 17, 1987) and Roscoe Mitchell (June 13, 1995); and several interviews from WKCR's Coltrane festival in 2004 (Rashied Ali and Sonny Fortune, by Carlos Kase, March 23; Jimmy Heath, by Phil Schaap, March 17; Wynton Marsalis, by Phil Schaap, March 24; Roland Alexander, by Phil Schaap, March 16).

Some quotations from George Russell, Jimmy Oliver, and Rashied Ali come from the five-hour 2001 radio series created by Steve Rowland and Larry Abrams, *Tell Me How Long Trane's Been Gone*. (Information on obtaining a copy on CD is available at www.artistowned.com.) Material from the Jazz at Lincoln Center panel discussion titled "Did John Coltrane Lose His Way?" from September 20, 2006, is from a video provided by Jazz at Lincoln Center.

Among the books owned by Coltrane which I have used in the text or looked at for background are Cyril Scott, *Music: Its Secret Influence Throughout the Ages* (London: Rider & Company, 1933); Richard H. Popkin and Avrum

Stroll, *Philosophy Made Simple* (Garden City, New York: Doubleday & Company, 1956); Alfred Jules Ayer, *Language, Truth and Logic* (New York: Dover Publications, n.d.); Edgar S. Bley, *Math Without Numbers* (New York: Sterling, 1961); Joseph Schillinger, *Kaleidophone: Pitch Scales in Relation to Chord Structures* (New York: M. Witmark, 1940 revised edition); and—in the realm of "possibly owned"—Hazrat Inayat Khan, *The Mysticism of Sound and Music* (Boston and London: Shambhala, 1996).

For information and material on Coltrane, jazz, and New York in the 1950s and sixties, and provocative directions, I thank Ravi Coltrane, Lewis Porter, Dan Morgenstern, Ran Blake, Joyce Johnson, Larry Appelbaum, Aaron Cohen, Ethan Iverson, Bruce Lundvall, Hal Miller, Bethany Ryker, Lorraine Gordon, George Avakian, Peter Keepnews, Ashley Kahn, Peter Watrous, August Blume, Joel Dorn, Phil Schaap, Eric Kulberg, Mike Canterino, Stanley Crouch, Toby Gleason, Garnette Cadogan, Bruce Boyd Raeburn, Allaudin Mathieu, Don Crews, Brent Edwards, David Wild, Kate Jennings, and my father, Marcus Ratliff.

A special order of thanks goes to Paul Elie. I'm grateful, too, to Neil Belton, Cara Spitalewitz, Abby Kagan, and Zoe Pagnamenta.

Other books which have supplied valuable information:

A. Alvarez, *Under Pressure* (Harmondsworth, Middlesex: Penguin Books Ltd., 1965).

Iain Anderson, *This Is Our Music: Free Jazz, the Sixties, and American Culture* (Philadelphia: University of Pennsylvania Press, 2006).

Molefi Kete Asante, *The Afrocentric Idea* (Philadelphia: Temple University Press, 1987).

Whitney Balliett, *American Musicians II* (New York: Oxford University Press, 1996).

Amiri Baraka, *The Autobiography of LeRoi Jones* (New York: Freundlich Books, 1984).

Richard Barksdale and Kenneth Kinnamon, eds., *Black Writers of America: A Comprehensive Anthology* (New York: Macmillan, 1972).

Paul F. Berliner, *Thinking in Jazz* (Chicago: University of Chicago Press, 1994).

James E. B. Breslin, *Mark Rothko: A Biography* (Chicago: University of Chicago Press, 1993).

Jack Chambers, *Milestones: The Music and Times of Miles Davis* (New York: Da Capo Press, 1998).

Bill Cole, *John Coltrane* (New York: Schirmer Books, 1976).

Harold Cruse, *The Crisis of the Negro Intellectual: From Its Origins to the Present* (New York: William Morrow, 1967).

Arthur C. Danto, *The Abuse of Beauty* (Chicago: Open Court, 2003).

Miles Davis and Quincy Troupe, *Miles: The Autobiography* (New York: Simon and Schuster, 1989).

William Duckworth and Richard Fleming, eds., *Sound and Light: LaMonte Young, Marion Zazeela* (Lewisburg, Pennsylvania: Bucknell University Press, 1996).

Gerald L. Early, *This Is Where I Came In: Black America in the 1960s* (Lincoln: University of Nebraska Press, 2003).

Ralph Ellison and Albert Murray, *Trading Twelves: The Selected Letters of Ralph Ellison and Albert Murray* (New York: Vintage Books, 2001).

Wayne Enstice and Janice Stockhouse, *Jazzwomen* (Bloomington: Indiana University Press, 2004).

John Gennari, *Blowin' Hot and Cool: Jazz and Its Critics* (Chicago: University of Chicago Press, 2006).

Joe Goldberg, *Jazz Masters of the Fifties* (New York: Macmillan, 1965).

Michael S. Harper, *Dear John, Dear Coltrane* (Champaign: University of Illinois Press, 1985).

Mike Heffley, *Northern Sun, Southern Moon: Europe's Reinvention of Jazz* (New Haven and London: Yale University Press, 2005).

Steven L. Isoardi, *The Dark Tree: Jazz and the Community Arts in Los Angeles* (Berkeley and Los Angeles: University of California Press, 2006).

Jane Jacobs, *The Death and Life of Great American Cities* (New York: Random House, 1961).

William James, *Writings 1902–1910* (New York: The Library of America, 1987).

Ashley Kahn, *Kind of Blue: The Making of the Miles Davis Masterpiece* (New York: Da Capo Press, 2000).

———, *A Love Supreme: The Story of John Coltrane's Signature Album* (New York: Viking, 2002).

———, *The House That Trane Built: The Story of Impulse Records* (New York: W. W. Norton, 2006).

Philip Larkin, *All What Jazz: A Record Diary 1961–1971* (New York: Farrar, Straus and Giroux, 1985).

Yusef Lateef, *The Gentle Giant* (Irvington, New Jersey: Morton Books, 2006).

D. H. Lawrence, *Studies in Classic American Literature* (London: Penguin Books, 1971).

Phil Lesh, *Searching for the Sound* (New York: Little, Brown, 2005).

John Litweiler, *The Freedom Principle: Jazz After 1958* (New York: William Morrow, 1984).

———, *Ornette Coleman: A Harmolodic Life* (New York: William Morrow, 1992).

Peter Nabokov, *A Forest of Time: American Indian Ways of History* (Cambridge: Cambridge University Press, 2002).

Babatunde Olatunji, *The Beat of My Drum: An Autobiography* (Philadelphia: Temple University Press, 2005).

Karen Painter and Thomas Crow, eds., *Late Thoughts: Reflections on Artists and Composers at Work* (Los Angeles: Getty Publications, 2006).

Art and Laurie Pepper, *Straight Life* (New York: Schirmer, 1979).

Jed Perl, *New Art City: Manhattan at Mid-Century* (New York: Alfred A. Knopf, 2005).

Paul Perry, Michael Schwartz, and Neil Ortenberg, *On the Bus: The Complete Guide to the Legendary Trip of Ken Kesey and the Merry Pranksters and the Birth of the Counterculture* (New York: Thunder's Mouth, 1997).

Gary M. Pomerantz, *Wilt, 1962: The Night of the 100 Points and the Dawn of a New Era* (New York: Crown Publishers, 2005).

Carter Ratcliff, *Out of the Box: The Reinvention of Art, 1965–1975* (New York: Allworth Press, 2000).

Larry Rivers with Arnold Weinstein, *What Did I Do?* (New York: HarperCollins, 1992).

Constance Rourke, *American Humor* (New York: New York Review of Books, 2004).

Edward Said, *On Late Style: Music and Literature Against the Grain* (New York: Pantheon Books, 2006).

Cuthbert Simpkins, *Coltrane: A Biography* (New York: Herndon House, 1975).

Susan Sontag, *Against Interpretation* (New York: Farrar, Straus and Giroux, 1966).

Arthur Taylor, *Notes and Tones* (New York: Perigee/Putnam, 1982).

J. C. Thomas, *Chasin' the Trane* (Garden City, New York: Doubleday, 1975).

Chris Villars, ed., *Morton Feldman Says: Selected Interviews and Lectures 1964–1987* (London: Hyphen Press, 2006).

Andrew White, *Trane 'n Me (A Semi-Autobiography): A Treatise on the Music of John Coltrane* (Washington, D.C.: Andrew's Musical Enterprises, Inc., 1981).

Oscar Wilde, *Plays, Prose, Writings and Poems* (London: Everyman's Library/Random House, 1991).

Martin Williams, *The Jazz Tradition*, second revised edition (New York: Oxford University Press, 1993).

Carl Woideck, ed., *The John Coltrane Companion: Five Decades of Commentary* (New York: Schirmer, 1998).

# index